Writing Space

Computers, Hypertext, and the Remediation of Print

Second Edition

Jay David Bolter
Georgia Institute of Technology

LEA LAWRENCE ERLBAUM ASSOCIATES, PUBLISHERS

2001   Mahwah, New Jersey   London

Lawrence Erlbaum Associates, Inc., Publishers
10 Industrial Avenue
Mahwah, NJ 07430

Cover design by Kathryn Houghtaling Lacey

Library of Congress Cataloging-in-Publication Data

Bolter, J. David, 1951-
Writing space : computers, hypertext, and the remediation
of print / Jay David Bolter—2nd ed.
     p.   cm.
Includes bibliographical references and index.
ISBN 0-8058-2918-0 (cloth : alk. paper)
ISBN 0-8058-2919-9 (pbk. : alk. paper)
1. Word processing. 2. Hypertext systems. 3. Electronic pub-
lishing. 4. Authorship—Data processing. 5. Text processing
(Computer science) I. Title.
Z52.4 .B65 2000
652.5—dc21

                                                    00-037663
                                                    CIP

Books published by Lawrence Erlbaum Associates are printed
on acid-free paper, and their bindings are chosen for strength
and durability.

Printed in the United States of America
10 9 8 7 6 5 4 3 2 1

For Christine and David

Contents

Preface

In the nine years since the first edition of this book was published, there have been enormous changes in the writing space offered by electronic technology. Those changes are due almost entirely to the development of the World Wide Web. When this book was first published, the World Wide Web was only about a year old and was still limited largely to research centers and universities, following Tim Berners-Lee's original vision of the Web as a space for scientific publication and exchange. Like many others, I had no idea that the Web would grow into a defining application for electronic communication. As a global hypertext system, the Web has provided the most convincing evidence of the computer's potential to refashion the practice of writing. For better or worse, the Web *is* hypertext for us today; all the earlier applications of stand-alone hypertext seem experimental or provisional in comparison. It seemed worthwhile to revise *Writing Space* to take the Web into account, simply because much of what I had written was made obsolete by this phenomenon.

If the Web has given us a definition of hypertext, it has also demonstrated the growing importance of graphics, animation, video, and audio. It was the explosion of multimedia forms on the Web and elsewhere that led me, indirectly, to the major change of emphasis in this version. After writing the first edition of *Writing Space*, I became increasingly interested in the audiovisual capabilities of digital technology. I realized that our culture was coming to value the computer not only as writing technology, but also as a device for presenting and manipulating sounds and images. Focusing on digital visual technologies, such as computer games, virtual reality, and graphics on the Web, my colleague Richard Grusin and I sought to explain the relationship between these new media and such earlier visual media as photography, film, and television. When we published *Remediation*, we did not include

any extensive consideration of the relationship of print technology to new media. This edition of *Writing Space* is meant to fill that gap: to show how hypertext and other forms of electronic writing refashion or "remediate" the forms and genres of print.

This edition is about 10,000 words shorter than the first, although certainly not because there is less to say about hypertext today. There is much more to say, and there must now be dozens of books and thousands of articles exploring the technical, economic, cultural, and aesthetic aspects of hypertext and the World Wide Web. Often I have been able to cite or summarize these works rather than provide my own, less adequate discussion. On literary hypertext and hypertext theory, in particular, there are the works of Jane Douglas (1988, 2000), Michael Joyce (1995, 2000), George Landow (1992, 1997), Richard Lanham (1993), Stuart Moulthrop (1989, 1991, 1992, 1994, 1997), Mark Bernstein (1998), and others, whom the reader will find repeatedly cited in the pages that follow.

Even prior to the success of the World Wide Web, some computer scientists had turned their attention to hypertext. The ACM had even created a special interest group, now called SIGLINK. In the 1980s and early 1990s, the discipline gave us important theoretical and practical work on which I have drawn. The practical systems included Hypercard, Notecards, Aquanet, and SEPIA. On the theoretical side, Jacob Nielsen's *Hypertext and Hypermedia* (1990) became a key work for understanding the utility and usability of hypertext applications. Frank Halasz and others developed the Dexter model, which served as the classic formal description for linking strategies for both hypertext and hypermedia. Many others have done foundational work in user interface design, information retrieval, hypertextual annotation, the creation of digital libraries, and so on, including John B. Smith and Stephen Weiss (Smith & Weiss, 1988; Smith, Weiss, & Ferguson, 1989), Gary Marchionini and Ben Schneiderman (1988), John Leggett (Leggett & Schnase, 1994), and Cathy Marshall (1998). All of this work has contributed to the maturation of hypertext as a computer technology.

I have also shortened this second edition by eliminating many prophetic claims that either did not come true or were simply made irrelevant by the development of hypertext in directions that I had not foreseen. I have revised and pared back the historical materials. The development of the Web and multimedia has foregrounded the relationship of word and image, so that the history of the tension between verbal and visual representation seems more important than ever. For that very reason, however, the history of phonetic writing seems to me less relevant now than it did nine years ago. Digital technology is not now elaborating on phonetic writing in interesting ways. Perhaps as speech recognition technology matures, the pendulum will swing back. At present, however, it seems to me that the computer is not leading to a new kind of orality, but rather to an increased emphasis on visual communication.

In this edition, I have made an effort to respond creatively to the criticism of the first edition—in particular on the question of technological determinism (see for example, Haas, 1996; Grusin, 1996). In the first edition, I often seemed to portray the computer and earlier technologies of writing as autonomous agents. I seemed to be suggesting that these technologies themselves could change the way we organized and expressed our literary and cultural forms and even the way we think. In this respect I had fallen into a rhetoric, which McLuhan, Ong, and others had pioneered and which remains popular. I have tried to incorporate the insights of these critics (who have also and more importantly criticized McLuhan and Ong themselves). In chapter 2 and elsewhere, I acknowledge that writing technologies do not alter culture as if from the outside, because they are themselves a part of our cultural dynamic. They shape and are shaped by social and cultural forces. In chapter 2 and elsewhere, I have depended on Haas (1996), Chartier (1994, 1995), Nunberg (1996), Duguid (1996), Hesse (1996), Drucker (1994, 1995), and others to explain the materiality of electronic writing. Electronic writing participates in our material culture, as do handwriting and printing: electronic writing and reading are physical and visual practices. And of course the World Wide Web and information technology (IT) are now major sites of economic exchange.

I expect further criticism in one area at least, because I have continued in this edition to use some terms interchangeably where others have made distinctions: electronic writing, digital writing, hypertext, and hypermedia. There may be useful distinctions to be made here. Some prefer the term "digital writing" to "electronic writing," on the grounds that the essence of these new forms is their digital method of representation. Electronic devices are used currently to embody the digital computer and, I think, will continue to serve as the basis for digital writing far longer in the future than this book will be read. Furthermore, the electronic components of digital writing are important to their current cultural construction. At present, electronic (or digital) writing describes a larger category than hypertext or hypermedia. Electronic writing includes word processing, e-mail, listservs, chat rooms, and MUDs and MOOs, none of which have the node and link structure of classic hypertext. I have argued, however, that all electronic writing shares important qualities with hypertext (flexibility, instability, interactivity), so that hypertext, once again in the form of the World Wide Web, serves a paradigm for our cultural experience with electronic writing. Hypermedia is multimedia hypertext, in which the defining characteristic remains the linking of presentational elements.

In revising this book, as I have noted, I have depended on the published work of many colleagues in literary hypertext and computer science, as the references indicate. In addition to drawing on their printed and electronic publications, I have also been privileged to know many, perhaps most, of the important figures in the field. I have benefitted from attending their conference papers and from e-mail discussions and private conversations. Many of them have shared with me their insights into and critiques of the first edition of *Writing Space*, and they have helped to shape my vision and correct my errors and excesses. They include Michael Joyce, Stuart Moulthrop, Nancy Kaplan, Jane Douglas, George Landow, Espen Aarseth, Terry Harpold, Janet Murray, Kate Hayles, and many other colleagues and students.

A final word regarding the reference system used in this edition. In addition to the standard references for printed works, included in parenthesis in the APA reference form, I have referred to Web sites by including the URL and (because Web site addresses can change arbitrarily) the date on which this URL was referenced. I have also included some internal references to indicate connections between various points in the text and to avoid repetition. The marker (=> p. 23) following a sentence indicates that the reader can find a related discussion on page 23. This is meant to be a printed version of a hyperlink, which seems to me appropriate for a book on hypertext. Richard Grusin and I first used the technique in *Remediation*. There is nothing radical about this technique of course, and it seems odd to me that a system of internal references is not used more often in contemporary books.

* * *

Portions of chapter 4 were adapted from my article "Ekphrasis, Virtual Reality, and the Future of Writing," pp. 253–272, which appeared in *The Future of the Book*, edited by Geoffrey Nunberg, © 1996, The Regents of the University of California.

Portions of chapter 7 were adapted from "The Rhetoric of Interactive Fiction," which appeared on pp. 269–290 of *Text and Textuality: Textual Instability, Theory, and Interpretation*, edited by Philip Cohen and published by Garland Publishing in 1997.

1

Introduction: Writing
in the Late Age of Print

THE LATE AGE OF PRINT

In a well-known passage in Victor Hugo's *Notre-Dame de Paris, 1482,* the priest Frollo sees in the invention of the printed book an end rather than a beginning:

> Opening the window of his cell, he pointed to the immense church of Notre Dame, which, with its twin towers, stone walls, and monstrous cupola forming a black silhouette against the starry sky, resembled an enormous two-headed sphinx seated in the middle of the city. The archdeacon pondered the giant edifice for a few moments in silence, then with a sigh he stretched his right hand toward the printed book that lay open on his table and his left hand toward Notre Dame and turned a sad eye from the book to the church. "Alas!" he said, "This will destroy that" (Hugo, 1967, p. 197).

The priest remarked "Ceci tuera cela": this book will destroy that building. He meant not only that printing and literacy would undermine the authority of the church but also that "human thought ... would change its mode of expression, that the principal idea of each generation would no longer write itself with the same material and in the same way, that the book of stone, so solid and durable, would give place to the book made of paper, yet more solid and durable" (p. 199). The medieval cathedral crowded with statues and stained glass was both a symbol of Christian authority and a repository of medieval knowledge, moral knowledge about the world and the human condition. The cathedral was a library to be read by the religious, who walked through its aisles looking up at the scenes of the Bible, the images of saints, allegorical figures of virtue and vice, and visions of heaven and hell (Yates, 1966, p. 124). In fact, the printed book did not eradicate the encyclopedia in stone; it did not even eradicate the medieval art of writing by hand. People continued to contemplate their religious tradition in cathedrals, and they continued to communicate with pen and paper for many purposes. However, printing did displace handwriting, in the sense that the printed book became the most highly valued form of writing. Philosophers and scientists of the later Renaissance used the medium of print to refashion the medieval organization and expression of knowledge. As Elizabeth Eisenstein has shown, the printing press has been perhaps the most important tool of the modern scientist (1979, especially pp. 520–574).

Hugo himself lived in the heyday of what we might call "the industrial age of print," when writers and publishers were taking advantage of mechanized presses to create mass-publication newspapers, magazines, and novels. Hugo's own popularity in France (like Dickens' in England) was evidence that such writers were reaching and defining a new audience. Today we are living in the late age of print. Word processing, databases, e-mail, the World Wide Web, and computer graphics are displacing printed communication for various purposes. In the 1980s, the computer and the printed book still seemed to serve different spheres of communication. Computers were well suited to scientific analysis and business data processing and possibly to forms of ephemeral writing, such as memos. Business letters and technical reports might also migrate to the computer, but literary, scholarly, and scientific texts of lasting value would remain in printed form. Now, however, the distinction between lasting texts and pragmatic communication has broken down, and all kinds of communication are being digitized. Major book publishers have for years put their texts in machine-readable form for photocomposition, so that even these texts pass through the computer on their way to the press. It now seems possible that many texts might never be printed, but simply distributed in digital form. The Internet and the World Wide Web have already expanded enormously the uses for digital communication: there are Web sites offering us Greek literature, avant-garde fiction, articles from medical journals, online magazines and newspapers, business materials and advertising for all kinds of products, and both written and visual pornography. Although print remains indispensable, it no longer *seems* indispensable: that is its curious condition in the late age of print. Electronic technology provides a range of new possibilities, whereas the possibilities of print seem to have been played out. As we look up from our computer keyboard to the books on our shelves, we may be tempted to ask whether "this will destroy that." The question does not have a definitive answer. What is characteristic of the late age of print is, rather, that we pose the question.

The phrase "late age of print" no doubt makes many readers think of Frederic Jameson and many other neoMarxists who have characterized ours as the age of "late capitalism." For Jameson (1991), late capitalism does not mean dead capitalism; it means instead a changed system that operates globally through and around traditional governments and cultures (pp. xviii–xxi). Jameson writes, "[w]hat 'late' generally conveys is rather the sense that something has changed, that things are different, that we have gone through a transformation of the life world ... " (xxi). This is also the best way to think of the late age of print, as a transformation of our social and cultural attitudes toward, and uses of, this familiar technology. Just as late capitalism is still vigorous capitalism, so books and other printed materials in the late age of print are still common and enjoy considerable prestige, especially for the humanities and some of the social sciences. On the other hand, with the rapid decline of socialism, capitalism now seems to have no serious rival as an economic system. The printed book has a rival; indeed, it has had a series of rivals in the visual and electronic media of the 20th century, including film, radio, television, and now digital media. It is these rivalries—especially the latest challenge from digital media—that are now defining how the printed book will function for our culture. Digital media are refashioning the printed book.

Because of the tension between print and digital forms, the idea of the book is changing. For most of us today, the printed book remains the embodiment of text. Both as authors and as readers, we still regard books and journals as the place to locate our most prestigious texts. Few authors today aspire to publish a first novel on the Internet (it is too easy); they still want to be in print. However, the printed book as an ideal has been challenged by poststructuralist and postmodern theorists for decades, and now the computer provides a medium in which that theoretical challenge can be realized in practice. Some groups (scientific researchers along with some in business and government) are already transferring their allegiance from the printed page to the computer screen. They think of the computer as their primary medium, print as a secondary or a specialized one. If our culture as a whole follows their lead, we may come to associate with text the qualities of the computer (flexibility, interactivity, speed of distribution) rather than those of print (stability and authority). As early as 1993, the historian Henri-Jean Martin was willing to claim that that shift in association had already occurred: "Books no longer exercise the power they once did; in the face of the new means of information and communication to which we will have access in the future, books will no longer master our reason and our feelings" (quoted in Chartier, 1995, pp. 13).

It is certainly true that we no longer rely on print exclusively in organizing and presenting scientific and academic knowledge, as we have for the past 5 centuries. The organization of such knowledge now depends on the interplay of printed and electronic forms. The shift to the computer may make writing more flexible, but it also threatens the definitions of good writing and careful reading that have developed in association with the technique of printing. In the heyday of print, we came to regard the written text as an unchanging artifact, a monument to its author and its age. We also tended to magnify the distance between the author and the reader, as the author became a monumental figure, the reader only a visitor in the author's cathedral. In the late age of print, however, we seem more impressed by the impermanence and changeability of text, and digital technology seems to reduce the distance between author and reader by turning the reader into an author herself. Such tensions between monumentality and changeability and between the tendency to magnify the author and to empower the reader have already become part of our current economy of writing.

THE FUTURE OF PRINT

Our culture's ambivalence in the late age of print is reflected in the contradictory predictions made about the future of the printed book and of printed forms in general. The question has been the subject for volumes such as *The Future of the Book* (Nunberg, 1996). The enthusiasts for electronic technology are not ambivalent, and they sometimes predict the end of the book, as Raymond Kurzweil (1999) does:

> ... [E]lectronic books [of the early 21st century] will have enormous advantages, with pictures that can move and interact with the user, increasingly intelligent search paradigms, simulated environments that the user can enter and explore, and vast quantities of accessible materials. Yet vital to its ability to truly make the paper book obsolete is that the essential qualities of paper and ink will have been fully matched. The book will enter obsolescence, although because of its long history and enormous installed base, it will linger for a couple of decades before reaching antiquity (pp. 297–298).

Sometimes the enthusiasts simply ignore print as they go on to imagine an era of pure and transparent electronic communication, characterized by interactive audio and video or even networked virtual reality. For example, some educators imagine a classroom in which books are replaced by virtual environments:

> Applications of virtual reality are being developed in such fields as architecture, medicine, and arcade games ... It is time to see how it could be applied to education and the development of virtual classes in the fullest sense as wraparound environments for learning where students as telepresences can see, hear, touch, and perhaps one day even smell and taste (Tiffin & Rajasingham, 1995, p. 7).

Nor are the critics of electronic writing always ambivalent. Some continue to insist on the division between literary and pragmatic communication—to argue that computers may be used for technical communication and for home entertainment, but that literature will continue to be printed. The novelist E. Annie Proulx claimed in the *New York Times* that "no one is going to read a novel on a twitchy little screen. Ever" (1994, p. A23). Taken literally, this claim is simply wrong. Such conventional novels as *Brave New World* and *Jurassic Park* have been digitized and read (or at least purchased) by an audience of hundreds or a few thousand. Such hypertext fictions as *afternoon* and *Victory Garden*, written exclusively for the twitchy little screen, have also won relatively small, but appreciative audiences. Proulx might be right, if we take her to mean that there will never be a mass audience for verbal fiction in this new medium, and in that case the scientific and literary communities would no longer share a space for publication or a forum for dialogue. Sometimes, too, critics will claim not to be Luddites, but only to be insisting on sensible limits to the computerization of culture: for example, Mark Slouka in *War of the Worlds: Cyberspace and the High-Tech Assault on Reality* (1995). Sometimes a critic will assert that no such limits are possible. In his *Gutenberg Elegies* (1994), Swen Birkerts assumed this fatalistic tone in discussing the eclipse of the printed book: "A change is upon us—nothing could be clearer. The printed word is part of a vestigial order that we are moving away from—by choice and by societal compulsion ... This shift is happening throughout our culture, away from patterns and habits of the printed page and toward a new world distinguished by its reliance on electronic communications" (p. 118). The inevitable was also lamentable: Birkerts spent much of his book, which was, after all, entitled an elegy, lamenting the passing of the traditional literary culture that he associated with print.

The questions that concern both the enthusiasts and the critics include: What is the nature of the challenge that digital media pose for print? Will digital media replace print? Does the advent of the computer announce a revolution in writing, or is the change less significant? Digital media may challenge traditions of writing at several levels. There is a challenge to print as a technology for delivering alphabetic text and a challenge to the genres and structures that we associate with printed books, newspapers, magazines, and so on. When Proulx complains about reading novels on "twitchy" screens, she assumes that the genre of the novel, which developed in the age of print, will continue to exist in its linear form and denies that computer screens will be the space in which such forms are read. She discounts the challenge that new electronic media might pose to the structure of fiction and nonfiction. In fact, linear forms such as the novel and the essay may or may not flourish in an era of digital media. Writers generally still write with a single, fixed order in mind, but the popularity of the World Wide Web and CD-ROM and DVD is leading some to exploring more fluid structures.

Digital media may also challenge alphabetic writing in any form—in a printed book or on a computer screen. Although printed books, newspapers, and magazines can and do combine graphics with text, new digital media seem often to favor graphics at the expense of text. If in the 1980s, the personal computer was a word processor, it has now become an image processor, which can manipulate and deliver static graphics, animation, and video (as well as audio). Computer graphics are refashioning conventional television and film. The question is whether alphabetic texts can compete effectively with the visual and aural sensorium that surrounds us. And if prose itself is being forced to renegotiate its cultural role, then the printed book is doubly challenged. It is not just that the computer as hypertext can challenge print as a mode of writing; it is also that the printed book is associated so strongly with verbal text. If prose loses its cultural warrant, then who will care about printed books, which are mostly prose? Can printed picture books hope to compete effectively with broadcast television and interactive video? Perhaps printed books will survive as the place for purely verbal texts and for that very reason be pushed to the cultural margin. Prose might in fact have a brighter future, if it could free itself from print technology. In electronic hypertext, for example, prose might combine with audiovisual presentation and perhaps share in the cultural prosperity of the image.

A whole set of cultural questions is connected with the changing status of the word. The importance of verbal literacy in education, the traditional canon, sex and violence on television, censorship in various media—these are all disputes over the appropriate balance between word and image. Much of what American conservatives think of as the "culture wars" is in fact an argument about modes of representation. The number and complexity of these questions suggest that we are at a critical moment in the history of writing. This moment is worth our consideration, no matter how the current tensions between print and digital technology are resolved in the coming decades.

Although it is very difficult to avoid all prediction (in practice, to avoid writing in the future tense), it should nevertheless be possible to resist the impulse to unify—to avoid merging individual predictions into a synthesis that is supposed to represent the one, true future. We should instead treat the predictions of both the enthusiasts and the critics as part of the ambiguous present that constitutes the late age of print. Their predictions reflect the struggles among various cultural factions that are trying to work out the relationship of digital technology to its predecessors. Although we need not try to decide whether the printed book will in fact disappear in 10, 20, or 50 years, we can try to understand the current relationship between print and digital media, which may show us why the future of the printed book seems so uncertain and the future of digital media so bright.

THE OLD AND THE NEW IN DIGITAL WRITING

In this late age of print, digital writing seems both old and new. Although we began in the 1980s by using word processors and electronic photocomposition to improve the production of printed books and typed documents, it has now become clear that we can use the computer to provide a writing surface with conventions different from those of print. A World Wide Web page already differs in some important ways from a conventional printed page. Electronic text takes on shapes that Web designers and other digital authors deem appropriate to the computer's capacity to structure and present information. In this respect authors and designers are performing the same service for electronic technology that printers performed in the decades following Gutenberg's invention.

As early as the 1450s and 1460s, Gutenberg and his colleagues were able to achieve the mass production of books without sacrificing quality. Gutenberg's 42-line Bible does not seem to us today to have been a radical experiment in a new technology. It is not poorly executed or uncertain in form. The earliest incunabula are already examples of a perfected technique, and there remains little evidence from the period of experimentation that must have preceded the production of these books. Gutenberg's Bible can hardly be distinguished from the work of a good scribe, except perhaps that the spacing and hyphenation are more regular than a scribe could achieve. Because early printers tried to make their books identical to fine manuscripts, they used the same thick letter forms, the same ligatures and abbreviations, and the same layout on the page (Meggs, 1998, p. 63). It took a few generations for printers to realize that they could create a new writing space with thinner letters, fewer abbreviations, and less ink.

The parallel to Gutenberg's period can be overstated, however, for Gutenberg inaugurated the new age of print, rather than the late age of the manuscript. At its invention, the printed book seemed familiar and yet was in many ways new, whereas the computer seems utterly new and revolutionary, when, at least as a writing technology, it still has much in common with its predecessors. Electronic writing is mechanical and precise like printing, organic and evolutionary like handwriting, visually eclectic like hieroglyphics and picture writing. On the other hand, electronic writing is fluid and dynamic to a greater degree than previous technologies. The coming of this new form in fact helps us to understand the choices, the specializations, that the earlier printed book entailed.

Those who tell us that the computer will never replace the printed book point to the physical advantages: the book is portable, inexpensive, and easy to read, whereas the computer is hard to carry and expensive and needs a source of electricity. The computer screen is not as comfortable a reading surface as the page, so that reading for long periods promotes eyestrain. Finally—and this point is always included—you cannot read your computer screen in bed. However, electronic technology continues to evolve. Machines have diminished dramatically in size and in price during the past 40 years, and computer screens are becoming more readable. Some portable computers already have the bulk and weight of notebooks, and it is not hard to imagine one whose screen is as legible as a printed page. In fact, specialized devices styled as electronic books are already commercially available (= > p. 79). We can also envision a system whose flatscreen display is built into the top of a desk or lectern (like those used in the Middle Ages and the Renaissance), where the writer can work directly by applying a light pen instead of typing at a keyboard.

Ease of use is only one measure of a writing technology. The great advantage of the first printed books was not that you could read them in bed. Gutenberg might well have been appalled at the thought of someone taking his beautiful folio-sized Bible to bed. For generations, many important printed books remained imposing volumes that had to be read on bookstands, so that people often read (and wrote) standing up. Mass production by the letterpress did eventually make books cheaper and more plentiful, and this change was crucial. However, the fixity and permanence that printing seemed to give to the written word was just as important in changing the nature of literacy. By contrast, our culture regards digital texts as fluid and multiple structures. If this fluidity seems to offer new possibilities of expression, then writers and readers will put up with some inconveniences to use it.

In place of the static pages of the printed book, the computer can maintain text as a dynamic network of verbal and visual elements. Although writers have been exploiting these dynamic networks for two decades, as long as we are living in the late age of print, electronic writing will seem to be in its infancy. The electronic incunabula include computer-controlled photocomposition, the word processor, the textual database, the electronic bulletin board and mail, and now Web sites. Word processors already demonstrate the flexibility of electronic writing in allowing writers to copy, compare, and discard text with the touch of a few buttons. Change is the rule in the computer, stability the exception, and, as was already realized in the 1980s, it is the rule of change that makes the word processor so useful. On the other hand, most writers have enthusiastically accepted the word processor precisely because it does not challenge their conventional notion of writing. The word processor is an aid for making perfect printed copy: the goal is still ink on paper. Like computer-controlled photocomposition, the word processor is not so much a tool for writing, as it is a tool for typography. (On the interplay between fluidity and fixity in word processing, see Balestri, 1988; Heim, 1987; Mullins, 1988.) The word processor treats text like a scroll, a roll of pages sewn together at the ends, while its visual structures are still typographic. A conventional word processor does not treat the text as a network of verbal ideas. It does not contain a map of the ways in which the text may be read; it does not record or act on the semantic structure of the text. Other forms of electronic writing do all these things, making the text from the writer's point of view a network of verbal elements and from the reader's point of view a texture of possible readings. They permit the reader to share in the dynamic process of writing and to alter the voice of the text.

REFASHIONING THE VOICE OF THE TEXT

Writing in the classical and Western traditions is supposed to have a voice and therefore to speak to its reader. A printed book generally speaks with a single voice and assumes a consistent character, a persona, before its audience. In today's economy of writing, a printed book must do more: it must speak to an economically viable or culturally important group of readers. Our culture has used printing to help define and empower new groups of readers: for example, the middle-class audience for the 19th-century British novel. But this achievement is also a limitation. An author must either write for one of the existing groups or seek to forge a new one, and the task of forging a new readership requires great talent and good luck. Even a new readership, brought together by shared interests in the author's message, must be addressed with consistency. Few publishers would accept a book that combined two vastly different subject matters: say, European history and the marine biology of the Pacific, or Eskimo folklore and the principles of actuarial science. It might even be difficult to publish a book that was part fiction and part nonfiction—not a historical novel, a genre that is popular and has a well-defined audience, but, let us say, a combination of essays and short stories that treat the same historical events. We might say that these hypothetical books lack unity. Yet our definition of textual unity comes from the published work we have read, or more generally, from the current divisions of academic, literary, and scientific disciplines, which themselves both depend on and reinforce the economics of publishing. The material in a book must simply be homogeneous by the standard of some book-buying audience.

This strict requirement of unity and homogeneity is relatively recent. In the Middle Ages, unrelated texts were often bound together, and texts were often added in the available space in a volume years or decades later. Even in the early centuries of printing, it was not unusual to put unrelated works between two covers (=> p. 77). On the other hand, it seems natural to think of any book, written or printed, as a verbal unit. For the book is already a physical unit; its pages are sewn or glued together and then bound into a portable whole. Should not all the words inside proceed from one unifying idea and stand in the same rhetorical relationship to the reader?

Our literate culture is choosing to exploit electronic technology in part to refashion the unified rhetorical voice of the text. Michael Heim (1987) has written, for example, that "Fragments, reused material, the trails and intricate pathways of 'hypertext,' as Ted Nelson terms it, all these advance the disintegration of the centering voice of contemplative thought" (p. 220). An electronic text may fracture the single voice of the printed text and speak in different registers to different readers. An electronic encyclopedia may address both the educated novice and the expert, just as the same corporate Web site may serve for general public relations, stockholder education, and even sales and marketing. In the ideal, if not in practice, an electronic text can tailor itself to each reader's needs, and the reader can make choices in the very act of reading.

Until recently, the printing press was a classic industrial machine, producing large quantities of identical texts. McLuhan (1972) called printing the first example of the assembly line and mass production (p. 124). Computer-controlled photocomposition has made printing more flexible, helping publishers to produce books more quickly and to target well-defined markets. However, hypertextual writing can go further, because it can change for each reader and with each reading. Authors can exploit the dynamic quality of hypertext to alter the nature of an audience's shared experience in reading. If all the readers of *Bleak House* or *Ulysses* could discuss these works on the assumption that they had all read the same words, no two readers of a hyperfiction can make that assumption. They can only assume that they have traveled in the same textual network. Fixed printed texts can be made into a literary canon in order to promote cultural unity. In the 19th and early 20th centuries, when the canon of literature was often taken as the definition of a liberal education, the goal was to give everyone the experience of reading the same texts—Shakespeare, Milton, Dickens, and so on. This ideal of cultural unity through a shared literary inheritance, which has received so many assaults in the 20th century, must now suffer further by the introduction of new forms of highly individualized writing and reading.

Critics accuse the computer of promoting homogeneity in our society, of producing uniformity through automation, but electronic reading and writing seem to have just the opposite effect. European and North American culture exploited the printing press as a great homogenizer of writing and of the literary audience, whereas that same culture now seems eager to use electronic technologies to differentiate genres and audiences as well as economic markets. In our current world of publication, electronic texts—Web sites, hyperfictions, CD-ROMs and DVDs for entertainment and education—are offered to us as fragmentary and potential texts, each as a network of self-contained units rather than as an organic whole in the tradition of the 19th-century novel or essay. This fragmentation need not imply mere disintegration, however. Elements in the electronic writing space need not be simply chaotic; they may instead function in a perpetual state of reorganization, forming patterns that are in constant danger of breaking down and recombining. This tension may lead to a definition of effective writing that supplements or replaces our traditional notion of the unity of voice and of analytic argument. What unity there is in an electronic text derives from the perpetually shifting relationship among its verbal elements. What unity there is in the audience for that text comes from the momentary constellation of different economic and cultural "special interests."

REFASHIONING THE WRITING SPACE

In addition to redefining the voice of the text, our culture is also redefining the visual and conceptual space of writing. Indeed, the spatial metaphor for writing and reading is as culturally powerful now as it has ever been. Cyberspace has become a term for characterizing almost anything to do with the Internet or electronic communication. When we browse the World Wide Web, we think of ourselves as traveling to "visit" the sites, although in fact the servers are delivering pages of information to our computer. The Internet and the Web, CD-ROMS and DVDs, and computer RAM constitute a field for recording, organizing, and presenting texts—a contemporary writing space that refashions the earlier spaces of the papyrus roll, the codex, and the printed book. The continuous flow of words and pages in the book is supplanted in electronic space by abrupt changes of direction and tempo, as the user interacts with a web page or other interface.

Each writing space is a material and visual field, whose properties are determined by a writing technology and the uses to which that technology is put by a culture of readers and writers. A writing space is generated by the interaction of material properties and cultural choices and practices. Moreover, each space depends for its meaning on previous spaces or on contemporary spaces against which it competes. Each fosters a particular understanding both of the act of writing and of the product, the written text, and this understanding expresses itself in writing styles, genres, and literary theories. The writing space is also a space for reading, as Roger Chartier reminds us (Chartier, 1994, p. 2; 1995): communities of readers help to define the properties of the writing space by the demands they place on the text and the technology. For ancient Greece and Rome, the space for writing and reading was the inner surface of a continuous roll, which the writer divided into columns—not because papyrus had to be used this way, but because ancient culture made this choice. The space of the papyrus roll defined itself in relation to earlier oral forms of communication and to stone or wood inscriptions (=> p. 77). For medieval handwriting and modern printing, the space was the white surface of the page, particularly in a bound volume, which was again a cultural decision of both the Latin and Byzantine Middle Ages. Initially, in late antiquity, the handwritten codex was in competition with the space of the papyrus roll and offered advantages that must have seemed important to contemporary readers. In the 15th century, the printed book defined itself in relation to the manuscript codex that it sought to displace. The space of electronic writing is both the computer screen, where text is displayed, and the electronic memory, in which text is stored. Our culture has chosen to fashion these technologies into a writing space that is animated, visually complex, and malleable in the hands of both writer and reader. In this late age of print, however, writers and readers still often conceive of text as located in the space of a printed book, and they conceive of the electronic writing space as a refashioning of the older space of print.

Because writing is such a highly valued individual act and cultural practice, the writing space itself is a potent metaphor. In the act of writing, the writer externalizes his or her thoughts. The writer enters into a reflective and reflexive relationship with the written page, a relationship in which thoughts are bodied forth. Writing, even writing on a computer screen, is a material practice, and it becomes difficult for a culture to decide where thinking ends and the materiality of writing begins, where the mind ends and the writing space begins. With any technique of writing—on stone or clay, on papyrus or paper, and on the computer screen—the writer may come to regard the mind itself as a writing space. The behavior of the writing space becomes a metaphor for the human mind as well as for human social interaction. Such cultural metaphors are in general redefinitions of earlier metaphors, so that in examining the history of writing, and in particular electronic writing today, we should always ask: How does this writing space refashion its predecessor? How does it claim to improve on print's ability to make our thoughts visible and to constitute the lines of communication for our society?

2

Writing as Technology

It is not difficult to recognize the printing press, the typewriter, and the Linotype machine as technologies. These industrial-age means of book production were complex and to a degree self-activating or self-directing. The mechanization of writing began in the 15th century with the letter press itself, which was the first text "processor," the first technology of writing to duplicate words en masse. (On the development of printing, see Steinberg, 1959.) In replacing the scribe who formed letters one at a time, the press registered several pages of text onto a large sheet of paper with each impersonal pull. As McLuhan recognized in *The Gutenberg Galaxy* (1972), "the invention of typography ... provid[ed] the first uniformly repeatable commodity, the first assembly line, and the first mass-production" (p. 124). Printing had the additional virtue that it could produce books that were nearly identical to the best manuscripts: the press rivaled handwriting in quality while far surpassing it in quantity. Elizabeth Eisenstein (1983) noted that "[t]he absence of any apparent change in product was combined with a complete change in methods of production, giving rise to the paradoxical combination of seeming continuity with radical change" (p. 20). This paradox made the mechanization of the word easier to accept, and scholars in the 15th century immediately saw the advantages of this new technology. Gradually, over several generations, printing did change the visual character of the written page, making the writing space technically cleaner and clearer. The book had taken on a different and more modern look by the late 18th century. In the 19th and 20th, steam and electric presses, and automatic typesetting brought further mechanization, further distancing the human controller from the printing process and defining an industrial age of print. The computer in turn adds new flexibility to the rapidity and efficiency of printing. The computer's capacity to adjust the text to each user's needs, which is uncharacteristic of the classic industrial machine, derives from the unmechanical materials of electronic technology. The computer's central processor itself contains no gears or indeed any moving parts above the level of electrons, and even the mechanical components of a computer system, such as disk drives and printers, are characterized by rapid movement and fine control. The digital computer suggests a new definition of the machine, as a complex interrelation of logical as well as physical parts that, unlike the steam engine and the dynamo, processes information rather than producing power. If the printing press was the classic writing machine, the computer constitutes a technology of writing beyond mechanization, a postindustrial form of writing.

The medieval manuscript and ancient papyrus roll in turn represent technologies of writing before mechanization. These preindustrial technologies also required devices—pen and paper or parchment in the Middle Ages or reed pen and papyrus in the ancient world. Working from such raw materials as rags, animal skins, or plants to produce a finished book certainly required considerable technical knowledge. Still, the manuscripts were produced at the relatively slow pace of the scribe's hand, not the insistent rhythm of the machine, and we can see on each page the variations in size and shape of letters that indicate direct human production. The development of mechanical printing and now writing by computer has affected our view of these previous writing techniques. A medieval manuscript, rubricated and bound in leather, would perhaps have struck a Greek in Plato's time as a complicated and ingenious device. When we admire the manuscript as art, however, what we admire is the apparent negation of technology, the fact that the codex is not a printed book and therefore not the product of a machine.

There are good historical (as well as etymological) reasons, however, for broadening the definition of technology to include skills as well as machines. The Greek root of "technology" is *techne*, and for the Greeks a *techne* could be an art or a craft, "a set of rules, system or method of making or doing, whether of the useful arts, or of the fine arts" (Liddell & Scott, 1973, p. 1,785). In his dialogue the *Phaedrus*, Plato calls the alphabet itself a *techne*. He would also have called the ancient book composed of ink on papyrus a *techne*; even Homeric epic poetry was a *techne*, as was Greek tragedy. All the ancient arts and crafts had this in common: that the craftsman must develop a skill, a technical state of mind in using tools and materials. Ancient and modern writing are technologies in the sense that they are methods for arranging verbal ideas in a visual space. The writer always needs a surface on which to make his or her marks and a tool with which to make them, and these materials become part of the contemporary definition of writing. Writing with quill and parchment is a different skill from writing with a printing press, which in turn differs from writing with a computer. However, all writing entails method, the intention of the writer to arrange verbal ideas in a space for later examination by a reader. In *Orality and Literacy* (1982) Walter Ong argued that writing is "interiorized" and that the process of interiorization makes it difficult for us to recognize writing itself as a technology (pp. 81–82).

Our technical relationship to the writing space is always with us as readers and writers. Literacy is, among other things, the realization that language can have a visual as well as an aural dimension, that one's words can be recorded and shown to others who are not present, perhaps not even alive, at the time of the recording. Literate people know that words can be placed in a visual space and have continued existence in that space. They always know this. Even when they are speaking, they know that their words can be written down. Students of culture as uncongenial as Walter Ong and Jacques Derrida have insisted that writing is a constant presence in our mental life. Cultures with a long tradition of literacy develop a standard literary language, so that men and women reveal their literacy when they are speaking as well as writing. Illiterates are denied access to that language, while those educated in the tradition tend to speak in a combination of colloquial and literary terms. They speak, as they write, in a variety of styles and levels, and they often structure their speech as they do their writing, talking in sentences and even paragraphs. They write in their mind as well as on paper or at a keyboard; indeed, they are writing whenever they think or verbalize in that methodical way characterized by writing.

There may be many such literacies at any given historical moment. A cultural elite may succeed in defining a high literacy, whose *techne* excludes various minorities. North American culture, for example, was relatively successful in maintaining such a high literacy until perhaps the Second World War: this *techne* was embodied in the literary canon that some traditionalists still wish to affirm as the basis for education. Minorities, however, may develop their own *technes*, their own internalized literacies. Spoken language can itself be a *techne*, for it can require method—most obviously in the varieties of oral poetry and storytelling that have been practiced for thousands of years and are still important today in much of the developing world. (On Homeric oral poetry, see Lord, 1968; Thomas, 1992, pp. 29–51. On the many other varieties of oral poetry, see Finnegan, 1977.) The oral poet applies method to language in order to create verse forms and story structures, although in this case the structures must be able to be appreciated by listening rather than by reading. The oral poet is a writer, who writes exclusively in the minds of his or her audience.

Despite its apparent immediacy, however, oral poetry is no more natural than writing, just as writing with pen and paper is no more natural, no less technological, than writing on a computer screen. Although the computer is a more complicated and fragile device than a pen, we could not isolate ourselves from technology by reverting to older methods of writing. The production of today's pens and paper also require a sophisticated manufacturing process. Without electricity, industrial organization, and networks of transportation and distribution, we could not provide ourselves with adequate supplies of these simple writing materials. It is not the complexity of the devices that matters so much as the technical or literate frame of mind. Writing technologies are never external agents that invade and occupy the minds of their users. These technologies are natural or naturalized only in the sense that they are constituted by the interaction of physical materials and human practices. No technology, not even the apparently autonomous computer, can ever function as a writing space in the absence of human writers and readers. And what Walter Ong characterized as the literate mind is simply another name for the collective decisions shared among writers and readers about how to exploit their materials in order to communicate.

WRITING TECHNOLOGIES AND MATERIAL CULTURE

As Christina Haas (1996) puts it: "Writing is situated in the material world in a number of ways. It always occurs in a material setting, employs material tools, and results in material artifacts" (p. 4). Roger Chartier has made the argument repeatedly in his work on the history of the book:

> "Whether they are in manuscript or in print, books are objects whose forms, if they cannot impose the sense of the texts that they bear, at least command the uses that can invest them and the appropriations to which they are susceptible. Works and discourses exist only when they become physical realities ... This means that ... keen attention should be paid to the technical, visual, and physical devices that organize the reading of writing when writing becomes a book" (Chartier, 1994, pp. viii–ix).

What Chartier says of books and manuscripts is certainly also true of digital technology (see also Duguid, 1996). The materiality of writing matters, as much for electronic writing as for earlier forms. Electronic writing still requires our physical interactions with terrestrial materials—with the keyboard, the mouse, and the computer screen. Despite the dreams of cyberpunk authors and virtual reality enthusiasts, repetitive stress injuries should serve as a reminder that computers are physical entities. Electronic writing is always involved in material culture and in contemporary economics. Computers are tangible objects with aesthetic and social significance, and digital devices and software are objects of important economic exchange. A single software program, an operating system, has made one man perhaps the richest private citizen in the world, but more important has had a significant impact on economic activity throughout the developed world.

Electronic writing may also be virtual, yet all previous writing technologies were virtual as well, in the sense that they invited writers and readers to participate in an abstract space of signs. This virtual or conceptual writing space forms a continuum with the material space of writing: it is both a reflection of contemporary materials and techniques and an expression of our culture's ambitions for its writing. Just as new digital media refashion the material conditions of print and handwriting, so the computer's virtuality refashions the writing space of the printed book and the manuscript. The electronic writing space may seem to be severed from the material world in a way that the space of print was not. Enthusiasts for the electronic writing space often promote as revolutionary its dynamic and apparently autonomous character—the fact that Web pages and multimedia applications can act as well as react, redefining themselves in ways that neither the author nor the reader can necessarily predict in advance. Yet those actions and reactions are grounded in the physics and computer science of the technology and are the result of specific interventions on the part of human writers (or programmers) and readers (or users). Our literate culture is simply using the new tools provided by digital technology to reconfigure the relationship between the material practices of writing and the ideal of writing that these practices express. It remains as true for the computer as for earlier technologies that the materiality of writing "must be acknowledged to fully appreciate the nature of literate acts" (Haas, 1996, p. 3). (For a discussion of materiality and theories of language and writing in the 20th century, see Johanna Drucker's *The Visible Word*, 1994, particularly pp. 9–47.)

Chartier reminds us that writing never exists only in the abstract:

> "Readers and hearers, in point of fact, are never confronted with abstract or ideal texts detached from all materiality; they manipulate or perceive objects and forms whose structures and modalities govern their reading (or their

hearing), thus the possible comprehension of the text read (or heard)" (Chartier, 1994, p. 3).

Each technology of writing involves different materials or different ways of deploying the writing materials, and these differences are significant. This is not to suggest, however, that the material conditions of writing determine in an exclusive fashion how a literate culture will read and write its texts. The relationship of the material techniques and the nature of writing—what Haas (1996) calls the Technology Question (pp. 3–23)—is far subtler and more interesting (see also Grusin, 1996). The very materiality of writing binds writing firmly to human practices and therefore to cultural choices. The technical and the cultural dimensions of writing are so intimately related that it is not useful to try to separate them: together they constitute writing as a technology. The technology of ancient writing is not only the papyrus, the ink, and the techniques of making book rolls; it is also the styles and genres of ancient writing and the social and political practices of ancient rhetoric. The technology of modern writing includes not only the techniques of printing, but also the practices of modern science and bureaucracy and the economic and social consequences of print literacy. If personal computers and palmtops, browsers and word processors, are part of our contemporary technology of writing, so are the uses to which we put this hardware and software. So too is the rhetoric of revolution or disaster that enthusiasts and critics weave around the digital hardware and software.

It is not a question of seeing writing as an external technological force that influences or changes cultural practice; instead, writing is always a part of culture. It is probably best to understand all technologies in this way: technologies do not determine the course of culture or society, because they are not separate agents that can act on culture from the outside. Yet the rhetoric of technological determinism remains common today. Popular writers often seem to suggest that technologies, especially digital information technologies, are agents in this sense. The World Wide Web, virtual reality, or computers are said to revolutionize our society, our economy, and even the way we think. More substantial writers such as McLuhan and Ong can also sound like technological determinists: McLuhan when in *Understanding Media* (1964) he explores media as "extensions of man", and Ong when he claims in *Orality and Literacy* (1982) that writing restructures consciousness. The very title of Elizabeth Eisenstein's massive book on the age of print, *The Printing Press as an Agent of Change* (1979), suggests that she too is guilty of technological determinism. On the other hand, it is possible to understand print technology is an agent of change without insisting that it works in isolation or in opposition to other aspects of culture. Even the Marxist sociologist of media, Raymond Williams, warned us to avoid economic or social determinism, just as we should avoid technological determinism (1975, pp. 130).

Individuals and whole cultures do mold techniques and devices to their own purposes, but the material properties of such techniques and devices also impose limitations on their possible uses. There are many things we cannot do with contemporary computers, even things that some would obviously like to do. For example, artificial intelligence has not provided us machines with the capacity to write stories or create fully autonomous graphic worlds, though many technophiles would like to have them. It also seems that a technique or device can render certain social constructions easier and or even possible. The hardware and software of the Internet made it possible to construct the World Wide Web. Our culture chose to turn the Web into a carnival of commercial and self-promotional Web sites, but that carnival would not be possible without the underlying hardware and software protocols. Yet even this way of putting it seems to create a false dichotomy between devices ("hard" technology) and social uses. Even in their brief period of development, the hardware and software of the Internet have clearly changed in response to social and economic pressures, and these social and economic pressures respond in turn to each new technical possibility. The open architecture of the World Wide Web allowed individuals to create sites and add them to the Web without the approval of any authority. This openness led to erotic Web sites, which in turn led to calls in the United States to block such sites because children might visit them. Some politicians wanted to censor these sites by law, and the ensuing struggle has also led to the development of software filters to allow parents to block certain sites. Wherever we start in such a chain of cause and effect, we can identify an interaction between technical qualities and social constructions—an interaction so intimate that it is hard to see where the technical ends and the social begins. When I speak of a technology of writing throughout this book, I will in general mean not just the hard technology, but the sum of the technical and social interactions that constitute a writing system. It is the contemporary technology of digital writing in this broad sense that we are trying to characterize.

In this characterization, the material properties remain significant. The properties of handwriting, of print, or of digital writing do each seem to favor certain kinds of expression and to prejudice others. The printed book favors linear writing; the computer makes associative linking easier. A technology, as it has been culturally constructed, can predispose us toward a particular definition of "natural" writing. Thus, if a writer chooses to display fixed, linear prose on a computer screen, she is working "against the grain" of the technology, just as Lawrence Sterne in the 18th or the dadaists and other avant-gardes in the 20th century have worked against the medium of print to create highly associative prose. The very fact that such writers exploit the technology in other than its "natural" mode gives their work its significance. Even in these cases, however, we do not have to argue that linear writing is inherently natural to print. The linear character of print is the outcome of the constant interaction between the properties of the printed book and the decisions that Western authors and readers have made about how to exploit those properties. In other words, we can reject the attempt to isolate the technical from the social aspect of technologies of writing, but we can still examine how these techniques and materials have been deployed by writers and readers at various cultural moments. Linear writing is appropriate to print technology both because the printed page readily accommodates linear text and because our culture expects that printed prose should be linear. Other styles may be appropriate to digital technology, where software systems like the World Wide Web are both expressions of and influences on our changing attitudes toward writing.

ECONOMIES OF WRITING

Each culture and each period has had its own complex economy of writing, a dynamic relationship among materials, techniques, genres, and cultural attitudes and uses. The earliest economies flourished in Mesopotamia and in Egypt, where complex word-syllable scripts were recorded on stone, clay, or papyrus (see Gaur, 1984; Gelb, 1963; Jensen, 1969; Sampson, 1985). The ancient Greeks and Romans borrowed both the materials and the elements of their writing economy: the Greek alphabet was taken from the Phoenicians, and papyrus from Egypt served as the chief writing material for the Greeks and the Romans. The ancient book was a roll, consisting of sheets of papyrus glued together at the ends. The paged book or codex, which came into use in the 2nd and 3rd centuries A.D., opened a range of new possibilities for writing, by offering a space both more varied and more accessible than that of the roll (See Chartier, 1995, pp. 18–20; Reynolds & Wilson, 1978, pp. 30–32) (=> p. 78). The codex was put to more sophisticated use in the Western European economy of writing. In the Middle Ages parchment provided a more durable and more attractive writing surface than papyrus, which in any case became hard to obtain from Egypt. Paper was introduced from the Far East as a cheaper replacement for parchment in the later Middle Ages. Although not as tough as parchment, paper made from rags could be produced in greater quantities and could therefore supply a growing demand for reading materials (see Febvre & Martin, 1971, pp. 39–60. See also Gaur, 1984, pp. 44–47). With these new materials, medieval scribes slowly refashioned the writing space they had inherited from the ancients; they employed word division, punctuation, rubrication (decorated initial letters), headings, and letter styles to organize the text visually on the page. They began to insert critical notes and glosses into the margins of the text, sometimes in several layers. In some scholarly medieval codices, the page became a web of text and interpretation, tradition and innovation. Finally, the invention of printing in the 15th century initiated the modern economy of writing with its highly organized and standardized space. During each of these periods, there have been numerous secondary technologies as well: wax tablets, chalkboards, typewriters, stenographs, dictaphones, and so on—each fulfilling needs that could not be easily met by the dominant technology (see, for example, Rouse & Rouse, 1989).

When in the history of writing a new technology appears, it may supplement an established technology or replace it. Papyrus was replaced in the Middle Ages by parchment and paper. In the late 19th and early 20th centuries, the typewriter replaced handwriting for business communications. At the same time American society was beginning to accept women into the work force so that the change created secretarial jobs for young women, who took the place of male clerks (see Zuboff, *In the Age of the Smart Machine*, 1988, pp. 115–116). Now the word processor has replaced the typewriter. Whenever a dominant technology is challenged, there may be a major refashioning of the culture's writing space. The three dominant technologies since ancient times, the papyrus roll, the codex, and the printed book, each participated in the fashioning of a rather different writing space. When the codex replaced the roll, it refashioned the writing space from the still relatively oral space of ancient culture to the progressively more visual and less oral space of medieval writing. When the printed book supplanted and marginalized the codex, the writing space took on the qualities of linearity, replicability, and fixity that we have associated with the printed book. Electronic and digital technology are helping to refashion the writing space again. In the late age of print, this refashioning is not complete, and we are now experiencing the tensions and inconsistencies that come from attempts either to reconcile the two spaces of print and digital technology or definitively to replace the one with the other.

In its role as a great refashioner, electronic writing is reintroducing characteristics that have belonged to a variety of marginal techniques of the past. Electronic writing shares with the wax tablet or chalkboard the quality of rapid and easy change. It shares with the typewriter its keyboard (at least at present), its method of discrete selection of alphabetic elements, and its mechanical uniformity; with improvements in speech recognition, electronic writing systems can function like a tape recorder in taking input through a microphone. The computer can serve as a copier, a note pad, a calendar, or a teletype machine. In fact, it is hard to think of a marginal technology in the history of writing that the computer cannot imitate, just as it is hard to think of a dominant technology whose elements the computer does not borrow and reinterpret. Electronic writing may therefore participate in the restructuring of our whole economy of writing. Of greatest importance, however, is the way in which our literate culture is using the computer to refashion the printed book, which, as the most recent dominant technology, is the one most open to challenge.

REMEDIATION

In about the 8th century B.C., the Greeks began to refashion the space of oral mythology and heroic legend into the more precise and linear space of the papyrus roll (and stone or wooden inscription), a process that, according to Eric Havelock (1982), lasted hundreds of years. In late antiquity the shift from papyrus roll to codex refashioned the space again, making more effective use of the two-dimensional surface to deploy text. In Western Europe the shift from handwritten codex to printed book was another such refashioning, and the shift to electronic writing is yet another. We might call each such shift a "remediation," in the sense that a newer medium takes the place of an older one, borrowing and reorganizing the characteristics of writing in the older medium and reforming its cultural space. Writing on papyrus remediated oral communication by involving the eye as well as the ear and so giving the words a different claim to reality. The other shifts too blatantly or subtly changed the terms on which we as readers approach the text and its mode of representing the world. Remediation involves both homage and rivalry, for the new medium imitates some features of the older medium, but also makes an implicit or explicit claim to improve on the older one.

Remediation is a process of cultural competition between or among technologies. For centuries, the Greeks and Romans conceived of their technology of alphabetic writing on papyrus roll in a dialectic tension with the oral tradition that writing only partly replaced. Ancient prose, even philosophy and history, was often highly rhetorical, as if the writing were still trying to imitate and improve on oral presentation. The shift from codex to papyrus roll was less problematic, with the result that the codex remediated the roll almost out of existence in a few centuries. In the Renaissance the printed book remediated the manuscript by appearing to provide the same visual space as the manuscript with the added benefits of mass production (= > p. 78). Over centuries, however, the printed book was a significant refashioning that defined a space in which fixity and accuracy were more highly prized than perhaps ever before.

Digital technology is turning out to be one of the more traumatic remediations in the history of Western writing. One reason is that digital technology changes the "look and feel" of writing and reading. A printed book could and did at first look like a manuscript, its appearance changing gradually over several decades. Chartier (1995) argues that the current shift from print to electronic technology, which he calls a revolution, entails a change greater than the one from manuscript to print:

> "Our current revolution is obviously more extensive than Gutenberg's. It modifies not only the technology for reproduction of the text, but even the materiality of the object that communicates the text to readers.... The substitution of screen for codex is a far more radical transformation because it changes methods of organization, structure, consultation, even the appearance of the written word.... The present revolution has only one precedent in the West: the substitution of the codex for the *volumen*—of the book composed of quires for the book in the form of a roll—during the first centuries of the Christian era" (pp. 15, 18).

Yet, until the 1980s, it was not apparent to most readers and writers that the computer was a writing technology at all. Before the advent of word processing on personal computers, our literate culture regarded computers as "number-crunching" tools for engineers or as electronic filing cabinets for bureaucratic data. In the past two decades, however, computers have been recognized not only as writing technologies, but as media for popular entertainment and expression, which we are using to refashion visual as well as verbal communication.

Remediation is not limited to technologies of writing. Richard Grusin and I have examined the ways in which new visual media, such as computer graphics, virtual reality, and the World Wide Web, define themselves by borrowing from, paying homage to, critiquing, and refashioning their predecessors, principally television, film, photography, and painting (Bolter &

Grusin, 1999). Computer games remediate film by styling themselves as "interactive movies"; virtual reality remediates film as well as perspective painting; digital photography remediates the analog photograph. The World Wide Web absorbs and refashions almost every previous visual and textual medium, including television, film, radio, and print. Furthermore, older media can remediate newer ones within the same media economy. Today, the traditional cinema is attempting to maintain its status by employing computer graphics in conventional linear films. And television is making such extensive use of new media that TV screens often look like pages from the World Wide Web. Remediation is a characteristic process not only for contemporary media, but for all visual media at least since the Renaissance with its invention of linear-perspective painting. Each medium seems to follow this pattern of borrowing and refashioning other media, and rivalry as well as homage seems always to be at work.

Furthermore, since the Renaissance, our culture has had two apparently contradictory expectations for its visual media. In one sense the goal of representation has been transparent presentation. The medium is supposed to function as a window through which the viewer can see the objects represented. That was in fact exactly how the artist and writer Leon Battista Alberti characterized linear-perspective painting in his treatise "On Painting": as a window on the world (Alberti, 1972, p. 55). Western artists and audiences have generally treated perspective painting, photography, film, and now virtual reality and three-dimensional computer graphics as transparent media. On the other hand, artists and their audiences do not always want the medium to disappear; they often want to be made conscious of and even surrounded by media. Instead of transparency, they strive for *hypermediacy*, an intense awareness of and even reveling in the medium. Contemporary television, for example, is often hypermediated, although it can sometimes function as a transparent medium as well. Among new digital media, the World Wide Web is most often characterized by hypermediacy. The same medium can strive for transparency in one case and hyper- mediacy in another, and in general today we swing back and forth between a desire for transparent contact with the ostensibly real (unmediated) world and a fascination with the possibilities that media offer us. Because the number of old and new, analog and digital, media available to us today is very great, we live in an environment that is conducive to hypermediacy. Yet the desire for a transparent medium remains strong.

What all media and media forms have in common for our culture is the promise of immediacy. Transparent media promise to disappear and leave us in contact with the unmediated world, although it is a promise that they can never entirely fulfill. Hypermediated media give up the attempt to present a world beyond themselves; instead, they offer themselves as immediate experiences. When one medium sets out to remediate another, it does so by claiming to do a better job. It can claim to be better at transparency. For example, virtual reality promises to be the ultimate transparent medium, better than painting or photography, because the viewer in virtual reality can actually step into the world viewed. Or the medium can promise a more elaborate hypermediacy, as World Wide Web sites do in combining painting, photography, graphic design, film, audio, and video into a sort of popular *Gesamtkunstwerk*. In either case the new medium is trying to convince us that it offers greater immediacy than its predecessors. Because our culture today is saturated with media, claims of greater immediacy are constantly being made, as new and older media vie for our attention.

The remediations of writing technologies are like those of visual media, particularly in the case of digital media where words and images combine and interact so freely (= > p. 47). Furthermore, throughout the 20th century, print has engaged in contests of remediation with photography, film, and television. All these visual technologies are still remediating print, while digital technologies are working their remediations too. The best way to understand electronic writing today is to see it as the remediation of printed text, with its claim to refashioning the presentation and status of alphabetic writing itself. The qualities that distinguish electronic writing from print, flexibility and interactivity, become the bases of the enthusiasts' claim that the computer can improve on the printed book. For the enthusiasts, these qualities can make the experience of reading sometimes more transparently real, sometimes more hypermediated, but always more immediate. As we shall see, to say that electronic writing is flexible and interactive is to say that it is hypertextual.

3

Hypertext and the Remediation of Print

If a decade ago the concept of hypertext was esoteric, today with the enormous success of the World Wide Web, the concept, if not the name, has become common cultural knowledge. A typical Web page consists of text and graphics like a page in a magazine or illustrated book. Unlike in a book or magazine, however, phrases in the text or portions of the graphics on the Web page can be "hot": clicking on them will bring up a new page. One page can be linked electronically to many others (Fig 3.1). In one sense this linking is simply the electronic equivalent of the footnote used in printed books for hundreds of years. Instead of looking to the bottom of the page or the end of the book, the reader positions the cursor, and the computer retrieves and displays the reference. There is this important difference, however: the second Web page can also contain linked phrases that in turn lead the reader to other pages. The process can continue indefinitely as the reader moves through a textual space that, in the case of the World Wide Web, can extend throughout the Internet. Although in a printed book it would be intolerably pedantic to write footnotes to footnotes, in the computer we have already come to regard this layered writing and reading as natural. Furthermore, the second page is not necessarily subordinate to the first. One linked phrase may lead the reader to a longer, more elaborate page. All the individual pages may be of equal importance in the whole text, which becomes a network of interconnected writings.

Such a network is called a hypertext, and it is the creation and presentation of such hypertextual structures that seem to constitute a new form of writing. We use the computer as hypertext to write with symbols that have both an intrinsic and extrinsic significance. That is, the symbols have a

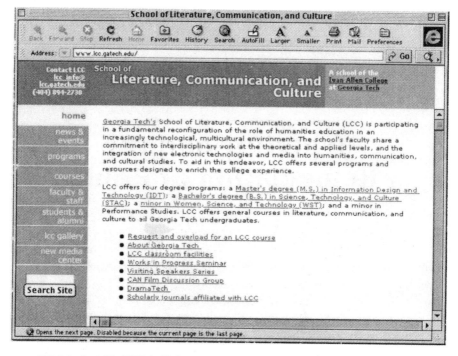

FIG 3.1   Each World Wide Web page is an episode in a global hypertext; the user can click on any linked word, phrase, or image to load a new page.

meaning that may be explained in words, but they also have meaning as links, as elements in a larger structure of verbal gestures. Both words and structures are visible, readable, and potentially writable in the electronic space. Web pages function as ordinary text, but they also function as places along a path.

Hypertextual links can serve many informational and rhetorical purposes, as George Landow (1997) and many others have recognized and as hundreds of thousands of Web sites demonstrate. Links can make the structure of the site transparent—with, for example, a list of links on the home page that functions as a menu to articulate for the reader the various areas of the Web site. Links can also function like printed footnotes to provide additional information or to document what is on the page. Such links may be circular, so that the reader returns to the original page after examining the note. Associative links can take the reader to other Web sites to explore related topics. The principal task of authors of hypertextual fiction on the

Web or in stand-alone form is to use links to define relationships among textual elements, and these links constitute the rhetoric of the hypertext.

What is true of the World Wide Web and of most stand-alone systems is that hypertext consists of discrete units—pages, paragraphs, graphics—and the links between them. We tend to conceive of hypertext spatially: the links constitute a path through a virtual space and the reader becomes a visitor or traveler in that space. We say that the reader or user "visits" Web pages in California, Germany, or Japan, when in fact we could just as easily say that the pages come to her. Technically, her computer's browser contacts the server that holds the pages of text and graphics, which the server then transmits to her machine for display. The pages must all be stored, at least temporarily, on her machine in order to be displayed on her screen. When we browse, however, we turn the situation around metaphorically. We think of the pages themselves as floating in a virtual space, which we vaguely associate with the various physical locations of computers on the Internet. Despite its apparently ephemeral and ethereal quality, electronic writing maintains a sense of place in the physical world.

WORD PROCESSING AND TOPICAL WRITING

A writer working with a word processor spends much of her time entering words letter by letter, just as she did two decades ago at the typewriter. Revising is a different matter. With a word processor, writers can delete or replace an entire word; they can highlight phrases, sentences, or paragraphs. They can erase a sentence with a single keystroke; they can select a paragraph, cut it from its current location, and insert it elsewhere, even into another document. In using these facilities, the writer is thinking and writing in terms of verbal units or topics, whose meaning transcends their constituent words. The Greek word *topos* meant literally a place, and ancient rhetoric used the word to refer to commonplaces, conventional units or methods of thought. In the Renaissance, topics became headings that could be used to organize any field of knowledge, and these headings were sometimes set out in elaborate diagrams (see Ong, 1958, pp. 104–130). Our English word "topic" is still appropriate for the computer because its etymology suggests the spatial character of electronic writing. Topics exist in a writing space that is not only a visual surface but also a data structure in the computer. The programmers who designed word processors recognized the importance of topical writing, when they gave us operations for adding or deleting sentences and paragraphs as units. They did not, however, take the further step of allowing a writer to associate a name or a visual symbol with each topical unit, which would give the unit a conceptual identity.

A traditional word processor, which imitates the layout of the typed page, flattens the text and offers a writer little help in conceiving its evolving structure. Although the word processor allows the writer to define a verbal unit in order to move or delete it, the definition lasts only until the operation is complete. But if the word processor offers the writer only temporary access to her structure, outline processors make structure a permanent feature of the text. The writer can think globally about the text, by treating topics as unitary symbols and writing with those symbols, just as in a word processor one writes with words. In an outline processor, now often included as part of a word processing suite, the prose remains, but it is encased in a formally operative structure (Fig. 3.2). With a pen or typewriter, writing meant literally to form letters on a page, figuratively to create verbal structures. In an electronic writing system, the figurative process becomes a literal act. (In fact one recurrent strategy in the electronic refashioning of the space of typewriting and print is this turning of the figurative into the literal.) By defining topical symbols, such as headings in an outline, the writer can, like the programmer or the mathematician, abstract herself temporarily from the details of the prose. The value of this abstraction lies in seeing more clearly the structural skeleton of the text.

It is no accident that the computer can serve so successfully as an outline processor. The machine was designed to create and track such formal structures, which are important for all its various uses. The computer's memory and central processing unit are intricate hierarchies of electronic components. Layers of software in turn transform the machine's physical space of electronic circuits into a space of symbolic information. The electronic writing space is shaped by the objects that occupy it: a computer programmer forms her space by filling it with elements and then by connecting these elements as the program requires. Any symbol in the space can refer to another symbol by using its numerical address. Such pointers constitute the structure of computer programs, so that programming itself might be defined as the art of building symbolic structures in the space that the computer provides—a definition that makes programming itself a kind of writing.

One such programming structure, which represents hierarchy, is called a tree. Trees (and their relatives such as lists, stacks, and networks) are ubiquitous in programs that must record and track large bodies of information or information subject to frequent change. Tree diagrams, in which elements are

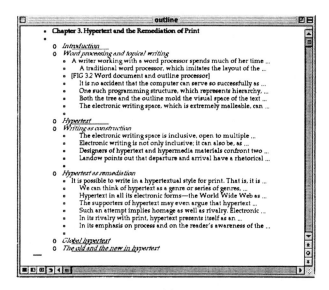

(a)

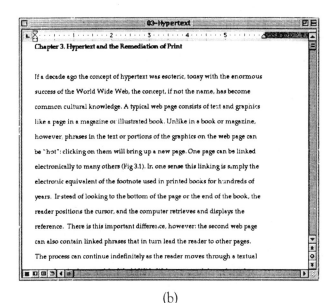

(b)

FIG. 3.2. (a) An outline processor can reveal or hide detail in a document; (b) a word processor flattens and obscures the structure of the document.

connected by branches as in a genealogical tree, have a long history in writing as well. They date back at least to the early Middle Ages and are not uncommon in medieval and Renaissance books, where they were used for the spatial arrangement of topics (Ong, 1958, pp. 74–83, 199–202, 314–318). A traditional outline is a strict hierarchy that can also be represented by a tree diagram.

Both the tree and the outline mold the visual space of the text in a way that is meant to reflect its structure. A printed page of paragraphs is by comparison a flat and uninteresting space, as is the window of a word processor. A writer can use a word processor to type an outline, and, if the word processor permits graphics, the writer can insert a tree diagram into the text. But the outline or diagram will then be stored as a picture, a sequence of bits to be shown on the screen; the picture will not be treated as a data structure and will not inform the space in which the writer is working. The writer will not be able to change the structure by manipulating the outline, as she can in an outline processor, through which she can intervene at any level of the evolving structure. And if the writer gives the reader a disk rather than a printed version, then the reader too gains immediate access to that structure. All this is possible, because the writing space itself has become a hierarchy of topical elements.

The electronic writing space, which is extremely malleable, can be fashioned into one tree or into a forest of hierarchical trees. In the static medium of print, the writer must normally settle on one hierarchy, one order of topics, although he may find that the topics could be arranged equally well in, say, three orders corresponding to three electronic outlines. Unlike the space of the printed book, the electronic writing space can represent any relationships that can be defined as the interplay of pointers and elements. Multiple relationships pose no special problem, so that a Web site, for example, may have three different organizations, each represented by its own home page with its own outline of links. The creator of the site may alter one outline while leaving the others intact; she may alter any of the outlines themselves without revising the text in any one of the topics. The structure of an electronic text is in this sense abstracted from its verbal expression. This multiplicity already suggests for the electronic writing space some cultural uses different from the ones that we have assigned to print.

HYPERTEXT

A common goal of writing for printed publication has been to create a perfect hierarchy, but it is not always easy to maintain the discipline of such a structure. All writers have had the experience of being overwhelmed with ideas as they write. It was a Romantic notion that the act of writing could it-self release a flood of thoughts—one idea suggesting another and another, as the writer struggled to get them down in some form before they slipped from his conscious grasp. (This sense of being overwhelmed from within was supposedly Coleridge's problem with his poem about Xanadu.) Perhaps the sense of the medium failing one's thoughts was a characteristic notion that cultures associated with handwriting as well as printing. "I only wish I could write with both hands," noted Saint Teresa, "so as not to forget one thing while I am saying another" (Peers, 1972, vol. 2, p. 88). Romantics like Carlyle founded their psychology of literature upon this experience. In the late age of print, however, we are concerned not that there is too much in our minds to get down on paper, but rather that there is too much informa-tion held in electronic media for our minds to assimilate. We are now over-whelmed from without rather than from within. (This new sense of being overwhelmed was Ted Nelson's problem with his electronic Xanadu.)

A writer today may still begin with a jumble of verbal ideas and only a vague sense of how these ideas will fit together. He may start by laying out topics in an arrangement less formal than an outline: he may organize by as-sociation rather than strict subordination. Teachers of writing often en-courage their students to sketch out topics and connect them through lines of association, an activity they have sometimes called "prewriting." What students create in prewriting is a network of elements. The computer can maintain such a network of topics and reflect the writer's progress as he trims his network by removing connections and establishing subordination, until there is a strict hierarchy. When the goal is a printed text, associative writing is considered only a preliminary. However, association is not really prior to writing, as the term "prewriting" suggests. Every text, no matter how rigid its hierarchical organization, must after all work though associa-tions of sound as well as ideas. Even if a writer begins with and remains faith-ful to an outline, the result is always a network of verbal elements. The hierarchy (in the form of paragraphs, sections, and chapters) is an attempt to impose order on verbal ideas that are always prone to subvert that order. The associative relationships define alternative organizations that lie be-neath the order of pages and chapters that a printed text presents to its reader. These alternatives constitute subversive texts-behind-the-text.

Previous technologies of writing, however, could not easily accommo-date such alternatives. The ancient papyrus roll, for example, was strongly linear in its presentation of text. Using first the codex and then the printed book, late medieval and modern writers have made better efforts to accom-modate association as well as hierarchy. In a modern book the table of contents (listing chapters and sometimes sections) defines the hierarchy, while the indices record associative lines of thought that permeate the text. An index permits the reader to locate passages that share the same word, phrase, or subject and so associates passages that may be widely separated in the pages of the book. In one sense the index defines other books that could be constructed from the materials at hand, other themes that the author could have formed into an analytical narrative, and so invites the reader to read the book in alternative ways. By offering multiplicity in place of a single order of paragraphs and pages, an index transforms a book from a tree into a network. There need not be any privileged element in a network, as there always is in a tree, no single topic that dominates all others. Instead of strict subordination, we have paths that weave their way through a textual space. If all texts can ultimately be regarded as networks of verbal elements, digital technology makes it much easier to record and present these networks to writers and readers. Just as the outline processor treats text as a hierarchy, the World Wide Web and other computer systems can refashion the space of the text into a general network or hypertext. Because of its distributed architecture, the World Wide Web is highly associative. The Web has only a loose administrative organization and no controlling conceptual hierarchy. Some so-called "portal" Web sites, of which the best known is Yahoo! (*www.yahoo.com* January 29, 2000), provide ad hoc tables of contents for the Web: portal sites present a hierarchy of topics that is constantly changing as the Web itself changes. Meanwhile a search site such as Alta Vista (*www.altavista.digital.com* January 29, 2000) serves as an dynamic index for millions of web pages—an index that the user constructs on the fly by specifying a word or phrase as a "search string."

The term "hypertext" was coined in the early 1960s by Ted Nelson. Working with mainframe computers at the time, Nelson had already come to appreciate the machine's capacity to create and manage textual networks for all kinds of writing. "Literature," he wrote, "is an ongoing system of interconnecting documents." By literature he meant not only humanistic but also scientific and technical writing: any group of writings on a well-defined subject. "A literature is a system of interconnected writings. We do not offer this as our definition, but as a discovered fact" (Conklin, 1987, pp. 22–23; see also Nelson, 1974; Nelson, 1984, p. 2/7). Actually this "fact" had been discovered independent of and long before the computer, but the machine provided Nelson with the technology that he believed was needed to realize writing as a network. Even before Nelson, the scientist and engineer Vannevar Bush had envisioned using electro-mechanical technology as a hypertextual reading and writing system. In 1945 in the *Atlantic Monthly*, Bush proposed (but never built) a device he called the "memex" to serve as an interactive encyclopedia or library. The reader of the memex would be able to display two texts on a screen and then create links between passages in the texts. These links would be stored by the memex and would be available for later display and revision; collectively they would define a network of interconnections. Because electronic storage was not yet capacious or reliable, Bush chose microfilm as the storage medium for his memex. Fortunately, the development of electromagnetic and optical devices has rendered microfilm obsolete for this purpose. But computer technology was already far enough advanced for Bush to see the possibility of hypertext and to proclaim nothing less than "a new relationship between thinking man and the sum of knowledge," as the editor of the *Atlantic Monthly* put it (Bush, 1945, p. 101).

Bush and Nelson had identified the key characteristics of hypertext long before practical systems were built. Whether realized on microfilm or in computer memory, a hypertext consists of topics and their connections, where the topics may be paragraphs, sentences, individual words, or indeed digitized graphics and segments of video. A hypertext is like a printed book that the author has attacked with a pair of scissors and cut into convenient verbal sizes. The difference is that the electronic hypertext does not simply dissolve into a disordered heap, because the author also defines a scheme of electronic connections to indicate relationships among the slips.

The connections of a hypertext constitute paths of meaning for the author and for the reader. Each topic may participate in several paths, and its significance will depend on which paths the reader has traveled in order to arrive at that topic. If in print only a few paths can be suggested or followed, in an electronic version the texture of the text becomes thicker, and its paths can serve many functions. In the electronic writing space, hierarchical and associative thinking may coexist in the structure of a text, because the computer can take care of the mechanics of maintaining and presenting both networks and trees. In the medium of print, the writer may use an index to show alternatives, but these alternatives must always contend with the fixed order of the book's pages. Although the canonical order of a printed book is defined by the pagination, and all other suggested orders remain subordinate, a hypertext need not have any canonical order. Because every path may define an equally convincing and appropriate reading, the hypertext's multiplicity (or overdetermination) suggests a changed relationship between the reader and the text. New rhetorical relationships are possible, as Landow, Joyce, and many others have suggested (Joyce, 1995, 2000; Landow, 1989).

A text as a network may have no univocal sense. It can remain a multiplicity without the imposition of a principle of domination. In place of hierarchy, we have a writing space that is not only topical; we might even call it "topographic." The word "topography" originally meant a written description of a place, such as an ancient geographer might give. Only later did the word come to refer to mapping or charting—that is, to a visual and mathematical rather than verbal description. Electronic writing can be both a visual and verbal description. It is not the writing of a place, but rather a writing with places as spatially realized topics. Topographic writing challenges the (logocentric) notion that writing should be merely the servant of spoken language. The writer and reader can create and examine structures on the computer screen that have no easy equivalent in speech. The point, which is obvious when the text is a collection of images stored on a video disk, is equally true for a purely verbal text that has been fashioned as a tree or a network of topics and connections. Topographic writing as a mode is not even limited to the computer medium, for it is possible to write topographically for print or even in manuscript. Whenever we divide our text into unitary topics, organize those units into a connected structure, and conceive of this textual structure spatially as well as verbally, we are writing topographically. Many literary artists in the 20th century have adopted this mode of writing (=> p. 121).

WRITING AS CONSTRUCTION

The electronic writing space is inclusive, open to multiple systems of representation. Some writing systems have operated simultaneously under conflicting principles. Hieroglyphics and cuneiform combined word signs, syllable signs, and even pure picture signs that had no phonetic value, and Japanese writing is still today a complex system including word and syllable signs represented in several different scripts. True phonetic writing, however, at least as embodied in the Greek alphabet, is remarkably uncomplicated. Subordinating writing to a single principle, it seeks to drain the pictorial meaning from the written sign. The Greek alphabet aimed at creating a uniform system of writing, in which there was nothing beyond a phonetic transcription of the spoken word. In this respect the Greek alphabet has been our model of writing for 2,700 years. The alphabet defines text as the phonetic transcription of prior speech and moves everything else away from the center of the writing space. Perhaps no writing system in human use can remain purely phonetic or even purely alphabetic. Even our alphabet is "contaminated" with word symbols such as "1," "2," "3," and "&." Nevertheless, the goal of alphabetic writing is to simplify by exclusion. Electronic writing by contrast is inclusive and for that reason resonates with and reminds us of the earliest forms of writing. Electronic writing seems in some ways to be more like hieroglyphics than it is like pure alphabetic writing. The computer welcomes elements that we in the West have long come to regard as inappropriate to writing; it constitutes electronic writing as a continuum in which many systems of representation can happily coexist. On the other hand, this new technology, like all its predecessors, does have margins. Such forgotten or demoted technologies as picture writing may gravitate back toward the center of electronic writing. What in turn threatens to become marginal is precisely that quality that has been central for the past 500 years: the fixed and monumental page of print, the book that exists in thousands of identical copies and heroically resists change.

Electronic writing is not only inclusive; it can also be, as Michael Joyce (1995) has indicated, constructive (pp. 39–59), because an electronic writer can build new elements from traditional ones. Hypertext depends on the computer's capacity to designate any unit of text as a new element in an expanding vocabulary of signs. The writer of a hypertext indicates these signs by defining a link (anchor on the World Wide Web) from one element to another. When she links one Web page to another, she is in effect creating two new writing elements, each of which has become a unitary sign. Whatever else the first element (page on the World Wide Web) means, it now has an added meaning as the source of a connection, and the second element now takes on meaning as a destination. The connection forms these two signs into a new sentence, which reads: "This element (page) leads to that one." The reader comes to understand the sentence by following the link. That movement, mediated by the computer, is the reading of the sentence. If the reader chooses to follow the link, she expects that the second page will comment on, elaborate, or explain the first. George Landow (1989) notes that:

> Designers of hypertext and hypermedia materials confront two related problems, the first of which is how to indicate the destination of links, and the second, how to welcome the user on arrival at that destination. Drawing upon the analogy of travel, one can say that the first problem concerns exit or departure information and the second arrival or entrance information (pp. 188–189).

Landow points out that departure and arrival have a rhetorical dimension; the presence of a link from element A to element B causes the reader to assume that B somehow explains A. Like a sentence of prose, the movement itself from A to B is taken by the reader as a rhetorical gesture. The movement is a meaningful juxtaposition of the two elements, which have become symbols in the hypertext. There are as many new symbols in each hypertext as there are sources and destinations for the links. Writers of hypertext create the elements of their writing system in the act of writing—by adding new composite elements to the alphabet, graphics, and icons available on their computers. Writing in the electronic medium can be challenging precisely because writers are compelled to define their own system as they proceed. Reading in the electronic medium can be challenging as well, for readers must decipher the system as they read.

GLOBAL HYPERTEXT

Although experiments had been conducted since the 1960s, workable hypertext systems such as the World Wide Web are relatively recent. It was not until the advent of personal computers and workstations that hypertext could be made available to a large audience of writers and readers. Stand-alone systems, such as Bill Adkinson's Hypercard, have existed since the 1980s. In the later 1980s and early 1990s, the study of hypertext began to become a legitimate discipline in computer science, and innovative systems were produced, such as Notecards (Halasz, 1989; Halasz, Moran, & Trigg, 1987; Trigg & Irish, 1989), Aquanet (Marshall, Halasz, Rogers, & Johnson, 1991; Marshall & Rogers, 1992), Trellis (Furuta & Stotts, 1989), and SEPIA (Streitz, Hanneman, & Thüring, 1989; Streitz et al., 1992). Frank Halasz and others offered theoretical models, such as the Dexter model, for understanding the nature of hypertextual linking (Halasz & Schwartz, 1990).

The principle of hypertext had been implicit in computer programming for decades. If we define hypertext broadly as the dynamic interconnection of a set of symbolic elements, then many kinds of computer applications (databases, simulation programs, even programs for artificial intelligence) are hypertextual. Hypertext shows how programming and conventional prose writing can come together in the space provided by the computer, by putting at the disposal of writers data structures that programmers have used for decades. We can also regard the programmer's data structures as formalized versions of the textual strategies that writers have exploited for centuries. Finally, the Internet itself constitutes a physical expression of hypertext: each host computer or router is a node, and the hypertextual relationships among these nodes are defined by the cables and microwave or satellite links.

On this architectural platform of the Internet, two global hypertext systems have been built. The first was the system of electronic mail that dates back to the 1970s, although this network was never explicitly recognized as hypertext (Rheingold, 1991, p. 7). Subscribers to electronic mail systems, listservs, and newsgroups write and read messages created by others within their local area network or elsewhere on the Internet. E-mail messages travel a path through the communications links until they reach their single, marked destination, while newsgroup and listserv submissions spread out to many nodes on the net simultaneously. At any one moment the network holds a vast text of interrelated writings—the intersection of hundreds of thousands of messages on thousands of topics. It is a hypertext that no one reader can hope to encompass, one that changes moment by moment as messages are added and deleted. Writing for such a network is by nature topographical, in the sense that relatively small units of prose are sent and received. The medium itself encourages brevity, since two correspondents can send and receive several messages in one day. The addresses of the messages provide a primitive system of links. To reply to a given message is to link your text to that message, and both the message and the reply may circulate for days around the network provoking other responses. No user is bound to read or reply to anything; instead, any message can refer to any other or ignore all previous messages and strike out in a new direction. This communications network is therefore a hypertext in which no one writer or reader has substantial control, and because no one has control, no one has collective responsibility. The situation is different for stand-alone hypertext systems for personal computers, where there is one author and one reader and the twin issues of control and responsibility are paramount.

The World Wide Web was an explicit hypertext system from the beginning. As early as 1989, Tim Berners-Lee, had characterized his proposal for information management as hypertext (see www.w3.org/History/1989/proposal.html October 15, 1999). Like other hypertexts, Berners-Lee's system divided information into topical units, specified links among the units, and gave the user control over the movement from one unit to another. (In an obvious remediation of print or typewriting, these units came to be called pages.) The great innovation of his World Wide Web was to define a protocol to make hypertext global. In the stand-alone hypertext systems of the 1980s, the links moved the reader among texts created by the same author or authors and all stored on a diskette or CD-ROM. Because an "anchor" on a Web page can define a link to any other server on the Internet, Web hypertexts are not limited in size or location. One Web page can take the reader to a dozen pages around the word, and the authors of these target pages may never be aware of these links. The Web is a vast network of links to pages that may remain the same for years or disappear tomorrow. Its popularity has meant that hypertext has become an integral feature of our culture's reading and writing.

We can date the enormous popularity of the Web not from its first implementation in 1990, but from the introduction of the first graphical browser, Mosaic, in 1993 (see Hafner & Lyon, 1996). Berners-Lee had conceived of the Web as research tool for physicists and others; he thought that scientists needed an easy and consistent interface for sharing drafts of their papers and data. His browser was entirely textual, although data and graphics could be transferred and viewed separately. In 1993, however, programmers at the University of Illinois created Mosaic, in which graphics could be integrated with text. Almost immediately the possibilities for global hypertext expanded tremendously, as designers and business people foresaw recreational, entertainment, and commercial uses that were not apparent when there was only text on the screen. The number of users of the Web and in turn the Internet increased extraordinarily rapidly, until by the beginning of 2000 an estimate by the *Computer Industry Almanac* put the world-wide total at more than 250 million (cyberatlas.internet.com/big_picture/geographics/article/0, 1323,5911_151151,00.html January 7, 2000). Mosaic transformed the Web from hypertext to hypermedia, in which multiple modes of representation constitute the units for hypertextual linking (see Fig. 3.3). At first the media were limited to text and static graphics, but by the mid-1990s users could connect to video and audio segments through Internet services in conjunction with the Web. Again, although stand-alone hypermedia systems existed in the 1980s, the Web has made hypermedia culturally ubiquitous. We now come upon the unwieldy URL addresses everywhere: on billboards, in magazines and newspapers, on television, and even on the radio. Meanwhile, multimedia on the Internet is helping to redefine the relationship of word and image, a process of redefinition that had already been going on in our culture's writing space for decades (=> p. 47).

HYPERTEXT AS REMEDIATION

It is possible to write in a hypertextual style for print. That is, it is possible to use print or handwriting to achieve many of the literary or rhetorical effects

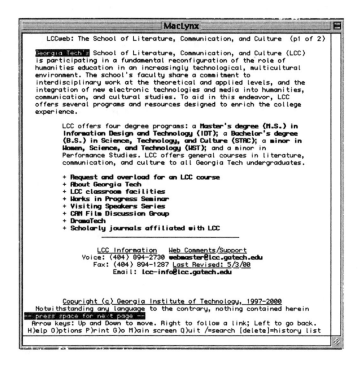

FIG. 3.3.   This Lynx browser displays only text, as did all browsers before 1993. Compare
this page to Fig. 3.1, displayed in Internet Explorer, a descendant of the first graphical
browser, Mosaic.

of hypertext, just as it is possible to write on the computer without taking
advantages of hypertextual linking. The conventional word processing document only hints at the potential for associative and flexible writing that we
have identified as hypertext. What, then, is the relationship between the
digital technology and hypertext?

We can think of hypertext as a genre or series of genres, including interactive fiction, applications for education and entertainment, Web sites (which
themselves constitute many different genres), and so on. These genres already have structures and conventions and generate expectations among
their authors and readers. Genres are associated with one medium or sometimes with a set of media. Hypertext is intimately associated with digital technology. Without this technology, hypertext would never have been
recognized as a set of genres. Without the genres of hypertext, however, electronic writing (which would be mere word processing) would not assert itself

as distinct from linear writing for print. What defines hypertext is the way that it distinguishes itself from other genres, in particular, those of print.

Hypertext in all its electronic forms—the World Wide Web as well as the many stand-alone systems—is the remediation of print. Writers and designers promote hypertext as a means of improving on the older medium, or more precisely on the genres associated with the medium of print, such as the novel, the technical report, and the humanistic essay. Where printed genres are linear or hierarchical, hypertext is multiple and associative. Where a printed text is static, a hypertext responds to the reader's touch. The reader can move through a hypertext document in a variety of reading orders. Whether multilinearity and interactivity really do render hypertext better than print, is a cultural determination. The question becomes: better in what sense, for whose purposes, and, as various contemporary critics would immediately ask, for whose economic benefit? This is the series of questions with which we are struggling in the late age of print, as we try to assign various cultural tasks to print materials and to digital forms. The apologists for hypertext and the apologists for print continue to search for the appropriate rhetoric to keep us on their side. Each group will claim that their writing space is more natural or truer to experience, which is a version of the claims of immediacy that we find are also made for and against digital visual media. Some of the enthusiasts for hypertext, or information technology in general, will also make the economic argument that new media mean new prosperity for our society.

The supporters of hypertext may even argue that hypertext reflects the nature of the human mind itself—that because we think associatively, not linearly, hypertext allows us to write as we think. Vannevar Bush entitled his article "As We May Think" and in justifying the memex wrote that " ... [t]he human mind ... operates by association. With one item in its grasp, it snaps instantly to the next that is suggested by the association of thoughts, in accordance with some intricate web of trails carried by the cells of the brain" (Bush, 1999, p. 33). Ted Nelson (1984) also seemed to suggest that hypertext was natural to the mind. He noted, for example, that " ... [t]he structure of ideas is never sequential; and indeed, our thought processes are not very sequential either. True, only a few thoughts at a time pass across the central screen of the mind; but as you consider a thing, your thoughts crisscross it constantly, reviewing first one connection, then another" (1/16). Sometimes Nelson argued that hypertext was natural or true to our tradition of literacy, as when he claimed to have discovered the fact that "literature" is a system of interconnected writing. By this logic, ironically, hypertext becomes a transparent form that actually captures and reveals the structure of the underlying written record. The supporters of print in this debate, such as Birkerts (1994) and Slouka (1995), may argue for the naturalness of print in a number of ways. Sometimes they claim that the linearity of print captures the true nature of historical, philosophical, or scientific argument or that novels need to be linear. Sometimes they will appeal to the apparent simplicity of print and the printed book. Printed books are portrayed as closer to nature, because one can read them out of doors or in places where it is hard to operate computers. The supporters of print will associate the computer with high technology, which is by definition distanced from nature or the human. They will challenge the hypertextual definition of interactivity: letting the reader choose links only gives the illusion of control, which is really withheld from the reader. If authors prescribe links, they deny the reader the choice of making her own associations, so that a printed novel or essay actually gives the reader greater freedom to interact with the ideas presented. This debate turns on the question: which form is better at constituting the real, the authentic, or the natural? Remediation is always an attempt to redefine these key cultural values.

Such an attempt implies homage as well as rivalry. Electronic hypertext certainly pays homage to the medium that it is seeking to refashion. A literary hypertext often consists of units of prose, each the size of a paragraph or longer. Web pages are, after all, called pages and are often modeled on the graphic layout of a magazine or newspaper (= > p. 68). Hypertexts remain linear and booklike at this level: they remediate the printed book as if by tearing out its pages and reordering them before the reader's eyes. The very notion of hypertextual reading and writing begins with the construction of the reader and writer as we have known them from 500 years of printing. In these ways, hypertext acknowledges its debt to its rival printed forms.

In its rivalry with print, hypertext presents itself as an intensification, a hypermediation, of the older medium. When Nelson gave the name *hypertext* to linked digital texts, he meant something like the "ne plus ultra" of text. In following hypertextual links, the reader becomes conscious of the form or medium itself and of her interaction with it. In contrast, print has often been regarded as a medium that should disappear from the reader's conscious consideration. Indeed, two levels of mediation are supposed to disappear, the printed page and the prose itself. In a traditional novel, the reader is supposed to forget that he is reading and simply "see" the events that the author describes. In an essay or monograph he is supposed to focus on the argument—not on the words and certainly not on the choice of type or the page layout. In contrast, the most compelling apologists for hypertext argue that it challenges the aesthetic of disappearance and requires that the reader pay attention to the process by which the text is presented and renewed on the screen. Hypertext is a process as much as a product, as Michael Joyce (1995) argues with his notion of constructive hypertext (pp. 39–59).

In its emphasis on process and on the reader's awareness of the medium, hypertext seems to belong to the literary tradition of modernism, and indeed modernist writers such as James Joyce can be regarded as forerunners of hypertextual writers such as Michael Joyce (= > p. 142). The early modernists in literature and the visual arts also created works whose surfaces drew attention to themselves, works that demanded the reader or viewer acknowledge the reality of the genre or medium itself. The reader of *Ulysses* does not lose himself in the story for long periods, as is (naively) supposed to happen with Victorian novels: *Ulysses* is not transparent in this sense, but rather hypermediated. Likewise the reader of Michael Joyce's hypertextual fiction *afternoon* does not lose herself in the story: what captures her is the experience of moving through the story on a trajectory partly determined by her own choices (= > p. 124).

THE OLD AND THE NEW IN HYPERTEXT

Many hypertext enthusiasts are also like modernist writers and visual artists in their dedication to the principle of the new. They characterize hypertext as a break with the past, a revolutionary form of writing, just as modernists often characterized their forms of prose, poetry, and painting as revolutions in the early 20th century. For example, John Slatin (1991) writes that " … hypertext is very different from more traditional forms of text. The differences are a function of the technology, and are so various, at once so minute and so vast, as to make hypertext a new medium for thought and expression—the first medium, after programming languages, to emerge from the computer revolution" (p. 153). Landow (1991) himself has written that "[h]ypermedia, which changes the way texts exist and the way we read them, requires a new rhetoric and a new stylistics" (p. 81). If the enthusiasts take the role of modernists, their critics, such as Laura Miller in the *New York Times Book Review* (1998), can assume the role of the defenders of sane tradition and simple pleasures against Bolshevik claims of the new:

> Readers like me stubbornly resist hyperfiction's efforts to free them from what [Robert] Coover calls 'domination by the author'…. [The] surrender

... and the intimacy to be had in allowing a beloved author's voice into the sanctums of our minds, are what the common reader craves. Hyperfiction's champions aren't the first self-styled revolutionaries threatening to liberate other people from their pleasures, but they make one of the weakest cases. The end of books will come only when readers abandon novels for the deconstructed stories of hypertext, and that exodus is strictly a fiction (p. 43).

Neither side has been moved by the arguments of the other in this debate over whether hypertextual writing is fundamentally different from and better than writing for print.

Understanding hypertext as the remediation of printed forms (and of earlier technologies and forms of writing) allows us to recast the debate. Electronic writing in general and hypertext in particular can be both old and new, because the process of remediation must acknowledge both their connection with and their difference from print. Electronic writing is new in precisely the same sense that each medium is new at its introduction. Each new medium claims to provide a new strategy—in this case the strategy involves interactivity and the unification of text and graphics—for achieving an authentic experience for its reader. Hypertexts such as the World Wide Web refashion the voice of the text as we have known it in print and in earlier technologies of writing; they turn vocal writing into spatial writing. The excitement and immediacy of the text is no longer an aural experience, as it was when texts were in manuscripts and as it has remained, however muted, in the printed book. Instead, the World Wide Web offers us the experience of moving through a visual and conceptual space different from the space of the book, although this experience still depends on our intuitive understanding of that earlier writing space. Indeed, we depend in a variety of ways on our knowledge of print in order to read and write hypertexts.

What is necessarily new about electronic hypertext is that it uses the printed book as its object of remediation. We evaluate hypertext over against hundreds of years of experience with print. The very fact that electronic writing must confront the tradition of print makes electronic writing different from print; it means that our culture will have at least some different uses for electronic texts. The World Wide Web now plays roles that only a few years ago were assigned almost exclusively to print, yet we do not experience the Web as a printed book. The Web seems different although—indeed precisely because—it appeals to print for its own definition. In the 15th century, the printed book depended for its self-definition and its strategy of remediation on the handwritten codex. The debate over those two media was less vehement than the current debate over electronic writing, however, because the remediation of the manuscript by the printed book was so respectful. Yet the printed book was also both new and old in its work of refashioning. New media are always new in their redeployment and refashioning of their predecessors.

In this late age of print, the two technologies, print and electronic writing, still need each other. Print forms the tradition on which electronic writing depends, and electronic writing is that which goes beyond print. Print now depends on the electronic too, in the sense that printed materials find it necessary to compete against digital technologies in order to hold their readers. For this reason print is becoming hypermediated, as it incorporates verbal genres and gestures in self-conscious imitation of and rivalry with electronic media, especially the World Wide Web. Although at this cultural moment print still seems "simple" and "natural" in comparison with electronic hypertext, print's ironic claim to being the natural medium of communication may not last. It seems increasingly natural to represent all sorts of information as hypertext on the World Wide Web.

In short, electronic hypertext is not the end of print; it is instead the remediation of print.

4

The Breakout of the Visual

Hypertext seldom exists as pure text without any graphics. Today, hypertext is usually hypermedia, as it is on the World Wide Web, and hypermedia offers a second challenge to the printed book. Digital media claim to achieve greater immediacy and authenticity by integrating images (and sound) with prose. Although printed books can also offer images—the ability to reproduce maps, diagrams, and eventually photographic images accurately was one of the great achievements of print—nevertheless, verbal text has usually contained and constrained the images on the printed page. On the World Wide Web, the images often dominate. In presenting animation and digitized video, a Web page can supplement or bypass prose altogether. In this respect hypermedia is participating in a process of remediation that has been going on for more than a century: the response of prose to the visual technologies of photography, cinema, and television. Print today is continuing to remake itself in order to maintain its claim to represent reality as effectively as digital and other visual technologies. This remaking is one of the important effects of our current fascination with hypermedia.

Scholars as radically different in their ideologies as E. H. Gombrich, W. J. T. Mitchell, and Frederic Jameson seem to agree that we are living in a visual culture. In the *Image and the Eye* (1982), Gombrich claims that "[o]urs is a visual age. We are bombarded with pictures from morning till night... No wonder it has been asserted that we are entering a historical epoch in which the image will take over from the written word" (p. 137). To Mitchell (1994) " ... we live in a culture dominated by pictures" (pp. 2–3), while Jameson (1991) remarks that: "My sense is that this is essentially a visual culture, wired for sound—but one where the linguistic element ... is slack and flabby, and not to be made interesting without ingenuity, daring, and keen motivation" (p. 299). If these very different theorists agree that our cultural moment—what we are calling the late age of print—is visual rather than linguistic, we might ask what is happening to print technology and to prose at such a moment. One answer is that print and prose are undertaking to remediate static and moving images as they appear in photography, film, television and the computer. Print and prose have undergone remediations in the past, but the task may be more difficult today in the face of the cultural success of analog and now digital visual media. What is happening is a readjustment of the ratio between text and image in the various forms of print (books, magazines, newspapers, billboards), and the refashioning of prose itself in an attempt both to rival and to incorporate the visual image. Remediation can be, perhaps always is, mutual: older technologies remediate newer ones out of both enthusiasm and apprehension. In this case, the ingenuity and daring, to which Jameson refers, are applied to the incorporation of visual media into print, while the keen motivation comes from the fear that the cultural significance of printed books and of writing itself is threatened.

Since its invention, printing has placed the word effectively in control of the image. Early printed books were in some ways not as visually sophisticated as medieval manuscripts, and printing perhaps never achieved the fluid relationship between the verbal and the visual that was characteristic of medieval illumination. Diagrams, illustrations, and maps did play an important role in the communicative power of printed books, especially with the refinement and increased use of copperplate engraving in the 16th century (Meggs, 1998, p. 105). Nevertheless, in traditional print technology, images were contained by the verbal text. Typographically, the containment came from the fact that the words and images were produced by different means. Although movable type served for the words, the images had to be generated separately by engraving or, later, lithography. Word and image tended to occupy separate visual as well as technological spaces. Growing alphabetic literacy reinforced the notion that what was important would appear in alphabetic texts and might then be supplemented by graphics. Writers in the age of print controlled the visual or sensory element by subsuming it into the text itself. Artistic prose and poetry did this through metaphor; discursive prose did it by subordinating the concrete to the abstract—techniques that writers inherited from ancient and medieval writers and further developed. In one sense, the history of Western prose might be understood as a series of strategies for controlling the visual and the sensory.

As the dominant technology of representation, print has been a voracious remediator since the 15th century; refashioning many of the functions of the manuscript, of oral communication (the homily, the scientific lecture or disputation, the occasional speech), and of visual art (through engraving). From the first, print was a mass production technology that generated hundreds or thousands of identical copies and so supported homogeneity and reinforced the sense of the author as an authority. On the other hand, print could be used in support of multiplicity and heterogeneity as well, because print increases the number of texts so that a single reader can collect and sample diverse points of view. In the 20th century, digital technology in the form of desktop publishing and computer-controlled photocomposition refashioned the practice of printing, and in comparison with the earlier mechanical techniques, digital printing seems to foster heterogeneity in both form and content. One reason is that the computer opens the printing process to small groups and even individuals. Amateurs can create their own camera-ready copy and make selective use of or ignore altogether the stylistic practices of professional typographers. Although breaking the rules may result in poor quality printing, it can also offer designers a new typographic freedom. For both amateur and professional typographers, digital visual media are suggesting new looks and functions for printed artifacts, as they compel printing to remake itself. This pressure to remediate is now expressed in two related ways. Printed books, magazines, and newspapers are changing typographically and visually by incorporating more elaborate graphics, while at the same time prose is attempting to remake itself in order to reflect and rival the cultural power of the image.

THE IMAGE AND THE PRINTED PAGE

We have today a spectrum of print styles that reflects every possible visual relationship between word and image: from traditional nonfiction in which the word dominates the image to art books or advertising billboards in which the image dominates. This spectrum is too varied to explore in detail here. The main point is that the relationship between word and image is becoming increasingly unstable, and this instability is especially apparent in popular American magazines, newspapers, and various forms of graphic advertisements.

   There remain domains, such as scholarly monographs and scientific journals, in which the image is still subordinated to the word and controlled by the idea of verbal communication. Control is not just a matter of the ratio of images to texts, but of the way in which text gathers around the image and supervises its reading. For example, the extremely influential books on graphic design and visualization by Edwin Tufte, *The Visual Display of Quantitative Information*, (1983); *Envisioning Information*, (1990); *Visual Explanations*, (1997) devote more space to graphics than to text, and yet there is no doubt which is in control, for in fact the graphics themselves are used textually. As Tufte (1983) put it, "[d]ata graphics are paragraphs about data and should be treated as such. / Words, graphics, and tables are different mechanisms with but a single purpose—the presentation of information" (p. 181). One of Tufte's favorite graphics is a tableau by the 19th-century designer Charles Joseph Minard, that "portrays the devastating losses suffered in Napoleon's Russian campaign of 1812" (p. 40). The map is a narrative, overwritten with words and numbers, in which every visual feature is related to one of the arguments: the dwindling size of the army, its location and direction of movement, or the outside temperature (Fig. 4.1). There is nothing left to be pictorial, nothing free of the hegemonic influence of the word. This "old-fashioned" view is still represented today in the hundreds of graphs and graphics that Tufte presents in his books and in the genres of graphic design of which he approves. In this view the ideal graphic is one whose pictorial elements reveal transparently the information that lies "behind" them—the equivalent in graphic design of Alberti's transparent window in perspective painting (= > p. 25).

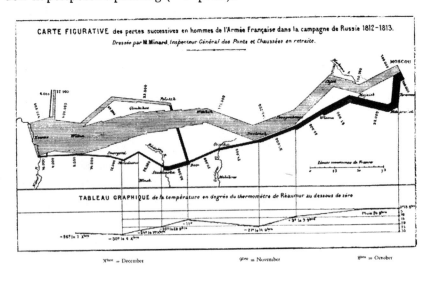

FIG. 4.1.   Napoleon's Russian campaign of 1812, described in a graphic by Charles Joseph Minard.

Very different from this philosophy of transparency is the design philosophy of popular publications such as USA Today. It is no surprise that Tufte considers the exuberant graphics like those in USA Today as "chartjunk" or even deceptive. Yet USA Today should not simply be dismissed as a deviation from the proper graphic style; it is an indication of a refashioning of the newspaper itself. In graphic form and function, the newspaper is coming to resemble a computer screen, as the combination of text, images, and icons turns the newspaper page into a static snapshot of a World Wide Web page. In many newspapers the index now consists of summaries gathered in a column running down the left-hand side of the page, and a small picture is often included with the summary. Anyone familiar with multimedia presentations can easily read such a picture as an iconic button, which the user would press in order to receive the rest of the story. USA Today in fact makes considerable use of "hypertextual" links back and forth throughout its pages, and these links are sometimes cued by small graphics. The purpose of these icons together with the other pictures and graphics is not merely decorative. Together they help to redefine the function of the newspaper, which is no longer only to transmit verbal information, but also to provide an appropriate visual experience and through that experience to dictate an appropriate reaction to the stories being told. On the other hand, the notion of photorealistic transparency remains popular today in such forms as Life magazine and the apparently candid photographs of People. The graphic design here is transparent, but not in Tufte's sense, and the image dominates the text, because the image is regarded as more immediate, closer to the reality presented.

Further along the spectrum of popular graphic design come magazines such as Mondo 2000 and WIRED. Their hectic, hypermediated style has its roots in collage and photomontage earlier in the 20th century. Just as collage and photomontage worked at the intersection of typography and the contemporary visual arts of painting and photography, the cybermagazines today are aggressively remediating the visual style of television and digital media. Every page of WIRED is a visual allegory for McLuhan's apothegm that the medium is the message. Similar, but more sophisticated, is the work of David Carson, whose designs for magazines such as Ray Gun were extremely influential in the 1990s. Like the typography of WIRED, Carson's typography is deliberately hard to read, violating the canon of the so-called International style of design from the 1930s and 1940s to the present (Kirschenbaum, 1999; Meggs, 1998, pp. 320–336, pp. 460–463). Carson might be considered Tufte's opposite number, because for Carson graphics are emphatically not visible texts, but, on the contrary, text itself becomes a pictorial experience. For Carson, words should be seen and not just (or not even?) read. The historian and designer Johanna Drucker (1994) has shown how words were treated pictorially in modern art and graphic design from the beginning of the century: among those practicing collage and photomontage, among the futurists, dadaists, and lettrists, and so on. The treatment of text as image becomes even more popular and more culturally compelling with the rise of digital media, because of the ease with which images and words can be combined.

Today's graphic design is characterized by the multiplicity of styles and by their juxtapositions and combinations. The transparent International style, derived ultimately from the Bauhaus, can still be seen in print advertising and it continues to influence Web designers today, as David Siegel illustrates in *Creating Killer Web Sites* (1997). Yet more hypermediated styles, such as punk design, are popular as well. No one seems surprised or disturbed to find on the Web a layered design in which the whole page is hypermediated and yet individual photographs or elements pursue a sentimental or naive version of transparency. Meanwhile, in contemporary typography and graphic design for print, verbal text does not enjoy its old hegemony, nor does pure imagery simply replace text. Instead, the spectrum of styles from transparency to hypermediacy and from pure text to pure pictorialism has become a register that the designer can vary without offending or apparently confusing most viewers or readers.

VISUAL METAPHORS

Every issue of *USA Today* offers three or four "USA Snapshots," colorful little graphs that tell Americans "who we are." In these graphs we can discern a tension between textual and visual modes of representation. The tension is apparent in Fig. 4.2, which illustrates how often American men shave on the weekend. This graph is a bar chart, and yet the bars are drawn as safety razors—apparently to convince the viewer that the graph is really about shaving. Distrusting the viewer's faith in numerical abstraction, the designers decided to draw two razors for the number of men shaving on both days and one for the number shaving on one day. The white lines behind the razors also indicate the designers' disdain of abstraction. Although these lines seem to define a Cartesian coordinate system, they do not correspond to any obvious numerical divisions. Instead the grid has become bathroom tiles: the need to make a visually interesting picture has overridden the

FIG. 4.2.   USA Snapshot: "Men's weekend shaving habits." © 1994 USA TODAY.
(*Reprinted with permission.)

needs of the graph. It is as if the designers no longer trusted the arbitrary
symbolic structure of the graph to sustain its meaning, as if writing as a texture of arbitrary signs were coming undone to reveal the icons that are assumed to lie "beneath" its surface.

The shaving man himself also has no function in the graph. His presence
transforms the graph into a picture, yet at the same time he gives the picture
much of its semiotic complexity. As he shaves, the man appears to be looking into a mirror, while we as viewers are on the other side of the mirror,
looking back at the man. As in other *USA Today* graphs and graphics, the
statistics embodied in this graph are supposed to be a mirror of American
life. Thus, the shaving man turns the graph into a verbal–visual pun, although it seems unlikely that the designers had this in mind. For them, the
humor probably lies in the Gestalt shifts between bars and razors, Cartesian
coordinates and grout lines between bathroom tiles. The caption of the
graph—"statistics that shape our lives"—is more ironic and appropriate
than the designers may have realized.

The pun in this graph recalls another technique that has become common even in those newspapers considering themselves more traditional and
more verbally sophisticated than *USA Today*. Headlines often draw out la-

tent metaphors in their subject: "Turbulent times ahead for United Airlines"; "Tobacco stocks are smoking"; "Mercedes slips earnings gears." In such headlines there is usually a visual or tactile image, and the point is to turn the analytic content of the headline into something sensual. The prose itself is straining to become iconic: to call forth through punning rhetoric an image that confirms what is being referred to in words.

Still another form of visualized rhetoric appears in glossy computer magazines such as *Byte*, particularly in advertisements. The headline of the advertisement will claim that a certain software product will give your company "a bigger piece of the pie." The picture will show an apple pie with a large slice being removed. A literal visual interpretation seems to lend the cliché greater conviction for the reader or viewer. The dialectic of word and image in such advertisements can be commonplace or sophisticated, but in each case there is a changed relationship in which the image is magnified at the expense of the prose. Words no longer seem to carry conviction without the reappearance as a picture of the imagery that was latent in them.

Throughout the history of writing, there have been visual puns and designs that combine words, icons, and pictures. For example, rebus and emblem poetry has been popular since the Renaissance. (Children today still enjoy rebus books, in which some of the nouns are replaced by stylized drawings. A young child can follow the story and become accustomed to the linearity of reading before he can actually decipher the letters that constitute alphabetic writing.) However, the contemporary examples of this visual play are more widespread and have greater significance, coming as they do after 500 years of printing. They can be seen as part of a trend to renegotiate the relationship between arbitrary signs and picture elements in communication.

The use of images for cultural communication is nothing new. Even before the invention of the printing press, the Middle Ages had developed a sophisticated iconography that served in the place of words for a largely illiterate audience. A medieval cathedral was indeed a complex, hypermediated text displayed in a sacred space for the community to read. However, there are obvious differences between the visual culture of the Middle Ages and our own visual culture. One is the sheer ubiquity of images today. In the Middle Ages, images must have had a sanctity not only because of their religious themes, but also because of their inaccessibility. A major source of such images, such as a cathedral, would have been available only to a fraction of the population. Most peasants would have attended parish churches that could hardly afford much stained glass and sculpture, and might have seen the interior of a cathedral only a few times in their lives. Even town dwellers fortunate enough to live near a religious center would have dragged themselves to church before or after an exhausting day's work and received a glimpse of the rich imagery. The images must have had a different status for them than the endless barrage that confronts the contemporary television viewer or Web user.

Furthermore, medieval society as a whole had a different relationship to verbal literacy: there was a small literate elite and a large class of illiterates. Our culture is by comparison postliterate, emerging out of the enormous experiment in mass literacy of the 19th and 20th centuries. In this historical context, visual representation too can be seen as emerging out of the alphabet and other symbol systems. The visual puns in USA Today, for example, depend upon centuries of exposure to statistical analysis and the Cartesian coordinate system. It is interesting to speculate how photography, film, television, and multimedia might have been developed and used, if Western culture could somehow have jumped over the technology of printing and gone directly from medieval iconography to photographic and electronic visual presentation. What did happen is that these visual technologies had to define themselves in a culture of printed materials, and in particular in a literary culture dominated by the printed novel. They had to assume the task of subverting the dominate model of prose, of breaking free of the constraints of verbal rhetoric.

That situation has changed. If, during the heyday of print in the 18th and 19th centuries, writers controlled the visual by subsuming it into their prose and poetry, popular prose today seems constantly to be trying to become more visual and sensuous. Eventually, the visual element not only rises to the surface of the text, but escapes altogether and takes its place as a picture on the printed page. It is not only newspapers and magazines that are renegotiating the verbal and the visual. Other forms, including "serious" and popular fiction and academic prose, are also changing, and in all cases verbal text seems to be losing its power to contain and constrain the sensory. Genres are either experiencing a breakout of the visual or reacting against it. It would be worthwhile, for example, to examine the history of artistic prose since the 19th century to watch how the sensory elements at first suffused the prose in late romantic and early modern writers and then began to bubble out of the writing altogether. One key to understanding this change would be to correlate it with the invention and spread of photography and then film—not because these new visual media "caused" prose to strive for the visual, but because both prose and the new media remediated each other. Traditionalists lament the death of prose, and they are right in the sense that prose must compromise its traditional power and authority in its effort to keep up with digital media. Prose today is indeed filled with dead metaphors and shouted metaphors, both of which are attempts to pierce through necrotic layers of contemporary language in order to awaken the senses, attempts to compete with the extraordinary noise level of contemporary video and graphic culture. In the late age of print, however, the death of prose will never be complete, because our culture will want to keep the patient alive, if moribund, so that the mutual remediation with digital media can continue.

EKPHRASIS

We have identified a process of reciprocal remediation between graphics and verbal text. Graphics in printed publications like USA Today are being used to replace text. They seem to bubble out of the prose and appear before our eyes, transforming us from readers into viewers. This process, as old as rebus poetry, is renewed for us by the techniques of animation and interactivity in digital media. The reciprocal process is equally old, in which prose tries to represent images (or sounds or sensory experience). In ancient rhetoric, this technique was called *ekphrasis*, and, in ancient rhetorical practice and still today, we can discern the ambivalence that belongs to ekphrasis as a strategy for remediation. Ekphrasis sets out to rival visual art in words, to demonstrate that words can describe vivid scenes without recourse to pictures. Ekphrasis also indicates that the writer is preoccupied with the visual, for in order to rival the visual, the prose must become descriptive in an effort to find the equivalent of what is "naturally" a visual experience. The attempt to make words do what pictures do might be taken to mean that pictures are primary and words secondary. However, earlier periods seemed more inclined to think that words were up to the task of bringing images under control. In ancient rhetoric the spoken word controlled the image; since the Renaissance it has been the written or printed word that was in control. Today, when neither the written nor the spoken word seems able to exert such power, ekphrasis may be too ambitious. Instead, as we have seen in digital media and even in print, we get a reverse ekphrasis in which images are given the task of explaining words.

The relationship between popular films and novels is further proof that the visual is now regarded as primary. It used to be, and often still is, the case that novels were made into films. In the classic Hollywood era, film sometimes borrowed the sense of legitimacy from novels by the device of showing a book cover and perhaps a page of text before dissolving into the first scene of the film. This device established a continuity between the novel and the film by suggesting that the film is the modern way to tell a story. At the same time, the device was an example of reverse ekphrasis, where the words turn into actual images. Today, when films are culturally more important than novels, we have the phenomenon of "novelization," where an already released film is repurposed as a paperback and sold in supermarkets or chain bookstores. The marketing of these novelizations reinforces a belief that the film is the more important form: the book must now do its best to recreate in words the experience of seeing the film. In general, our cultural assumption seems to be that while prose may not be very good at recreating images, there is nothing else that prose could or should be doing. The belief seems now to be widespread that to read a novel is to run a film in one's head and some readers even claim that they visualize all prose. When the text says simply that a character walks into a room, they imagine a room completely furnished. When the text introduces a character, they form a mental image. They ignore the fact that even in the most minutely descriptive novel there must be infinitely many visual details that are never provided.

Both ekphrasis and reverse ekphrasis are manifestations of what the literary critic Murray Krieger has described as the "desire for the natural sign." (On Krieger's notion of ekphrasis, see also Scott, 1993.) Krieger remarks:

> "In speaking of ekphrasis, or at least of the ekphrastic impulse, I have pointed to its source in the semiotic desire for the natural sign, the desire, that is, to have the world captured in the word.... This desire to see the world in the word is what, after Derrida, we have come to term the logocentric desire. It is this naive desire that leads us to prefer the immediacy of the picture to the mediation of the code in our search for a tangible, 'real' referent that would render the sign transparent" (Krieger, 1992, 11).

If, as Krieger suggests, we connect this desire with Derrida's logocentrism, then we could say that the desire comes into existence with the invention of writing itself (Derrida, 1976b). For Derrida, as soon as culture invents an arbitrary sign system, there arises a yearning to close the gap between the sign and the signified. We would add that this yearning can take different forms depending on the available technologies of representation. In Plato's Greece, when oratory and drama were the defining arts, the spoken word was treated as the natural sign. In one sense Plato himself created the dialogue form in order to bring his writing closer to the natural sign. Printed literature since the Renaissance has faced a different and more difficult situation, because the techniques of representation to which print has been responding have been visual rather than oral. Print managed to establish an equilibrium with representational painting, but that equilibrium began to erode perhaps with the invention of photography. Just as photography contributed to a crisis in painting, so it and the technologies that followed (film, television, and computer graphics) also called into question the power of prose. Thus, in the 19th and 20th centuries, the desire to capture the world in the word has been gradually supplemented by the more easily gratified desire to see the world through visual technologies. Under these conditions, ekphrasis becomes a greater and greater challenge. Ekphrasis may still be found in various guises, but in order to compete with film, television, and computer graphics, popular prose must now "speak the language" of these media: it must try to turn back into picture writing or pure imagery.

Because pictures or moving pictures are popularly believed to have a natural correspondence to what they depict, they can satisfy more effectively than prose the wish to cut through to a "natural" representation that is not a representation at all. So the desire for the natural sign may lead to the desire to curtail arbitrary symbol systems, such as alphabetic writing. The breakout of the visual is the expression of that desire. In the USA *Today* graph, there is an effort to render arbitrary symbols as images. The grid of the graph becomes bathroom tiles, and the bar charts become razors. In a similar graph on airline safety, the line defining the number of passenger miles flown each year becomes the smoke tail of a jet that flies up and to the right. Such tricks are not limited to newspapers or magazines. Everywhere we look in our media-saturated environment, we see efforts to "render" the symbolic—to color in and make figures out of arbitrary symbols.

The breakout of the visual, the ekphrastic impulse, is at its most vigorous in the electronic writing space, where new media designers and authors are also redefining the balance between word and image. Like the older visual media of photography, film, and television, new digital media remediate the book, the newspaper, and the magazine by offering a space in which images can break free of the constraint of words and tell their own stories. Designers of hypermedia employ images as well as sound in an effort to provide a more authentic or immediate experience than words alone can offer. This strategy of remediation cuts deeply into the history of writing itself—beyond alphabetic writing to earlier forms. Hypermedia can be regarded as a kind of picture writing, which refashions the qualities of both traditional picture writing and phonetic writing.

PICTURE WRITING

If alphabetic writing is regarded as secondary writing, in the sense that it refers the reader to another system (spoken language), picture writing seems to be primary. The signs in picture writing, stylized images, seem to constitute their own silent language. Although the writer and reader may use words to describe and interpret the pictorial message, two readers could explain the same message in different words, and speakers of different languages could share the same system of picture writing. Picture writing is perhaps constructed culturally (even today) as closer to the reader, because it does not depend upon the intermediary of spoken language and seems to reproduce places and events directly. As we look back through thousands of years of phonetic literacy, the appeal of traditional picture writing is its promise of immediacy.

By the standard of phonetic writing, however, picture writing lacks narrative power. The picture elements extend over a broad range of verbal meanings: each element means too much rather than too little. If the writer is drawing a battle, the writer's own comrades might not be distinguished from the enemy, and victory may be hardly distinguishable from defeat. When we look at this representation of a battle between tribes of native North Americans (Fig. 4.3), we have exactly this experience. We cannot tell whose side the writer is on. The explanatory text below the figure removes the ambiguity, but reading the verbal text keyed to portions of the picture is an utterly different experience from reading the picture itself. The description puts the picture elements in a logical and chronological order, whereas a viewer can examine the picture itself in many ways, starting at the left or the right. The picture is nearly symmetric, and there is nothing to indicate that the right or Ojibwa side is favored over the left or Sioux side. How could the viewer, even a 19th-century Ojibwa, guess that Shahâsh'king, the figure at b, is the author of this picture text? Nothing in picture writing corresponds to a first-person narrative, because picture writing has no voice. There is also no indication of the passage of time: the Ojibwa march seems contemporary with the battle at the river.

Shahâsh'king's text captures meaning, as pictures must, at a level prior to the word. When we examine this picture, we are not reading about a skirmish that occurred on a particular day in the year 1858; instead, we are seeing the schema of that battle. In order to get a text to our (still print-bound) way of thinking, in order to instantiate the schema, we must return to the writer. The picture elements themselves are generic signs for men, tepees,

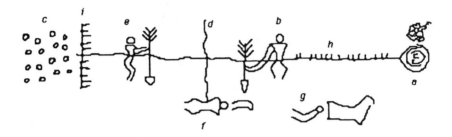

FIG. 4.3. "In 1858, a war party of Mille Lacs Ojibwa Indians, a, under the leadership of Shahâsh'king, b, went to attack Shákopi's camp, c, of Sioux at St. Peter's River, d. Shákopi is represented at e. The Ojibwa lost one man, f, at the St. Peter's River, while the Ojibwa killed five Sioux, but succeeded in securing only one arm of an Indian, g. The line h is the trail followed between Mille Lacs, a, and Shákopi's camp, c. The spots at c designate the location of the lodges, while the vertical line with short ones extending from it, i, signifies the prairie with trees growing near the camp" (taken from Mallery, 1972, vol 2, pp. 559–560; see also Jensen, 1969, p. 41).

and weapons. As we gaze at the picture, it comes to represent not so much a particular battle as a fragment of the conceptual world of the writer who produced it, an image from the cultural rather than the physical landscape of the Ojibwa. Traditional and postliterate picture writing has often had this suggestive power.

The bridge from picture writing to phonetic writing was the realization that picture elements could be identified with sounds in the language—a realization made by the Sumerians in the 4th millennium B.C., by the Egyptians perhaps independently, by the Chinese, and possibly by the Mayans centuries later (Sampson, 1985, pp. 46–47). The first step would have been to establish a correspondence between pictures for objects and the names of those objects, so that the pictogram became a logogram, a coded element telling the reader to pronounce a word in his or her language. Initially, the logogram was a double sign, referring both to an idea and to a word in the reader's language, but the principle was established that picture writing would function in the service of spoken language. The picture element stood in place of a word, and the task of the reader was to revive the sound of that word as he or she read. With logographic, syllabic, and finally alphabetic systems, this phonetic principle refashioned the writing space and redefined the immediacy offered to the reader. Alphabetic writing attempts to capture a different aspect of reality: it is no longer visual reality, but the reality of the voice. Even in the late age of print, defenders of literacy in general and print in particular emphasize that their technology can deliver to us the voice of great authors of the past. The voice of the text can tell us a story, which we may then visualize, but the voice is the primary experience.

After phonetic writing, picture writing survived only for special purposes: to communicate to people without a common language, to make a public display, and conversely to keep a secret. It survived in religious symbols, such as the Egyptian cross, the star of David, and the several varieties of the Christian cross, and in magical symbols such as the signs of the zodiac and of alchemy. Heraldry in medieval and modern Europe constituted an enormously complicated system of picture writing. Traditional trade signs and trademarks have existed for thousands of years and are now more important, or at least more prestigious and lucrative, than ever. A company may now spend millions of dollars developing or changing the picture sign by which it will be identified to tens of millions of consumers. Then there are airport signs, road signs, and a variety of public warning signs, which may combine words and images (see Wills, 1977). Picture elements in such systems as these are designed to identify objects (restaurants, bathrooms, gas stations) and situations (slippery when wet) rather than to tell a story in time: that task is left to phonetic writing. Modern examples of picture writing are in fact simpler in intent, although more sophisticated in execution, than Shahâsh'king's preliterate Ojibwa text.

ELECTRONIC PICTURE WRITING

For us today, electronic writing shares qualities with both postliterate and preliterate picture writing. By combining alphabetic writing with images and diagrams, Web and CD-ROM or DVD designers are defining the computer as a writing space that vacillates between intuitive and abstract modes of representation. An electronic text, such as a Web page, may now be a scattering of alphabetic signs among picture elements with various sizes and functions, static or animated elements that address the writer and reader without reference to speech. Connected to the Internet, the computer can also provide a video stream to the user. In the animated visual space of the computer, the verbal text must therefore compete for the reader's attention with a variety of pictorial elements, any or all of which may be in motion. Although pictures and verbal text have been combined in previous technologies of writing, the spoken word has perhaps not faced

such determined visual competition since the introduction of the phonetic principle.

We can see the eclectic and animated qualities of the computer's picture
writing in the now familiar desktop GUI, or graphical user interface, which
was pioneered by Douglas Englebart and later by Alan Kay and others at
Xerox PARC and popularized by Apple's Macintosh computer (see Barnes,
1997; Hiltzik, 1999; Johnson, 1997, pp. 42–104.) Through the controlling
visual metaphor of the business office, the user manages files and activates
programs. Files, in the shape of sheaves of paper, are contained in directo-
ries, represented as folders, while a program for word processing may look
like a hand writing on a piece of paper. When the user wants to get rid of a
file, she drops it into a metaphorical trash can. Every image is a reification of
some aspect of information processing. We noted that Shahâsh'king's picture writing was generic and presented to the reader the conceptual world
of the Ojibwa Indian. The desktop is similarly generic. It gives us the world
as an information processing environment—an efficient office in which
documents and data are effortlessly produced and consumed.

The defining element of the desktop GUI is the icon, which, although it
often has a name, is above all a picture that performs or receives an action.
These actions give the icon its meaning. As elements in a true picture
writing, icons do not merely remind the user of documents and programs,
but function as documents and programs. Reorganizing files and activating programs is writing, just as putting alphabetic characters in a row is
writing. Rather like the religious relics after which they are named, computer icons are energy units that focus the operative power of the machine
into visible and manipulable symbols. Computer icons also remind us of
the cultural functions of Hebrew letters in the Cabala or of alchemical and
other signs invoked by such Renaissance magi as Giordano Bruno (see
Frances Yates, *Giordano Bruno and the Hermetic Tradition*, 1964). Magic
letters and signs were often objects of meditation, as they were in the logical diagrams of the medieval Raymond Llull (1985), and they were also
believed to have operational powers. As functioning representations in
computer writing, electronic icons realize what magic signs in the past
could only suggest. The function of icons is to tie together elements in the
computer's writing space: to show how documents are grouped and to
connect documents to the programs that create them. As in the traditional Ojibwa picture writing, the spatial relationship of the icons is significant. It may show, for example, which documents are stored together on
the same disk. Although the spatial arrangement of words has always been

a feature of diagrams in printed texts, the desktop GUI is a representation that takes full advantage of its two-dimensional surface for images as well as words. Indeed, even the words on the screen, set above, beside, or beneath images, serve as visual units and enter into the larger spatial structure. Although diagrams are the exception on the printed page, they become the rule in electronic writing, which invites us to read the whole computer screen as a moving, evolving diagram.

In all picture writing, before and after literacy, the elements exist at the margin between linguistic and pictorial meaning. Sometimes, particularly when the picture text is a narrative, the elements seem to aim for the specificity of language. Sometimes, these same elements move back into a world of pure form and become shapes that we admire for their visual economy. The elements oscillate between being signs and being images, or rather it is the reader who oscillates in her perception of the elements. Whenever she find herself admiring the simplicity of computer icons, she has ceased to examine these elements as signs in a text. In the next instant she may resume her role as reader and treat the elements as arbitrary signs, as glyphs in an electronic alphabet. This oscillation is a characteristic of reading in the late age of print (=> p. 184).

In the representational art of the West, the picture space may be formal, but it is usually not rigidly codified. At least from the Renaissance to the 19th century, paintings tended to pursue the strategy of transparency—to provide the viewer with a window onto the real world or a possible world (=> p. 25). Artists and their viewers assumed that the space of the picture should reflect the space of nature and that the picture's elements should be arranged as they appear in nature. In a verbal text, where the visual space is wholly conventional, learning to read means learning the conventions of that space. Pictorial space and verbal space are therefore apparent opposites: the one claims to reflect a world outside of itself, and the other is arbitrary and self-contained. The situation becomes more complex when painters put words into the space of their pictures—an intermittent practice in Western art, although common in both Chinese landscape and ancient Greek vase painting. In these traditions, the juxtaposition of word and image creates a pleasing tension. The words seem to be trying to transform the world of the picture into a writing space, while at the same time the picture invites the viewer to consider the words as images or abstract shapes rather than signs.

We could also say that the space of the text was trying to remediate the image into discursive meaning, while the image was insisting on the formal significance of the word itself as an image. In Chinese writing the word signs are shapes whose function is to decorate as well as signify. The space of picture writing has always carried this ambiguity between the written and the pictorial, or the conventional and the apparently natural, between what Richard Grusin and I have called the hypermediated and the transparent (=> p. 25). Modern systems seem more conventional and arbitrary, whereas in preliterate systems the conventions are often less obvious because there is less technical refinement. In the Ojibwa text Shahâsh'king tried to make his picture correspond to the geography of the battlefield; however, he also apparently expected his readers to see that the picture elements constituted a message and to understand textual conventions in his writing. Every element in the picture was a sign, but many of the elements were drawn, however crudely, to be images as well. In electronic picture writing, the message conveyed by the images (icons, diagrams, graphs) is much more precise, but even here the images are often compelling as pure forms. A defining quality of picture writing is its capacity to unite two radically different spaces. Traditional picture writing co-opts the "pure" image in order to tell a story, record facts, or give a warning. As electronic picture writing, hypermedia refashions phonetic writing by reasserting the status of pictorial elements: hypermedia claims that it can communicate more effectively or more vividly with the user by embedding these elements in an interactive text.

The graphical user interface itself constitutes such a text. Because pictures and verbal text in the interface belong to the same space, pictures may cross over and become textual symbols. The unified character of the electronic space is unusual, though not unprecedented in the history of writing. The development of phonetic writing, although it did not eliminate pictures altogether from the writing space, did create a dichotomy between image and phonetic sign. If phonetic writing pulls the writer and reader toward the pure linear space of spoken language, pictures, diagrams, and graphs pull them back to a pictorial space that is at least two-dimensional and whose visual meaning is not strictly codified. Different writing technologies have mediated this tension in different ways.

In Egyptian writing, for example, there was an intimate relationship between images and text, both in wall-painting and on papyrus (see Davies, 1987). Because hieroglyphs were themselves small stylized images, Egyptian writing could blend smoothly with illustrative images both visually and conceptually (see Weitzmann, 1970, pp. 57–69). The Greek and Roman writing space was not as friendly to pictures. The ancients seem generally to have regarded writing as an instrument for holding spoken words in a fixed form until they could be revived by the voice of the reader. Book decoration was, therefore, an insignificant art in antiquity (see Nordenfalk, 1951, pp. 9–20). From the pure alphabetic space of early Greek inscriptions, it took several hundred years for the Greeks to readjust and admit pictures and diagrams fully into the writing space (see Weitzmann, 1970, pp. 97ff). The growing importance of pictures in late antique books continued in the Middle Ages, when codices presented a complex space of words and images, illustrations and ornamentation—the most complex prior to the electronic medium. In medieval books, pictures were sometimes separated from the text and given prominence as full-page miniatures. But the writing space was also decorated with the illuminated letters that were unique to the medieval writing.

Like computer icons, medieval illuminated letters functioned simultaneously as text and picture. Medieval illumination threatened to turn letters back into images or abstract designs and sometimes made the letters all but impossible to read (see Alexander, *The Decorated Letter*, 1978, p. 8). Perhaps the best-known instance is the *Book of Kells*, where, for example, the Greek letters chi-rho-iota (standing for "Christ" in Matthew 1.18) occupy a whole page. Although the design is so intricate that the shapes of the letters are almost completely obscured, these letters remain part of the verbal text: they have to be included in order to read the verse. The chi-rho-iota thus shows how the pictorial and verbal spaces interpenetrate. Medieval illumination embodied a dialectic between writing and the visual world; it was a means by which writing could describe or circumscribe the world—not symbolically through language, but visually through the shape of the letter itself.

Printers with their new technology favored a stricter separation of the verbal and pictorial writing spaces. Although diagrams and illustrations were as popular as ever, for technical reasons these images were not as well integrated with the words, as they had been in the best medieval traditions (see Tufte, 1983, pp. 181–182). Woodcut illustrations were segregated from the printed text as a product, and the wood revealed much more the hand of the craftsman. Many printed books contained no illustrations at all, just as many medieval manuscripts contained none. The ideal of the printed book was and is a sequence of pages containing ordered lines of alphabetic text. When the woodcut was replaced by the copper engraving, more elaborate and finely drawn images became part of the printed book. Printers and authors became more ingenious in putting words and images together. The 17th and 18th centuries were an age of allegorical frontispieces and illustrations. Today, although photolithography allows any image to be taken onto the page, the pictorial and verbal spaces are still not as subtly combined as they were in medieval illuminated manuscripts. Most books for adult readers still segregate blocks of text from blocks of pictures, and color plates are often gathered together in the middle of the book to lower production costs. On the other hand, today's magazines, newspapers, advertising tabloids, and billboards all tend to subvert the cultural primacy of linear verbal text; they work against the ideal established by the printed book.

So, from the nadir of early Greek writing, in which there was no room for pictures, the writing space of the papyrus roll, the codex, and the printed book have permitted a variety of relationships between picture and text. Pictures have been decorative, explanatory, and allegorical. They have commented on the text, and the text has commented on them. But only in the medieval codex were words and pictures as thoroughly unified as they are on the computer screen. On the screen, as on medieval parchment, verbal text and image interpenetrate to such a degree that the writer and reader can no longer always know where the pictorial space ends and the verbal space begins. In uniting the verbal and the pictorial, the screen constitutes a visual unit that depends on but also attempts to surpass the typography of the printed page.

THE ELECTRONIC PAGE

Typography in conventional printed books begins with the letter and never goes much further. Once the typefaces and styles (and perhaps colors of ink) have been chosen for a book, there are relatively few decisions left to be made. Each page will be a rectangle of text surrounded by white space. Illustrations will occupy blocks reserved within the rectangle, in the margins, or on separate pages altogether, and in any case illustrations will be relatively rare in "serious," discursive books. Although advertising and magazines present many possibilities for creative visual design, the layout of a book is as conservative as is the choice of fonts appropriate to the book. Many typographers would agree that the decisions of layout all flow from the letter, so that the printing press is really a letter processor.

In some ways the earlier handwritten page offered more freedom of design than the printed page. Already in the Carolingian period, scribes used a different script (uncial) to indicate titles and demarcate sections. By the 13th century, scribes had developed a number of visual cues to help the reader locate text and keep his orientation. Such cues as different styles and sizes of letters and different colors of ink were pioneered in the Middle Ages and then standardized in the age of print. Probably the most important visual structure in the medieval codex was the marginal note. Medieval texts were often arranged into two or more layers on the page: the center of the page contained the more ancient and venerable text, and the margins offered explanation and commentary added by one or more scholars. With this layout, it was relatively easy to move back and forth between text and notes, certainly much easier than it was for the reader in the ancient world to juggle several papyrus rolls. Marginal notes told readers what to look for and provided constant support in the task. Many Renaissance or later readers found these notes to be a hindrance, the weight of centuries of misreading of the text, and printers began to clear the page of this interpretive material, allowing the text to occupy the whole of the writing space and therefore to speak for itself. Notes moved to the foot of the page and often to the back of the book. But in banishing the notes, modern printers have sacrificed both the immediacy of reference and the sense of visual and intellectual context that marginal notes provided to their medieval readers.

In the modern printed book, the space is simple and clean. Different texts do not compete in adjacent spaces for the reader's attention, as they still do in a magazine or newspaper. In a magazine the text is divided into blocks of varying shapes and sizes, and readers find themselves pulled back and forth among the blocks. The page layout reflects the topical nature of the material—a combination of advertisements, notices, and long and short articles. A magazine or newspaper is in this respect closer in spirit to the topographic writing space of the computer, where the "typography" also mirrors the topical nature of the text itself. Larger units of text together with images can be isolated on the computer screen. The screen becomes a magazine page in which units rearrange themselves to meet various needs.

In the GUI the window is the defining feature of computer typography. A computer window is a framing device that marks out a space for a particular unit of verbal text, graphics, or both. It frames the writer or reader's view of that space, which is an indefinite two-dimensional plane. Other windows may contain graphics or video, so that the whole electronic writing space is constituted by a collection of tiled or stacked windows, each a view into a verbal or graphic space. The computer window recalls the page in a printed book, which is also a stack of two-dimensional planes. An important difference is that printed pages stay in one order. Working at the computer, the writer or reader can move one window aside in order to view parts of the windows below; she can reorder the stack by plucking one window from below and placing it on top. Ultimately the GUI's window metaphor owes as much to painting as to printing. Like perspective painting, which offers the user a window onto a world, each GUI window also contains a world—it may be a world of text, a graphic image in two or three dimensions, or a live video feed. The GUI presents the entire world of digital information through a set of such manipulable, paned views. If, in reading a printed book, we are offered only one view, one page at a time, the GUI is a hypermediated world in which multiple windows offer heterogeneous views at the same time.

If we are viewing a hypertext, the windows also take on a structural significance. In a hypertext, like the World Wide Web, there will be operational links from verbal and graphic elements within and between windows. Following a link can make windows appear, disappear, or rearrange themselves. Even within a single window, objects (images and verbal text) can be stacked: text can slide underneath a graphic, or the graphic itself may be moved to reveal another graphic. The layout of the screen may always change, and the reader may participate in those changes. Like the text itself, the typography is not determined prior to the reading, but is instead a manifestation of the act of reading: it is one aspect of interactive text. The screen enters into a series of configurations, and that evolving series is the visual expression of a particular reader's journey through the text. No one configuration is likely to be as attractive as a page that a professional typographer can produce for print. But no one configuration lasts very long, and it is the movement from one to the next that carries much of the meaning in a hypertext. In a conventional printed text or manuscript, although the reader's eye moves along the letters and possibly back and forth among images, the letters and images themselves are static. In an electronic text, however, both the reader's eye and the writing surface can be in motion. Electronic readers therefore shuttle between two modes of reading, or rather they learn to read in a way that combines verbal and picture reading. Their task includes activating signs by typing and moving the cursor and then making symbolic sense of the motions that these movements produce.

THE WORLD WIDE WEB AND THE
REMEDIATION OF GRAPHIC DESIGN

The World Wide Web has been a form of picture writing since 1993, when the introduction of "inline" images transformed and greatly expanded the uses of the Web (= > p. 40). It became apparent that the Web could be a new field for advertising and other commercial activities as well as for entertainment, none of which had been important in Berners-Lee's original vision for the Web. The sharing of texts for scientific research became one of the Web's many special uses. If Berners-Lee envisioned the Web as global hypertext, the developers of the graphical browser redefined it as global hypermedia. And if the Web as hypertext is the remediation of the printed book, the Web as hypermedia is the remediation of other, more ephemeral printed materials, the magazine and the newspaper. In the years since the development of the graphical browser, Web page design has borrowed its aesthetic and economic principles from graphic design for print.

The ongoing development of the "hypertextual markup language" (HTML) reflects the shift from conceiving of the Web as an electronic book to conceiving of it as an electronic magazine. The term "page" for the fundamental unit of Web design suggests that the originators were setting out to remake the book, but magazines and newspapers also have pages, which are laid out as a two-dimensional space of words and images. The original HTML tags did not afford the designer much control over the visual layout of the page: they provided for text that flowed in one dimension down the page, as it had in word processors. Images were simply inserted into this unidimensional flow. Graphic designers, however, have insisted on controlling the horizontal placement of images and texts, not just the vertical flow. They have exploited the HTML tags available and campaigned for new tags, and indeed whole new formats, in order to obtain that control. As a result, some of the most compelling Web pages began to look like magazine advertisements, with striking visual metaphors, display fonts, drop-shadowed texts, color gradients, and the pixel-by-pixel construction of gridded spaces (Siegel, 1997).

Graphic design itself was a form that arose when social and economic needs and technical improvements converged in the 19th and early 20th centuries (Meggs, 1998, pp. 126–205). (On the development of visual trademarks and advertising, in particular, see James Beniger, *The Control Revolution*, 1986, pp. 269–278.) Photolithography, the pantographic punch cutter, and other innovations greatly expanded the range of images and type styles that could be used on a page. At the same time, a new form of capitalism was seeking new ways to generate desire for its products among a public of consumers. Mere words no longer seemed adequate; they had to share their space with images. At the same time, graphic design was also distinguishing itself from high art, as designers associated with Russian Constructivism, the Bauhaus, and de Stijl influenced and were influenced by the work of modernist artists (Meggs, 1998, pp. 231–336). Graphic designers sought to show that a combination of word and image offered an experience that was more authentic than the conventional printed page could offer alone. Their claim to improvement lay in combining words, graphics, and photography. The Web now claims to supersede traditional graphic design by adding the interactivity and immediacy of global hypertext. Designers for the Web, like David Siegel (1997), now call for a rhetoric that simultaneously respects and overturns their heritage in graphic design for print.

This graphic rhetoric is an expression of the breakout of the visual that has assaulted print and prose genres since the beginning of the 20th century. The development of the graphical browsers (Mosaic, Netscape Navigator, and Internet Explorer) assured that the Web would also adopt this rhetoric, because the new HTML tags gave the same visual and operational status to the image as to verbal text. When clicking on a verbal phrase opens another window to reveal an image, that image seems to emerge from and overwrite the text (Fig. 4.4). In the dynamic typography of HTML, any juxtaposition is possible: images can also be linked to text, and images directly to other images. The image therefore slips out of the control of the word and makes its own claim to presenting the authentic and the real. It becomes hard to imagine how traditional prose could successfully compete with the dynamic and heterogeneous visual experience that the Web now offers.

Furthermore, Web design has not remained frozen at this stage of remediation of graphic design for print. Animation, streaming audio and video, and multimedia-style programmed interaction are all finding their way onto Web pages. The Web also remediates photography, film, radio, and television, and each of these technologies of representation have their cultural constructions and their own design principles—principles that Web designers will necessarily refashion as they incorporate these media in their pages and sites. The eclecticism of the Web will continue to challenge designers, who will have to combine disparate media in ways for which there are few obvious parallels. All of their remediations will be in pursuit of the same goal: greater authenticity and immediacy of presentation. Just as the Web has offered to traditional graphic designers a more dynamic space for their work, so it offers to producers of films, television, and radio a space that responds to the viewer. It remains to be seen whether interactive film and television will diminish the popularity of their traditional counterparts. But in any case, streaming technologies and animation will distance the Web further from the strategies of the printed book. They will reinforce the

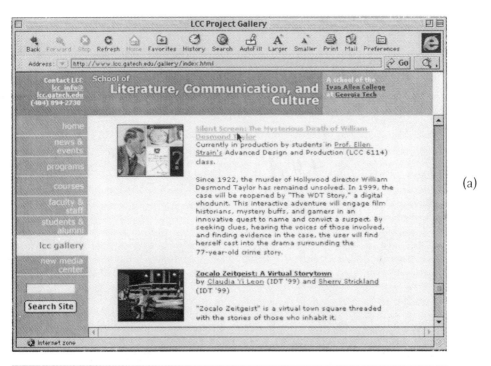

(a)

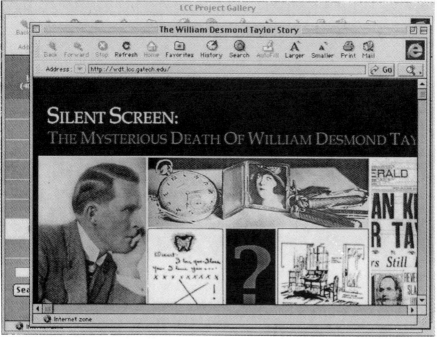

(b)

FIG. 4.4.   Text in Web pages is often linked to images. When the user clicks a phrase (a), an image breaks out of and dominates the text (b).

breakout of the visual on the Web, as in other forms of electronic writing, as they displace and threaten to overwhelm the text on the Web page.

TEXT IN CYBERSPACE

Text is by no means absent from digital media: the World Wide Web alone includes many millions of words of text. However, both in stand-alone multimedia and on the Web, text is often displaced in favor of graphic presentation. In multimedia, particularly in CD-ROM (or DVD) applications, but also in certain genres of Web pages, graphics dominate the screen, while the words themselves serve either for titles or merely to identify buttons. Multimedia applications are in fact often characterized by their "buttoned style." Pushing buttons or clicking on image maps call forth new images or activate videos, and this ongoing chain of visual and aural effects takes the place of discursive prose. In the buttoned style, to place more than a sentence or two of text on a screen is an admission of failure, for the assumption is that the designer should be able to deploy a graphic, a video, or perhaps an audio segment to communicate any idea she has. A paragraph of prose is a last resort—to be used when she runs out of ideas, time, or production resources.

The buttoned style is about writing with images rather than words. When multimedia does recall the earlier writing tradition, it often ends up in parody. Figure 4.5, for example, a splashscreen for a multimedia presentation on the state of Arkansas, is a unconscious parody of medieval illumination. The images pasted inside the letters remind us of the way in which large initial capitals in medieval manuscripts defined a space for decorative or figural art. Here, however, the word Arkansas has been dislocated, its letters jumbled and the images inside the letters straining to get out. The multimedia frames that follow this one in the application soon abandon words altogether for colorful images of the state.

On the Internet, electronic mail and newsgroups remain among the most widely used applications. Although these applications have been purely textual, they are not likely to remain so, as the technology improves for transmitting graphics and digitized audio and video over the network. Even in their purely textual form, e-mail and newsgroups are beginning to show signs of the breakout of the visual. One of the peculiar characteristics of writing for e-mail and newsgroups is the use of ASCII characters to form iconic faces. For example, the sequence :-) represents a smiling face and adds some ironic nuance to the previous sentence or paragraph (see Table 4.1). Such icons are meant to put the verbal text in context, as the writer tries to enforce a univocal interpretation on prose that is otherwise open to

FIG. 4.5.   A splash screen for a multimedia presentation on Arkansas.

many interpretations. The desire to contextualize in this way shows that the implicit model is not written or printed text at all, but face-to-face conversation or perhaps conversation on the telephone. Handwritten letters and especially printed prose have always faced the problem of decontextualization. However, at least in Western writing in the past several hundred years, these difficulties have not led to the development of icons designed to fix authorial intent. With some important exceptions (such as Sterne and Blake), writers in print have depended almost entirely on the prose itself to manipulate their own and their readers' perspectives. Often, they have exploited this decontextualization to produce texts that are explicitly polyvocal, as Bakhtin and others claimed for the genre of the novel. The use of icons in e-mail and newsgroups suggests that contemporary electronic writers are not interested in the distancing and ambiguity that prose offers and instead want to give their prose the immediacy of a single voice and if possible a face. As Internet technology develops, it seems likely that synchronous and asynchronous video will replace e-mail for many purposes, precisely because video offers to our visual culture the apparent and univocality that prose cannot. Text need not vanish from electronic communication, however: many kinds of documents may continue to be transmitted, but these documents may well be appended to video messages, just as they are appended to ASCII e-mail today. Verbal text will be further marginalized in the quest for immediacy.

MUDS AND MOOS

The text-based virtual environments called MUDs and MOOs constitute a more complicated case. It has often been noted that MOOs and their predecessors, interactive adventure games, have much in common with hypertextual fiction. Although MOOs seldom employ the techniques of distancing and self-reference found in mature hypertextual fictions such as *afternoon* (Joyce, 1990) and *Victory Garden* (Moulthrop, 1992), a MOO is nevertheless an interactive verbal text, in which the reader follows electronic links from screen to screen and so constructs the text in the act of reading. On the other hand, if in hypertextual fiction the reader is repeatedly made aware of the artificial character of reading and writing fiction, MOOs function more simply. They embody the assumption of transparency: that to read a descriptive or narrative text is to look through a window onto another world. With current network technology, a MOO is an example of *ekphrasis*, the attempt to capture pictures in words (= > p. 56). What is unusual is the collaborative character of the ekphrasis. Many writers may

TABLE 4.1
Emotions and Their Intended Meanings

ASCII icon	Representation
:-)	Smiling face
;-)	Winking and smiling
:-D	Laughing
:-I	Indifferent
:-O	Surprised
:-(	Frowning, unhappy
O:-)	Angelic face
}:-)	Devilish face
:-P	Tongue sticking out

work together to create the textual world of a MOO, often imagined as a building with a room devoted to each activity or belonging to each user. These same and other users then occupy the rooms synchronously and asynchronously, leaving behind their textual traces. In a typical MOO, each user adopts a persona, consisting of a name and set of characteristics. If she types a sentence in quotation marks at her keyboard, that sentence is broadcast as her utterance to the other characters in the same room (and appears on the corresponding users' computer screens). The remark becomes an element of dialogue in a collective story generated by the users in the room (=> p. 199).

MOOs may be stories, but they are not sophisticated fictions, in which the reader moves back and forth between an awareness of the text as text and the act of losing himself in the story. Any text may be regarded not only as a window on another world, but also as a rhetorical structure of allusions and references—just as a painting may be treated as a window onto a world (immediacy) or as a set of brush strokes on a canvas (hypermediacy). The reader may then oscillate between looking *at* the textual structure and looking *through* it (=> p. 184). However, most MOOs do not set up an oscillation between rhetorical awareness and forgetfulness. They do not ask their users to look *at* the text, but only *through* it to the scene that is being described.

The verbal MOO is an heroic attempt to recreate in prose what many, perhaps most, of its users would already prefer to be a sensory experience. For most users, it is probably true that the words only get in the way. Anyone who watches participants in a MOO, seated at their keyboards typing furiously, can see the intense involvement that such participation can require. Repetitive stress syndrome is almost a vocational hazard among MOO users, as they seek to sustain the rhythms of the visual and auditory illusion entirely in typed prose. So, along with e-mail and newsgroups, MOOs seem destined to become video experiences. The first graphical MOOs already appeared in the mid-1990s. The Palace is an early example, although it only places simple graphic backdrops behind the two-dimensional characters (www.thepalace.com September 17, 1999). There may not be much visual depth or movement in this environment, but each player is at least represented by a cartoonlike icon that gives her a location to occupy in the space of the room (Fig. 4.6). Rather unexpectedly, the Palace remediates the printed comic book: the drawing is simple and colorful, the backgrounds are static, and, when the characters speak, balloons appear above their heads containing their words. This remediation is a technically clever solution, for

FIG. 4.6.   The Palace, a graphical MOO. (Used by permission of Communications.com.)

by imitating the static form of the comic book, the Palace can function over even the lowest bandwidth connections on the Internet. The cultural effect, however, is once again to subordinate the text, as comic books or so-called "graphical novels" do in print. Other more graphically sophisticated MOOs will no doubt eventually exploit full-motion animation and video, and in the process they will remediate film and television and further diminish the status of any text that appears in this electronic environment.

5

The Electronic Book

THE CHANGING IDEA OF THE BOOK

At various periods, Western cultures have chosen to embody writing in various technological forms, and these choices have in turn affected the organization, style, and genres of writing and our expectations as authors and as readers. The physical unit of a writing technology helps to define the conceptual unit—what comes to be regarded as a written volume. For centuries in the ancient world, the papyrus roll, about 25 feet long, constituted a volume. (Our word "volume" comes from the Latin *volumen*, which means roll.) The codex, which replaced the roll, was more effective in enclosing, protecting, and delimiting the writing it contained. A whole work could be contained in a single codex, which was less often the case with the smaller papyrus roll, which might hold only segments or "chapters" of a work. The writer was and still is encouraged to think of his codex as a unit of meaning, a complete verbal structure. The codex has been associated with the idea that writing should be rounded into finite units of expression and that a writer or reader can and should close his text off from all other texts.

The papyrus roll was poor at suggesting a sense of closure, and in fact closure does not seem to have had the significance for ancient writers and readers that it acquired, for example, in the industrial age of print. In the ancient world, authors, especially poets, would often perform their works before an audience of listeners, who did not have their own copies. The writing on the roll served as a script, to be consulted when memory failed. The character and the length of these ancient texts were not determined by the size of the roll, but rather by the needs of performance. Because Greek epic poets were probably illiterate, their poetry was not determined by writing at all. The *Iliad* and *Odyssey*, each far too long to fit on one papyrus roll, were in a sense unbounded poems, fragments of a network of stories that could be extended indefinitely. Each Greek tragedy, on the other hand, was too small to fill up one roll, because its length depended on the conventions of the Greek dramatic festivals. The tragedian did, however, have to write down his play in order to convey it to the actors, so that tragedy remained halfway between orality and full literacy. Even when prose writers like Plato wrote for individual readers, the oral character of ancient writing remained strong. Perhaps for that reason the ancients were content with the papyrus roll, which was better suited to reading aloud than to silent reading and study. Throughout the ancient period, the papyrus roll remained too short to meet its own culture's need as a grand unit of expression, so that a major work by a philosopher, historian, or poet typically occupied several rolls. The papyrus roll did not contribute to any cultural sense of closure, and it is no coincidence that many ancient poetic and historical texts do not have climactic endings. They often simply fall silent, leaving the impression that there is always more to say. Perhaps it is characteristic of a primarily oral rather than written culture that its texts are often incomplete in this sense.

The development of the codex corresponded to a set of new possibilities for writers and readers. In place of a script for performing the text aloud, it provided a space that was visually more sophisticated and finished. A codex could hold several times as much text as a roll. The early Christians apparently preferred this new technology, because one codex could hold all the New Testament writings. Pagan texts followed in being transferred to the new medium (see Reynolds & Wilson, 1978, pp. 30–32). The physical presence of the book also began to matter more as public performance was replaced by individual study. Silent reading became common by the later Middle Ages, but long before that books were set before individual readers—monks in their libraries, for example (see Saenger, 1982). Writers and readers were encouraged to identify the physical book, which they held in their hands, with the text and to regard the end of the book as the end of the text. The importance of the book as an object perhaps reached its zenith in the Middle Ages, when illuminated manuscripts were examples of multimedia writing at its finest, in which all the elements functioned symbolically as well as aesthetically to define a verbal–visual meaning. In this one sense, printing was not an improvement, for it destroyed the synthesis that medieval manuscripts had achieved. On the other hand, Renaissance culture used print technology to strengthen the idea of the book as a complete and closed verbal structure. Although in medieval codices and early printed books, unrelated texts were often bound together, standardization and economies of scale eventually encouraged printers and publishers to put one text in each volume.

In the centuries following the invention of printing, then, it became the goal of serious writers to add another volume to the world's library. The paged book became the physical embodiment, the incarnation, of the text it contained. Incarnation is not too strong a metaphor, because, through printing, Western culture came more and more to anthropomorphize books, to regard each book as a subject with a name, a place (in the library), a voice, and a bibliographic life of its own. Modern printing includes the making of the binding and dust jacket, so that every edition of a book has its own visual identity. Although today you can tell a book by its cover, this was not the case in early printing, when books were often bound after they had been transported and sold (Febvre & Martin, 1971, p. 159). The unique identity of each publication has come to be sanctioned and even required by copyright law. Each book must be different enough from all other books to deserve its own place in the library, and it should be complete in its own terms. Each book strives to assert its identity, while at the same time entering into a cascade of relationships with other books. The relationships are attractive and repulsive, as the book refers the reader to some books and warns him against others.

As we refashion the book through digital technology, we are diminishing the sense of closure that belonged to the codex and to print. Various electronic devices (desktop, laptop and palmtop computers, digital assistants, pagers, and so on) pay homage to the printed codex and other paper-based materials, while at the same time aiming to supersede them. Portable computers present themselves as new and improved books: "notebook" has become a generic term for these devices, while Apple Computer has had lines called "Powerbooks" and "iBooks" and Hewlett Packard has sold "Omnibooks." These full-fledged computers are hybrid books, in which we can read and write texts and process numerical information. Here as elsewhere in the late age of print, we see the move to heterogeneity and hybrid forms, including on-demand printing from digital databases, printed books and magazines that refer to Web sites, Web sites that preview and sell books, and so-called "information appliances" that combine the characteristics of books, notebooks, and calendars (see Donald Norman's *The Invisible Computer*, 1999). All such hybrids work against closure, because both in form and function they refer their users to other texts, devices, or media forms.

One class of information appliances is positioned explicitly to replace the paged book: an example is the Rocket eBook. As its Web-based advertising indicates (Fig. 5.1), the eBook appropriates and refashions many of the physical properties as well as the "interface" of a traditional book. It is lightweight and easy to carry; the reader can write notes in its margins and underline passages as in a printed book. Unlike desktop computers, the eBook tries to imitate the physical presence of the codex. In addition, it offers its users texts that have already appeared in print: principally books, but potentially newspapers, magazines, or other materials. The designers of the eBook wanted to give their users a new way to approach the heritage of print. As with any remediation, however, the eBook must promise something more than the form that it remediates: it must offer what can be construed as a more immediate, complete, or authentic experience for the reader. One innovation is that the eBook turns any text into a hypertext, in which the reader can search for the occurrence of words and phrases

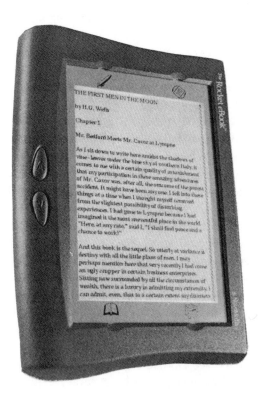

FIG. 5.1.   The Rocket eBook. © 1998–2000 NuvoMedia, Inc. (Used by permission.)

throughout the text, so that the whole text becomes immediately available to the reader in a way a printed book is not. The second, and ultimately more important, innovation is implied in the exhortation to "let the Rocket eBook put a world of books in the palm of your hand." Unlike a printed book, which can only contain one fixed text, the eBook is designed to be re-loaded. Because its texts are downloaded from the Internet, the eBook is connected to a growing world of materials available online. The eBook becomes not only a stand-alone device, but also a portal that leads the reader into cyberspace. In fact, most of the new information appliances are or will be networked: they will connect to the Internet at least for getting or sending data and may then disconnect for periods of personal use.

Such ersatz electronic books reflect our growing ambivalence about closed forms. (On closure in electronic texts, see Landow, 1997, pp. 79–88.) We remain under the influence of the tradition of print and its definition of closure. These electronic books look like closed forms, and as portable devices they assert their physical identity as strongly as traditional bound volumes. The designers of the eBook, with its strong lines reminiscent of Art Deco, sought to make the device stand out as a consumer object. On the other hand, the pull of the Internet is now culturally and economically overwhelming. Designers and their corporate managers want to connect almost every electronic device to the Internet, and such a connection works against the separate identity of electronic book forms and their contents. Thus, electronic books become information structures that reach out to other structures, not only metaphorically, as printed books did, but also operationally. An electronic book does not join itself to other books end-to-end, as printed books do when we set them on a shelf; instead, merging into the network of the World Wide Web, the electronic book invites exploration as part of a network of texts. The openness of such networked devices reflects our growing desire to construct writing in a way that breaks down the traditional distinctions between the book and such larger forms as the encyclopedia and the library.

GREAT BOOKS

The desire to make a great book, to set down all verbal knowledge in one place, was a dream shared by medieval writers and by the Greeks and Romans. In the cultures of the papyrus roll and of the codex, that desire expressed itself in two complementary forms: the library and the encyclopedia. A library amasses books, while an encyclopedia condenses them.

Both seek to organize and control texts in order to make them available to the reader.

The encyclopedic impulse was strong in later antiquity, when editors produced numerous handbooks or miscellanies on subjects important to their culture, such as rhetoric, poetry, natural history, and medicine. The impulse was also strong at times among Byzantine scholars and during the Middle Ages in Western Europe. Because Western medieval scholars attached great importance to authoritative texts (such as the Church fathers and later Aristotle), they felt the need to collect and summarize those texts in handbooks of their own. The most influential encyclopedias (by Martianus Capella, Isidore of Seville, and later Vincent of Beauvais) became authoritative texts themselves. These compilations were great books, and they encouraged philosophers and even poets to produce their own great books in response. Philosopher-theologians produced *summae*, which were encyclopedic in ambition—attempts to join the major philosophical and theological traditions into a convincing whole. This joining and reconciling of written authorities was a central task of medieval scholarship, as Ernst Curtius (1973) pointed out:

> For the Middle Ages, all discovery of truth was first reception of traditional authorities, then later—in the 13th century—rational reconciliation of authoritative texts. A comprehension of the world was not regarded as a creative function but as an assimilation and retracing of given facts; the symbolic expression of this being reading. The goal and the accomplishment of the thinker is to connect all these facts together in the form of the "summa." Dante's cosmic poem is such a summa too (p. 326).

The encyclopedic impulse diminished somewhat in the age of print. As books multiplied, it became harder to aspire to the goal of a book that would encompass all important works, even in a single field. Although more encyclopedias and handbooks were produced than ever before, the aim of the encyclopedists became more utilitarian: to report more accurate information rather than to synthesize all knowledge. The French *Encyclopédie*, whose first volume appeared in 1751, was perhaps both the last successful encyclopedia in the medieval sense and the first modern encyclopedia, because it was a statement of the ideals of the Enlightenment as well as a compendium of technical information. In the 19th and particularly in the 20th century, making encyclopedias became a business rather than a philosophical or scholarly endeavor. Major encyclopedias now maintain permanent editorial staffs, which revise the volumes continuously to furnish up-to-date information in a convenient package. Their concern is to provide information on subjects of popular interest, not to demonstrate the interrelations of all subjects. Today, however, the ideal of the encyclopedia as a synthesis of knowledge has reemerged in a new form. Many works on CD-ROM or DVD and on the World Wide Web explicitly remediate the printed encyclopedia, while in a larger sense the millions of pages hyperlinked on the World Wide Web are being read by our culture as an electronic compendium of knowledge, both a new encyclopedia and a new library.

ENCYCLOPEDIC ORDER

Prior to the invention of the printing, the population of books grew and declined along with the associated culture. In some periods manuscripts were plentiful; in other periods few manuscripts were read or copied, and many works were lost altogether. A great period of loss of ancient texts, for example, occurred from the 6th to the 8th centuries—both in the Latin West and in the Byzantine East (see Reynolds & Wilson, 1978, pp. 47–48, 75–76). Each period of sustained growth created a "textual overload," when there were many more books than a reader could afford to own or had the time or dedication to read. The opposite problem was a lack of books during periods of literary cultural decline. Whenever texts have become inaccessible—either because the available technology was too successful at producing texts or because the culture went into a literary decline—readers have turned to encyclopedias and handbooks. At the time of Pliny the Elder's *Natural History*, in the 1st century A.D., for example, readers had to confront an enormous quantity of scientific and literary texts produced by the Greeks of the classical and Hellenistic periods. By the time of Martianus Capella's allegorical encyclopedia of the liberal arts in the 5th century or Isidore of Seville's *Etymologies* in the 7th, the problem was scarcity. Vincent of Beauvais' *Speculum* appeared in the 13th century, when the already large medieval library was again being supplemented by Aristotle and other ancient texts. Three hundred years of printing created a vast textual space for the French *Encyclopédie*. Indeed, printing made textual overload a permanent condition: more books were produced in each succeeding century, and new editions preserved all books that changing cultural norms continued to regard as important (Eisenstein, 1979, vol. 1, pp. 181ff). What many have called the "information revolution" ushered in by the computer is only the most recent manifestation of a problem that is now 500 years old. (Geoffrey Nunberg has even suggested that the notion of quantifiable information was particularly well suited to what I have called the industrial age of print and that electronic technology ushers in not the beginning, but the end of this "information age." See Nunberg, 1996, pp. 103–133.)

The encyclopedia offers a solution for both conditions of surplus and scarcity. When there are too many books, it offers to control information that has gotten out of hand. When books are not available, the encyclopedia summarizes information that the reader cannot get from original sources. In either case, the encyclopedia puts textual elements in a place where the reader can be sure to find them and in this sense performs a therapeutic as well as a bibliographic function. An encyclopedia reassures its reader that the texts in the contemporary writing space are under control. The key to any encyclopedia is therefore its organization, the principles by which it controls other texts, and the choice of organizing principles depends on both the contemporary construction of knowledge and the contemporary technology of writing.

Ancient and medieval encyclopedias were organized at first simply by association and then by progressively more elaborate hierarchies of topics. Pliny the Elder constructed his *Natural History* on principles of association. He began with the stars and planets, then moved to the geography of the Earth, then to humans, animals, plants, and finally minerals. His intuitive approach was appropriate both for his Roman readers, who were not scientifically sophisticated, and for the highly linear papyrus rolls on which his work was recorded. After the invention of the codex, encyclopedists (such as Martianus Capella, Isidore of Seville, Hugh of St. Victor, and Vincent of Beauvais) gradually developed more elaborate categories and deeper hierarchies (Châtillon, 1966; Lemoine, 1966). The motive in all cases was to provide a framework that would be familiar or accessible to an educated reader. The codex form of these encyclopedias with its "random access" made the reader's work easier and allowed the author to develop a more elaborate outline of knowledge. The outline in turn solved the problem of textual overload by providing categories for all the elements of learning and so suggesting that one book could indeed encompass the textual world.

Hierarchies continued to be used in the Renaissance and after, but the cumulative medieval systems became less and less appropriate for categorizing new scientific knowledge. Francis Bacon responded by trying to derive his topics from first principles. In the second book of the *Advancement of Learning* he offered a system based upon three mental faculties: memory, imagination, and reason. To the faculty of memory belonged historical experience and writing, imagination was responsible for art, and reason for

philosophy and natural science. Bacon went on to elaborate these categories and include the traditional disciplines in this new hierarchy. After Bacon, however, as the printing press and scientific discovery continued to
generate materials that needed to be accounted for in any great book, there
was a growing trend toward neutral methods of "information processing"—alphabetization and indexing, which unlike topical outlines did not
presuppose a shared body of knowledge or worldview among the readers.
The shift from hierarchical to alphabetic organization in dictionaries and
encyclopedias was an acknowledgment that such systems as the seven liberal arts, which could be possessed by all educated readers, could no longer
accommodate specialized knowledge in physics, anatomy, geography, and
mathematics. Most encyclopedias from the 18th century to the present
have been alphabetical, because access to information, understood in an increasingly technical sense, has become more important than philosophical
vision. A good contemporary encyclopedia exploits every technique of
print technology (including tables of contents, indices, headnotes, side-
notes, and various type sizes and styles) to help the reader find the relevant
articles, paragraphs, and even finer units of text. Thus, printing, which had
made possible a new degree of textual overload, also offered the solution of
alphabetical order and precise indices.

Editors of encyclopedias, however, have perhaps never been entirely
happy with this solution, for the obvious reason that those who set out to
make encyclopedias are writers who want to impose an intellectually satis-
fying order on the world of texts. Alphabetic ordering does not define a writing space that clarifies the relationships among topical elements. The
editors of the *Encyclopédie* printed their articles alphabetically, but they did
not wish to deny the philosophical value of a hierarchical arrangement of
knowledge. D'Alembert wrote in the "Preliminary Discourse" that such an
arrangement:

> ... consists of collecting knowledge into the smallest area possible and of
> placing the philosopher at a vantage point, so to speak, high above this vast
> labyrinth, where he can perceive the principal sciences and the arts simulta-
> neously.... It is a kind of world map which is to show the principal countries,
> their position and their mutual dependence, the road that leads directly from
> one to the other (D'Alembert, 1963, p. 47).

Diderot and D'Alembert included in their preface a tree of knowledge
based on Francis Bacon's. Articles in the *Encyclopédie* contained references
to indicate their place in this tree, although readers could not easily use the

tree to organize their reading. The *Encyclopaedia Metropolitana* (1849) in the 19th century also tried to have it both ways: it was a "Universal Dictionary of Knowledge on an original plan, projected by the late Samuel Taylor Coleridge, comprising the twofold advantage of a philosophical and an alphabetical arrangement." Coleridge himself saw the encyclopedia as an educational tool: the reader should be introduced to all knowledge through the proper method, which consisted "in placing one or more particular things or notions, in subordination, either to a preconceived universal Idea, or to some lower form of the latter ... " (p. 22). Coleridge seems to have imagined the ideal reader starting at page one of the encyclopedia and working straight through. So, although he believed strongly in the topical arrangement that goes back to the Middle Ages, Coleridge's encyclopedia was clearly a product for the industrial age of print, in which the text is laid out in one ideal order.

More than a century later, the 15th edition of the *Encyclopaedia Britannica*, first issued in 1974, became another curious hybrid, a book straining to break free of the limitations of print. Mortimer Adler gave the *Britannica* both a topical and an alphabetic arrangement. The main articles were printed alphabetically in volumes called the Macropaedia. A separate volume, the Propaedia, was a vast outline, in which all knowledge was arranged into ten parts, the parts into some 140 divisions, the divisions into sections, and so on. The Propaedia outline was not adventurous or idiosyncratic: it was "constructed and corrected in the light of detailed recommendations, directions, and analytical contributions from scholars and experts in all the fields of knowledge represented" (*Encyclopaedia Britannica*, 1974–1987, vol. 1, p. 6). The most original aspect of Adler's outline was that it was meant to be a guide for reading the Macropaedia articles. The reader who pursued topics through the outline was eventually referred to pages in the Macropaedia. The Propaedia therefore served to reorder the articles of the Macropaedia: to show their relationships in Adler's structure of knowledge. There might be no single extended essay in the *Britannica* on creation myths in various cultures, but the reader could construct such an essay by finding that topic in the Propaedia and following the references. The Propaedia referred the reader to paragraphs, sections, or articles in the Macropaedia from which the essay could be fashioned. In this sense, the Propaedia turned the encyclopedia into a hypertext whose parts could be assembled by the reader.

The problem was that the references were hard to follow in a printed work of 30 folio volumes. Most readers of the *Britannica*, unwilling to go to the trouble of constructing their own essays, were content to read the articles in the conventional order. In any library that possessed the *Britannica*, the Propaedia could immediately be identified as the shiny new volume among the well-used and worn ones. In fact, the *Britannica* was trying to deny what modern culture had construed as the defining qualities of the printed book—its fixity and its linear order. If an encyclopedia is to be an alphabetical sequence of articles, the reader expects that each article will be a self-contained essay. The *Britannica* tried to create both a sequence of articles and a set of instructions for dismantling and reassembling those articles to make new readings. Eventually, the editors of the *Britannica* decided to add a conventional index and take most of the references out of the Propaedia. The Propaedia remained an outline of knowledge, but was no longer a blueprint for alternate readings of the rest of the work, when in the mid-1980s the *Britannica* became again a conventional printed encyclopedia.

THE ELECTRONIC ENCYCLOPEDIA

In spite of or indeed because of its inconsistencies, the 15th edition of the *Britannica* can be regarded as a forerunner of the electronically refashioned encyclopedia. The system of references in the Propaedia, which seemed irrelevant to readers of a printed book, would make more sense in an electronic edition, where the computer can facilitate the task of moving through the encyclopedic outline and among the various articles. The computer can take over the mechanical aspects of consultation: by getting the reader to the article and letting her read, by transferring her from one text to another, and by keeping her aware of her current position within the structure of the encyclopedia. In general the structure of an electronic encyclopedia can be both deeper and broader than that of its printed counterpart. If a printed book is generally divided into chapters or headings within chapters, in an electronic version the visible and useful structure may extend to the paragraph or even the sentence, and the computer can permit the reader to manipulate text at a variety of levels. In this way the computer might restore some of the legitimacy of topical arrangements for great books like the encyclopedia. At least, it answers the modern objections: that the world of textual knowledge is now too complex to be organized by topics; that any topical outline may be arbitrary or confusing; and that the reader will not be able to find topics because she will not know their place in the editor's outline. All this is true for a printed encyclopedia but not an electronic one. The problem of finding information in an electronic encyclopedia is facilitated by the fact that searching can be partly or wholly automatic, and such searching can cut across any categories established by the editor. In an electronic encyclopedia, alphabetical order is not the single canonical order of the text, as it is with a printed encyclopedia. Outlines or other topical arrangements can coexist with the alphabetical order, so that an electronic encyclopedia can be organized in as many ways as the editors and the readers can collectively imagine.

Any single topical outline today must seem arbitrary, because it reflects one editorial view of the organization of knowledge, which the reader may not share or even comprehend. The problem was less serious in the Middle Ages, when there was much broader agreement about the available structures of knowledge. But by the time of the *Encyclopédie*, D'Alembert recognized that there were many possible structures. When he compared the encyclopedia to a world map, he went to say that " ... one can create as many different systems of human knowledge as there are world maps having different projections.... There are hardly any scholars who do not readily assume that their own science is at the center of all the rest, somewhat in the way that the first men placed themselves at the center of the world" (D'Alembert, 1963, p. 48). When the encyclopedists were forced to choose one map, they preferred one validated by Bacon. In the *Britannica*, 200 years later, Mortimer Adler felt compelled to defend himself against this charge—by pointing out that his Propaedia outline was certified by contemporary experts. Adler's other defense was that his outline was not rigid: the topics could be displayed in a circle around which the reader could move associatively. However, the circle as a structure is the antithesis of the printed book, which wants to be linear in presentation and hierarchical in organization. In a printed book, the reader is certainly not invited to begin anywhere and move to any related section. By allowing multiple organizations, the *Britannica* anticipated an attitude toward knowledge that belongs to the late age of print, where the circle and the line are equally at home.

As it now moves into electronic media forms, the encyclopedic impulse is being directed in two channels. The first is the explicit remediation of the printed encyclopedia or handbook. Numerous CD-ROM and DVD products—such as the *Britannica DVD 99*, *Encarta Encyclopedia Deluxe 99*, *Year 2000 Grolier Multimedia Encyclopedia* (1999), and the *World Book CD Multimedia Encyclopedia*—have sought to appropriate the cultural significance of the printed encyclopedia. Many, like the *Britannica DVD 99*, depend on the reputation of the printed version and are excellent examples of the ways in which hypertext and hypermedia remediate print. If the printed *Britannica* has the reputation of being the premier general encyclopedia in the English language, its DVD counterpart suggests that it can bring the sophistication and knowledge of the original into cyberspace. The Web page advertising the DVD proclaims: "Discover the world's most authoritative source of knowledge, *Encyclopædia Britannica*, brought to life with the world's most advanced digital technology, DVD-ROM" (see www.eb.com/bookstore June 22, 1999). The electronic version promises greater immediacy (it is "brought to life") through multimedia, including "hundreds of new videos, thousands of new images, sound files and more." Immediacy of information is also guaranteed by hyperlinks among the articles and by the search capability, which allows the reader to retrieve articles that contain a key word or phrase. Finally, the topical organization of knowledge championed by Adler for the 15th edition is offered here as the "circle of learning" (a literal translation of the Greek for encyclopaedia): "More than just another multimedia encyclopedia, *Britannica DVD* turns information into understanding through its unique circle of learning, so you can see how facts and ideas combine to form the big picture." *Encarta* also remediates the printed encyclopedia, but in this case it borrows its cachet not from a venerable printed version, but from the reputation of Microsoft as a high technology computer company. It too depends on search capabilities, hyperlinks, and multimedia to suggest that it is an improvement on printed encyclopedias. Some version of the strategy of remediation is followed by the numerous handbooks and specialized encyclopedias also offered in CD-ROM or DVD format. Furthermore, the *Britannica*—like many others, including *Funk and Wagnalls, Grolier, World Book,* and the *Columbia Encyclopedia*—also exists in a Web version available by subscription. These online editions of the great book add to their claim of immediacy by connecting their user to cyberspace, which is itself already construed as a vast encyclopedia.

The other channel for the encyclopedic impulse lies in fact in the organization of cyberspace itself—in the many so-called portal Web sites that provide access to for the millions of pages on the World Wide Web. The Web is a textual universe that is by definition growing out of control; the distributed nature and economic potential of the Web ensure that designers will be constantly adding and deleting pages and sites without the knowledge of any central authority. Cyberspace is a universe that needs to be organized in order to be useful, and portal sites, such as Yahoo! (www.yahoo.com), provide that organization by refashioning the two principal organizing structures of the printed book: the table of contents and the index. A Web search engine functions like an index, permitting the user to retrieve Web pages that contain word or phrases of interest. Such a search facility lies at the heart of portal sites and gives a purely technical solution to the problem of control. Some portal sites like Yahoo! also provide a topical organization, a structure of nested menus that point the user to various categories of sites. This topical organization does not appear to come from any Baconian first principles or from consultation with scholars and scientists. At the top of its hierarchy, for example, Yahoo! currently offers 14 categories: Arts & Humanities, Business & Economy, Computers & Internet, Education, Entertainment, Government, Health, News & Media, Recreation & Sports, Reference, Regional, Science, Social Science, and Society & Culture (www.yahoo.com June 22, 1999). This menu is thoroughly ad hoc. Even in its heterogeneity, however, it constitutes a contemporary encyclopedic vision, a map of cyberspace and to some extent of our culture in the late ages of capitalism and print. It is our equivalent of Vincent of Beauvais or Pliny the Elder.

The organizational flexibility of hypertext together with the enormous capacity of electronic storage, especially on the Web, thus changes the scope of the encyclopedia. The encyclopedic vision has always been that the great book should contain all symbolic knowledge, although the making of such a great book has never been possible because of the inevitable limitations of the editors as well as the limitations of the available technology of writing. Even the World Wide Web must contain only a fraction of recorded symbolic knowledge. Thus, editors of encyclopedias have always made explicit or implicit exclusions: the mechanical arts, for example, were not represented in the early medieval encyclopedias of Martianus and Isidore, and biographies were excluded from the first *Britannica*. Encyclopedias in the Middle Ages were often statements of high learning; the utilitarian value of encyclopedias has been emphasized only in the past 200 years. In this century American encyclopedias have cut out scholarly subjects in favor of articles of popular interest in order to maintain the largest possible readership. The electronic encyclopedias are following that trend, while the World Wide Web considered as an encyclopedia is an utterly eclectic collection of texts and images.

Our culture's understanding, however, is that the computer can hold so much information that there is little need to be selective: the reader need only look at a tiny portion at any one time. Furthermore, the attitude toward knowledge structures reflected in electronic encyclopedias is opportunistic because of the temporary character of electronic information. This was not the case for an encyclopedia in manuscript or in print, where the technology encouraged more or less permanent structures of knowledge. What we have today is a view of knowledge as collections of (verbal and visual) ideas that can arrange themselves into a kaleidoscope of hierarchical and associative patterns—each pattern meeting the needs of one class of readers on one occasion.

THE LIBRARY AS A WRITING SPACE

The library as a great book adopts a strategy complementary to that of the encyclopedia. If the encyclopedia absorbs and digests other books, the library attempts to control knowledge by collecting as many books as possible within one conceptual and physical structure. The library is the physical realization of a culture's writing space of books. What the reader does metaphorically in the encyclopedia, he or she can do literally in the library—move into and through a textual space.

The space of the library has evolved along lines similar to those of the encyclopedia, but the principles of organization for libraries have generally been more ad hoc and utilitarian. Ancient Greek and Roman libraries of papyrus rolls were arranged by subject and then by author (Jackson, 1974, p. 23). It was common in the Middle Ages and even later to divide the books by university faculty: law, medicine, theology, and the arts. Within each division the organization was roughly alphabetical. However, unlike modern encyclopedias, modern libraries did not adopt a completely alphabetical arrangement. They continued to classify books by topic, and, as we would expect, the classifications became more complicated and more apparently arbitrary. When Conrad Gesner published his *Pandects* in 1548, he still suggested classing books under the seven liberal arts as well as by university faculty (Jackson, 1974, pp. 128ff). But by the end of the 19th century, the founders of modern classification, C. A. Cutter and Melvil Dewey, claimed to reject anything but utility as their criterion. Describing his system, Dewey wrote: "[t]he impossibility of making a satisfactory classification of all knowledge as preserved in books, has been appreciated from the first, and nothing of the kind attempted. Theoretical harmony and exactness have been repeatedly sacrificed to the practical requirements of the library ... " (Jackson, 1974, p. 388). The Library of Congress call numbers now used in research libraries in the United States follow a topical system that few users bother to learn. Apart from knowing that books on psychology or books on German literature are shelved together, the user simply treats the call number as a street address, a means of locating the book.

The call numbers in fact constitute a system of addresses, a mapping of the conceptual library onto the building, which is itself a physical hierarchy of floors, stacks, and shelves. At the same time the library's computerized catalog provides different conceptual views of the library: by author, by title, by subject, and so on. The library is a single physical hierarchy that is reorganized or "written over" in several ways by its catalog system. In current libraries the catalog, often available as a Web site, makes it relatively easy for the user to jump back and forth among views and to search for keywords in titles or subjects. The user can therefore rearrange the conceptual library with relative ease. Because the books themselves are still printed, the user must eventually leave the electronic world and set out on a physical journey among the stacks.

In a fully digital library, in which the books themselves are stored in machine readable form, the library would no longer be need to a building that the reader had to visit. The computers, storage devices, and communications equipment must be housed somewhere, but the reader has no need to see the equipment, any more than he or she needs to see the physical plant of the local telephone company. In such a library, the books could rearrange themselves at the reader's request. The same book could in effect appear on different shelves: for example, a book on the history of theories of mind could appear in the psychology section and in the philosophy section. It is often claimed that a principal advantage of a physical library is that the reader can browse and come across interesting books by chance. But an electronic library could give the reader the same opportunity. A graphical interface could even display the spines of the books on shelves and allow the reader to reach in and open the books, if that is really the best way for the reader to browse. Although a major library of printed books is always changing, as new books come in, and the physical shelving is expanded or redone, the ideal of such a library is not change, but preservation. Libraries have seemed venerable because they preserved what was created by past writers and valued by past readers. Francis Bacon called libraries " ... shrines where all the relics of the ancient saints, full of true virtue and that without delusion or imposture, are preserved and reposed" (Bacon, 1955, p. 233). No one would apply this rhetoric to an electronic library that reorganizes texts as readily as it preserves them.

The reverence accorded to the traditional library of manuscripts and printed books was reflected in the fact that the building itself was a kind of monumental writing, a writing and reading space in stone. In the industrial age of print, the library itself became the replacement for Victor Hugo's cathedral: the entry hall or reading room of more than one great library was built to resemble the nave of a cathedral, with the circulation or information desk as the altar. Because the physical libraries continue to fulfill a variety of institutional and cultural purposes, it seems unlikely that they will be dismantled in the near future. Instead, in the late age of print, academic and public libraries are becoming hybrids, combinations of printed texts with electronic facilities, accessed through terminals and computers onsite or online through the Internet. These hybrids are already remediations of the traditional printed library, as they both pay homage to print and offer new electronic services. In a larger sense, however, our culture also treats the World Wide Web or cyberspace itself as a library.

DIGITAL LIBRARIES

The electronic library is already decades old, in the sense there have been bibliographic and textual databases since the 1970s. At first these databases were expensive and were therefore restricted to medicine, law, the physical sciences, and government agencies. But now all kinds of information are being put into commercial and public databases, many of which are available through the Web, such as newspaper and journal articles, airline schedules, enormous amounts of government data, and scholarly bibliographies. As full texts become available online, we see the impulse to create "universal" databases: to have all U.S. Court decisions, all archaeological data from pre-Columbian America, all medical journals, or all medieval English literature in one electronic place. For several years, the National Science Foundation and research institutions have participated in a "Digital Libraries Initiative": to create the underlying technology, to collect the texts, and to study the user-related issues in the remediation of the research library (www.nsf.gov/pubs/1998/nsf9863/nsf9863.htm June 21, 1999); (see also Fox & Marchionini, 1998). The emphasis of this initiative has been on scientific and technical literature, but for the humanities, too, there exist electronic text repositories, of which the best-known in the United States is probably the Center for Text in the Humanities, CETH (www.ceth.rutgers.edu June 22, 1999).

With its low costs of production and distribution, the World Wide Web permits the publication of specialized libraries designed for small communities of users. For example, Perseus Project (www.perseus.tufts.edu June 26, 1999) calls itself "an evolving digital library" (or is it an encyclopedia? the distinction becomes harder to draw) of materials for classical studies: it provides millions of words of ancient texts in Greek and Latin and in translation, together with grammatical notes, a Greek dictionary, an historical atlas, diagrams, and pictures of archaeological sites. Perseus seeks to place before the reader all the materials of a small research library and to link these materials hypertextually. Perseus still has great scope to grow; nevertheless, because the textual and archaeological remains of classical antiquity are (relatively) limited, the goal of a universal scholarly library of antiquity becomes thinkable. Scholars of other literatures are pursuing similar collections.

Once they are on the Internet, such individual collections become steps toward the greater goal of a universal library. The desire is always to extend the collection, to incorporate new texts, to bring new fields into the same electronic structure, which for us today is the Web. Something like the Web as universal library was envisioned years ago under the appropriate name "Xanadu" by Ted Nelson, who also coined the word "hypertext" (= > p. 43). Xanadu was to be an electronic subscription library. Although users would pay to participate, Nelson expected that everyone would see the value of participation and that the library would become the universal writing space. Nelson labeled his project: "A Piece of Software that Proposes a New Era of Computers, a New Form of Instant Literature and a Whole New World." The Xanadu system structured information in the computer in such a way that any text could be referenced by any other, these references could in turn be referenced, and so on. Nelson explained that "[b]y using links to mark and type data elements, and to represent typed connections between the data elements, the Xanadu system provides A UNIVERSAL DATA STRUCTURE TO WHICH ALL OTHER DATA MAY BE MAPPED ... " (Nelson, 1987, p. 1). Nelson had much more in mind than a computer data structure. He saw writers and readers throughout the world working in the same conceptual space. Xanadu was "a plan for a worldwide network, intended to serve hundreds of millions of users simultaneously from the corpus of the world's stored writings, graphics and data" (Nelson, 1987, p. 1; see also *Literary Machines* by Nelson, 1984). Xanadu was a vision for the macrocosm: millions of texts were to be managed and ultimately joined into one world network. The result would be far larger than any library realized in print or manuscript, or indeed through today's World Wide Web. Nevertheless, what appealed to Nelson in imagining Xanadu still appeals to us today in our cultural construction of the Web as a universal library.

The historian Roger Chartier (1995) has aptly described how electronic technology figures the dream of the universal library:

If all existing texts, manuscript or printed, were digitized (in other words, converted into electronic text), then the universal availability of the written inheritance would become possible. All readers, wherever they might be, with the sole condition that it be before a reading post connected to a network for the distribution of computerized documents, could consult, read, study any text, regardless of the original location (p. 21).

Elsewhere Chartier (1994) writes:

... the library of the future is inscribed where all texts can be summoned, assembled, and read: on a screen. In the universe of remote communications made possible by computerized texts and electronic diffusion, texts are no longer prisoners of their original physical material existence.... The opposition long held to be insurmountable between the closed world of any finite collection, no mater what its size, and the infinite universe of all texts ever written is thus theoretically annihilated (p. 89).

This passion is a familiar one: what other goal have librarians ever had than to bring all books under their systematic control? The goal of a universal collection goes back at least to Alexandria, where the authorities apparently ordered that rolls found aboard ships entering the port were to be seized for their library. The modern equivalents of the Alexandrian library are the great national collections, such as the Library of Congress, the British Library, and the Bibliothèque Nationale de France, which are supposed to receive by law copies of all books printed in their respective countries. These national libraries are already building electronic extensions of themselves. In the 1990s the Library of Congress initiated the American Memory Project, collections of materials in machine-readable form, and since 1995 has had a National Digital Library as its goal (lcweb.loc.gov/loc/ndlf/digital.html June 22, 1999). The Bibliothèque Nationale de France has combined a massive new physical building (Tolbiac) with the beginnings of a digital collection, with some of the texts preserved as digital images and some in ASCII format (www.bnf.fr October 17,1999). The great national libraries of course want to maintain their physical presence. They are seeking to show that digital technologies do not make traditional libraries obsolete, but rather that these organizations with their long traditions of cataloging and control can now effectively colonize cyberspace. At the Bibliothèque Nationale de France, for example, the building now functions almost as a portal to cyberspace. If the physical collection validates and anchors the shift into the electronic medium, the electronic collection is meant to ensure that the great national library will not become obsolete.

In the late age of print, working libraries continue to be hybrids: combinations of machine-readable materials, computer services, and familiar printed books and journals. The example of earlier periods of remediation suggests that the transfer of materials from physical to electronic form may never be complete. The shift from papyrus roll to codex apparently left many ancient pagan texts behind, as did the shift from uncial to minuscule script in the Middle Ages, and the shift from manuscript to print. With considerable effort our culture could probably transfer all or almost all texts and images, but the question is whether we will ever make the effort. Each such shift in the past has been an occasion for weeding out texts that no longer seemed culturally relevant. Although we are likely to retain a broader variety of texts than ever before, texts that appeal to small or economically disadvantaged groups may still be neglected. On the other hand, for most readers and for most purposes, cyberspace itself in the form of World Wide Web may come to be treated as if it were a universal library. Readers will turn to the Web for information, and if they cannot find it there and are not willing to look elsewhere, then cyberspace may become by default the universal book, encyclopedia, and library all in one.

REFASHIONING THE BOOK OF NATURE

> ... the end of the *codex* will signify the loss of acts and representations indissolubly linked to the book as we now know it. In the form that it has acquired in Western Europe since the beginning of the Christian era, the book has been one of the most powerful metaphors for conceiving of the cosmos, nature, history, and the human body. If the object that has furnished the matrix of this repertory of images ... should disappear, the references and the procedures that organize the 'readability' of the physical world, equated with a book in the *codex* form, would be profoundly upset as well (Chartier, 1994, pp. 90–91).

Networked information appliances can be seen as first attempts to break down the limits of the traditional volume or codex and to put the whole world of writing into one book. At the same time, such devices take the book out into the world. Writers carry their devices everywhere. When they write on (or talk to) their portable computers, the information moves back and forth through a network that blurs the distinction between the world of nature and the world of texts. For writers in their cars or, better still, seated under the trees, beaming information to other writers and readers, the world has become an enormous volume in which they can leave their electronic marks. They are writing in and on the world.

As Chartier notes, the metaphor of the world as a book is not peculiar to the late age of print. Throughout the history of writing, the book has served as a metaphor for nature as a whole and for the human mind in particular. Scholars such as Curtius have traced a series of analogies among the ideas of mind, book, encyclopedia, library, and the world of nature. The metaphor of the book of nature appealed to the Middle Ages, precisely because of the importance of venerable texts and textual authorities for the medieval mind. For the medieval scholar, the world was made intelligible through such key works as those of Augustine and Aristotle. The very structure of the world was supposed to be mirrored in such books, and conversely the universe itself came to be viewed as a great book—hence the importance of encyclopedias and summae that brought the whole textual world under control. As Gellrich puts it in *The Idea of the Book* (1985), the ambition of encyclopedists and theologians was nothing less than " … to gather all strands of learning together into an enormous Text, an encyclopedia or summa, that would mirror the historical and transcendental orders just as the Book of God's Word (the Bible) was a speculum of the Book of his Work (nature)" (p. 18). Curtius argued that the poet Dante could invoke the same metaphor. At the end of the *Paradiso*, Dante's ultimate vision is of the universe as an enormous book that has finally been put together properly: " … all that has been scattered throughout the entire universe, that has been separated and dissevered, like loose quaderni [quires], is now 'bound in one volume.' The book—[in which all is contained]—is the Godhead" (Curtius, 1973, p. 332). Dante's poem itself has been called a summa, an attempt to encompass all knowledge between two covers. In the same way, the *Encyclopédie* or the 15th edition of the *Encyclopaedia Britannica* can be understood as modern secular attempts to encompass the book of nature in the technology of print. We recall that D'Alembert described the *Encyclopédie* as a world map (D'Alembert, 1963, p. 47).

Contemporary projects and proposals for hypertextual encyclopedias and digital libraries remediate this vision, although the metaphor has changed in response to the new technology. In the age of the manuscript and especially in the age of print, the book was valued for its capacity to preserve and display fixed structures. It was a technological reflection of the great chain of being, in which all of nature had its place in a subtle, but unalterable hierarchy. The hierarchical divisions of knowledge by Hugh of St. Victor or even Francis Bacon belonged on the written or printed page. Even as late as Coleridge, an encyclopedist thought that the purpose of his great book was to demonstrate how each notion is subordinated "to a preconceived universal Idea" (*Encyclopaedia Metropolitana*, 1849, p. 22)—in other words, to present hierarchies of knowledge. The passion for hierarchy finds expression in the elaborate table of contents of modern encyclopedias and other great books in print. The table of contents is both hierarchical and linear: it shows subordination and superordination, and it also shows the reader the order in which he or she will encounter these ideas in reading from first page to last.

Electronic structures are less rigid. Menus in an electronic information system can indicate a hierarchy of topics, as Yahoo! does, but only provisionally, and there is no single, linear order of pages to determine how the reader should move through the hierarchy. Our culture is defining the electronic encyclopedia, and electronic books in general, to reflect a different natural world, in which relationships are multiple and developing. It is a world in which the distinctions between nature and culture and between information and medium are unstable, as Donna Haraway (1991, 1997), N. Katherine Hayles (1999), and many others have argued. In fact, the metaphor of the book of nature is now moribund. Electronic writing technologies suggest a different metaphor: cyberspace, which blurs the distinction between nature and our networked culture. Cyberspace is not, as some enthusiasts have argued, divorced from the natural and social world that we know; rather, it is an expression and extension of both. Cyberspace is a great book of cultural choices that overlap and coincide with the "natural" order (= > p. 201). This new metaphor is yet another way in which digital technology suggests a refashioning of the tradition of the great book.

6

Refashioned Dialogues

THE READING PATH

A written text is a structure in space that also implies a structure in time: in some sense writing turns time into space, with a written text being like a musical score. The score is a visual pattern of barlines, notes, rests, and dynamic markings, but the pattern only makes sense when read as a sequence of measures. Most of us can read music, if at all, only by playing it on an instrument, but a good musician can read the score directly, activating the musical signs in his or her head. Those who can only read music by playing it are like people who read verbal texts by saying the words aloud: they are almost entirely absorbed by the unfolding temporal structure of the music. The musician, however, can appreciate the second dimension, the "vertical" structure of the score as well. A thorough reading of text or music may require attention to the space as well as the time of the writing. Once again, the writing technology used plays its role in defining the relationship between the time and space of the text. In a medieval codex the spatial structure is the pattern of rubrication and various sizes of letters; in a printed book it is the arrangement into paragraphed pages; in today's computers it is the pattern of text windows and images on the screen. The temporal dimension of a text is created by the reader's moment-by-moment encounter with these structures.

When a reader is reading a novel or an essay, the words create a rhythm of expectations. One word alludes to something earlier in the text or looks ahead to something to come. Expectations, explicit references, and allusions are also part of the purely oral arts of storytelling and public speaking. But one important difference between listening to a story and reading a book is that, although listeners simply allow the words to come to them,

99

readers must themselves make the words move. What the reader sees on the page is a pattern of signs, and he takes in some portion of the pattern in each glance. Practiced readers of printed books take in whole words or phrases at a glance (Levin & Addis, 1979). But whether the working unit is a single letter or an entire phrase, the reader's task is to thread these units into a sensible order: to read is to activate verbal elements in time. The English "read" comes from the Anglo-Saxon *raedan*, which also means "to give counsel, to interpret." This etymology reflects a belief that reading is a derived form of speech, that the reader is an interpreter who can make mute texts speak. The Latin word *lego*, which gives the Romance languages their words for reading (*lecture* in French, *lettura* in Italian), has a more interesting etymology. *Lego* literally means "to gather, to collect," and one of its figurative meanings is "to make one's way, to traverse." This etymology suggests that reading is the process of gathering up signs while moving over the writing surface. The reader on a journey through a symbolic space—this image, which fits all technologies of writing, is particularly appropriate to our culture's construction of electronic writing.

To read is to follow one path from among those suggested by the layout of the text. In confronting an ancient papyrus roll, the reader had few choices. The earliest ancient writing was strictly linear: it was simply a concatenation of letters that the reader turned back into sound. In fact, some early Greek inscriptions were written in a style called *boustrophedon* ("as the ox turns"), in which the line ran from left to right, bent around, and then continued from right to left with individual letters also drawn backwards. The technique was perfectly linear: the text defined letter by letter a continuous path for the reader to follow. At the other extreme are the numerous paths offered by the modern newspaper, in which several stories are laid out on each page and therefore compete for the reader's attention. A printed encyclopedia lies between these extremes, because each article is meant to be read linearly, but the alphabetized articles themselves can be read in any order.

The codex and the printed book both allow the writer to suggest many paths through the same work. But in most paged books as in the papyrus roll, one path dominates all others—the one defined by reading line by line, from first page to last. For the literate cultures of Europe and North America, the paged book has had a canonical order (for Japanese or Hebrew readers, of course, a different canonical order), even though there are many books that we may not read in that order. Although most of our reading today (newspapers, newsletters, magazines, sheets of instructions, memos, etc.) may not be in book form at all, our cultural construction of print—due perhaps in part to years of schooling in which we learned from text-books—remains shaped by the idea of the codex book to be read in one fixed order. Once that order is established, and indeed because it is established, a creative writer may want to suggest alternatives. The writer may incorporate in the text references and allusions that cause the reader to jump back and forth, at least mentally, as he reads. The printed book makes these acts of reference easier through the use of footnotes and page references. A writer using a papyrus roll was more likely to repeat himself just because it was hard to refer the reader back to a previous passage. In each historical moment, with each writing technology, and with each text, the question is: how and to what extent does the writer control the reader's experience of reading? To what extent does the reader actively participate in choosing his path through the text?

The question of control can also be posed in the absence of writing—in purely oral forms of storytelling and poetry. The orally composed Homeric poems have sophisticated structures of expectation and fulfillment (= > p. 77). Like all oral texts, however, they have no visible structure: nothing in Homer can depend on holding a text in one's hands and moving back and forth through the copy. Because Homeric poets as well as modern storytellers do not set out to create books, there may be no canonical order to their story. Although the storyteller's tale may be strictly linear, it need not be fixed from one telling to another. The teller is free to deviate from the storyline without the fear that a written text will prove him or her wrong. There may be, as in Homeric poetry, a network of established heroes and their adventures, but that network can allow for additions and deviations. Indeed, "deviation" is the wrong word, for it is impossible for the oral poet to deviate from the path, because the poet makes the path as he or she goes. The story still has a temporal structure, a rhythm of expectations and fulfillments. The poet can digress from the main story and hold the audience in suspense, but the awareness of a tension between the fixed, visible text and the flow of spoken language is not available to oral poets or their audience. For example, there is nothing in storytelling that quite corresponds to the reader's sense that in turning the pages he is coming to the end of the book.

The Homeric storyteller chooses what events to tell and the pace of the telling, and the storyteller can adjust the tale in order to suit what he or she conceives to be the wishes of the audience. Because the storyteller and the audience are in immediate contact, the audience too has a measure of control over the telling of the tale. We cannot say how Homer's original audience exercised that control: they may have shouted advice, or they may simply have shown greater or less interest as the performer proceeded. We know how our own children express their approval or disapproval of the way a story is told. In any case, writing changes the intimate relationship between the creator and the audience. It is no use shouting at a novel whose plot is heading in a direction we do not like, for the book obviously cannot adjust itself to our wishes as readers. If in that sense the reader loses control, in other ways the reader is more powerful than the listener, because each reader determines the pace of his own reading and can at least try to change the path through the text by scanning or skipping a paragraph, a page, or a whole chapter. In nonfiction or anthologies of stories, readers can read the chapters or sections in orders other than the one suggested. However, they must always be conscious that the book itself implies the preferred reading order.

It may in general be harder to hoodwink a reader than a listener, because the reader can stop at any time, reflect, and refer to a previous section of the text. The difference becomes obvious whenever we have the chance to compare oral and written presentations of the same material. When a politician or a scholar speaks (reads a speech), it may be harder to find the flaws. If we later read the text in a newspaper or in a journal, we may see nothing but flaws in the argument. Whenever we do have both the written text and an oral performance, we become aware of a tension between the two.

Plato was acutely aware of the tension between oral and written discourse, and he created a genre of writing that both embodied and profited from that tension. His dialogues combined the permanence of writing with the apparent flexibility of conversation. Each was the record of an impossibly artful philosophical discussion, and whatever its proposed subject, each dialogue was also about the difference between philosophy as conversation and philosophy as writing. Plato's Socrates prefers conversation to writing. In the *Phaedrus*, he tells a story that seems to condemn writing as a vehicle for any true philosophy. Socrates and Phaedrus have been examining the nature of rhetoric and public speaking. Toward the end of the discussion, Socrates tells the story of the Egyptian god Theuth, a great benefactor of the human race. Theuth was an avid inventor, who gave us arithmetic, geometry, astronomy, draughts and dice, and the alphabet. The king of Egypt was another god named Thamus, and so Theuth took his inventions to the king and explained the purpose and value of each. Of the alphabet, Theuth said, "this invention ... will make the Egyptians wiser and will improve their memories, for it is an elixir of memory and wisdom that I have discovered" (*Phaedrus*, 274E in Plato, 1919, p. 563). But the king replied that writing would have just the opposite effect: " … this invention will produce forgetfulness in the minds of those who learn to use it, because they will not practice their memory. Their trust in writing, produced by external characters which are no part of themselves, will discourage the use of their own memory within them. You have invented not an elixir of memory, but of reminding; and you offer your pupils the appearance of wisdom, not true wisdom" (275A, p. 563). Socrates goes on to explain that written words on a page are dead things. They cannot, as he puts it, answer questions we pose of them; they cannot explain themselves or adjust themselves to various readers. The process of adjustment and explanation is possible in philosophical conversation, the kind of questioning and answering that Socrates himself practices. The best writing, Socrates tells Phaedrus, is that of the living word, written in the mind of the student by a wise teacher, for this word is active: "it knows to whom it should speak and before whom to be silent" (276A, p. 567).

The ultimate failure of writing did not prevent Plato himself from becoming one of the most influential authors in the ancient world. Plato's dialogue was a nostalgic form looking back to a time when Greek culture could do without writing, for he lived in a period of transition in the history of literacy. Although the alphabetic writing was by no means new, literacy had taken centuries to work its way into the fabric of Greek culture. By Plato's time, children were going to school principally to learn to read and write, and the lawcourts were beginning to rely on written documents rather than hearsay. Plato understood that a whole way of life was finally passing, a way of life based on the spoken rather than the written word (see Havelock, 1982; Lentz, 1989, pp. 11–34). Nostalgia, however, was not the key for Plato; the key was rather the question of control in the new space that writing created. Platonic dialogue was a consciously literary attempt to imitate philosophical conversation. As the Phaedrus points out, such conversation is spontaneous, capable of going in any direction in order to pursue a problem, and the dialogue itself seems to share that spontaneity. Plato appeared to abdicate control of his text by reporting conversations between Socrates and his followers, yet this apparent abdication gave him a subtler control over his reader. Plato led and instructed his readers in the same devious way that Socrates led and instructed his partners in the discussion—by getting them to acquiesce until they were too deeply implicated in the argument to reject it.

Nevertheless, Plato the writer seemed to envy Socrates the oral philosopher, because Socrates could adjust his questioning to his audience. He could guide his interlocutor along the proper path, securing agreement at each step. Plato as writer set up his path, but he could not be sure that the reader was following. The reader was free to make all sorts of misunderstandings that the text separated from its author could not correct. The text could not ensure that it would be read properly (in accordance with the author's wishes), because the text no longer belonged to its author. For Plato, then, writing was both too rigid and too free. Readers even today may feel it as a limitation of the dialogue form that they cannot truly enter into the staged conversation. Exasperated when Socrates brings his audience to some particularly outrageous conclusion, readers may want to break in and change the course of the discussion, but they would only be shouting at a text. What is true of all writing is sometimes painfully obvious in a Platonic dialogue: the form invites the reader to participate in a conversation and then denies him or her full participation.

FROM DIALOGUE TO ESSAY TO WEB PAGE

A Platonic dialogue is a hybrid, a compromise between oral and written controlling structures. Such hybrids were common in ancient writing, where many genres were intended for oral performance—including speeches, dramatic and lyric poetry, and much historiography. Writers in these genres used structures that could be appreciated in reading aloud or in reading to others who do not have their own texts. So, for example, such early prose authors as Herodotus made use of a technique called "ring composition." Herodotus would proceed to tell a story, then digress on an interesting detail, and then notify the reader or listener that he was resuming the original storyline. The narrative proceeded as a straight line with occasional digressive loops. In early ancient works of fiction and nonfiction, the dominant structure was usually the line. Plays took the reader step by step through events; history was written chronologically (with digressions). If early writing was paratactic, rhetorical writing later became periodic, favoring elaborate sentences with many subordinate clauses. But both the paratactic and periodic styles were oral, not visual: they depended for their effect on hearing rather than seeing the text. Gradually in the ancient world, forms developed that were remote from the oral performance: the treatise, the encyclopedia, the handbook. Poets began to offer books of short poems that could be sampled; historians and academics began to write essays on scholarly subjects. Except perhaps in some branches of philosophy, however, ancient texts continued to be strongly linear. And the papyrus roll with its simple visual layout suited this linear structure.

After the invention of the paged book, linear structure of course survived, and writers still created narratives to be read straight through. The oral character of the text increased and diminished throughout the Middle Ages depending on the genre. Heroic and lyric poetry was destined for performance, and medieval encyclopedias, like their ancient counterparts, were designed to be consulted by single readers. In general, however, the new form of the book placed greater emphasis on the second visual dimension. It became more common to make hierarchical structures visible on the page by using different letter sizes and forms as well as different colors of ink, a trend reinforced with the invention of printing. Printing standardized the table of contents, which is a hierarchical description of the contents of the book.

Hierarchy can be expressed in a tree diagram (= > p. 31), and such diagrams appeared frequently in printed books from the 16th century on (see Ong, 1958, pp. 74–83, 199–202, 314–318). In the centuries following the invention of printing, the paragraph assumed its modern form both typographically and conceptually. Even today our major forms of nonfiction—the essay, the scientific article, and various genres of bureaucratic reports—are expected to be hierarchical in organization as they are linear in presentation. This is the paradigm for scholarly and scientific as well as business and technical writing. A scholarly essay should lead the reader step by step through its argument, making clear how each piece of evidence is relevant. The backbone of a technical report is supposed to be a careful outline of topics, which not only shows how each piece fits, but also directs the reader's movement through its parts. Whether we are told to write deductively or inductively, the result is still supposed to be a hierarchy of ideas and a carefully controlled reading.

This need to establish a hierarchy and to direct the reader is more than a matter of style: it still defines the professional activity of academic writers. All scholarly research is expected to culminate in writing. The historian or scholar does research not for its own sake, but in order to have something to write, and the same can be said of many of the social and even the hard sciences. In order to be taken seriously, both scholarly and scientific writing must be nonfiction in a hierarchical-linear form. Thus, although Foucault and others in the past three decades have tried to redefine historiography, the traditional historian's task remains to establish causes and effects: to provide the reader with a consistent, analytical path through some aspect of history. Even the highly theoretical, critical writing, which remains the standard in many humanistic disciplines, is generally far more hierarchical than is assumed by its conservative critics. For their part, social or physical scientists set up controlled experiments in order to exclude all but one or a few factors. When they write up their results, the goal is to tell a story of cause and effect, although in today's complex sciences this ideal may not always be achieved. The linear-hierarchical style of argument is still privileged in orthodox writing today, and this orthodoxy is approved by and built into our institutions of learning and research.

If linear and hierarchical structures dominate current writing, our cultural construction of electronic writing is now adding a third: the network as a visible and operative structure. The network as an organizing principle has been present in many forms of writing; indeed, Homeric oral poetry shows that the network is older than writing itself. Established by repetition in the minds of both the poet and the audience, the Homeric network contained all the mythological characters and their stories. The poet drew upon that network to tell each tale. After the invention of writing in the ancient world, it became the writer's task to establish his own network comprised of references and allusions within the text and connected to the larger network formed by other texts in the culture. From that time until the advent of electronic writing, the referential network has often existed "between the lines" of the text—that is, in the minds of readers and writers.

Now, however, the network can rise to the surface of the text. In pages on the World Wide Web, the network is visualized as a set of "anchor" phrases or "hotspots" that (in a typical browser) cause the cursor to change into a pointing finger as the user passes over them. The computer can not only represent associations on the screen; it can also grant these associations the same status as the linear-hierarchical order. It becomes as easy for the reader to follow an electronic footnote as it is to scroll to the next screen (= > p. 27). On the Web, readers probably move to a new page more often by choosing some link in the middle than by scrolling to the bottom and following a linear link to the "next" page. The previous invisible network of associations becomes visible and explicit to an extent never before possible. (The network can never be fully explicit, because the verbal ideas of the text will always reach out beyond any given electronic text to all other texts that the writer and reader know.) The electronic writer still has available the techniques of hierarchical organization from the technology of print, but she may choose to embed hierarchical structures within larger networks, or networks within hierarchies. The line, the tree, and the network all become visible structures at her and her reader's disposal.

THE END OF THE LINE?

"I generally approach a question not like this: x→ , but like this x 〰️. I shoot again and again past it, but always from a closer position" (Wittgenstein in Baker & Hacker, 1980, p. 23).

Although Plato was unwilling to set out his philosophy as a treatise, as a linear progression in which the writer assumes overt control of the argument, for the past 200 years, academic writers have been reluctant to accept any form other than the treatise. If in those 200 years our literate culture has used the printing press to reinforce that attitude, we are now beginning to use digital technologies to call it into question. Why should a writer be forced to produce a single, linear argument or an exclusive analysis of cause and effect, when the writing space allows a writer to entertain and present several lines of thought at once? This question was posed even before the invention of the computer and the advent of electronic communication by writers, who felt constrained by conventional structures in both fiction and nonfiction. Two decades ago, Susan Sontag observed that:

> ... a distinctive modern stylistics has evolved, the prototypes of which go back at least to Sterne and the German Romantics—the invention of antilinear forms of narration: in fiction, the destruction of the "story"; in nonfiction, the abandonment of linear argument. The presumed impossibility (or irrelevance) of producing a continuous systematic argument has led to a remodeling of the standard long forms—the treatise, the long book—and a recasting of the genres of fiction, autobiography, and essay. Of this stylistics, Barthes is a particularly inventive practitioner (Sontag, 1982, pp. xiv–xv).

Roland Barthes was assiduous in breaking down linear form (=> p. 179). At every level, from the sentence to a whole book, his texts were characterized by fragmentation and interruption—in his classic S/Z, for example, a commentary on a short story by Balzac. If a commentary is by nature a series of interruptions, in this case Barthes' comments overwhelmed the story and pried it apart, both typographically and conceptually. Barthes' writing was also decadent in the sense that it was a decline or falling away from an ideal form of writing for the age of print. The great monographs of the 19th-century essayists and historians showed what printing could achieve; by comparison, Barthes was intentionally playful and perverse. These are traits he obviously shared with such earlier writers as Kierkegaard, Nietzsche, and Wittgenstein, each of whom in his own way challenged the development of systematic, linear argument. We could also point to the many poststructuralist and feminist or postfeminist theorists of the past several decades (Lacan, Foucault, Derrida, Irigaray, Judith Butler, and so on) whose fragmentary or elliptical style has also tested the limits of sanctioned academic discourse.

Wittgenstein's dissatisfaction with linear argument is well known. Like Socrates, Wittgenstein was an influential teacher and a kind of antiauthor. Unlike Socrates, Wittgenstein did write, although he published little in his lifetime and at least in his later years agonized over the task of writing. He filled notebooks with short, unconnected paragraphs. When he sought to put these paragraphs together for what would become his *Philosophical Investigations*, he was frustrated. Wittgenstein claimed he wanted to produce a conventional treatise. He wrote in his Preface that he had considered it essential to set his ideas "in a natural order and without breaks" (Wittgenstein, 1953, p. ix). But he found that:

> ... my thoughts were soon crippled if I tried to force them on in any single direction against their natural inclination.—And this was, of course, connected with the very nature of the investigation. For this compels us to travel over a wide field of thought criss-cross in every direction.—The philosophical remarks in this book are, as it were, a number of sketches of landscapes which were made in the course of these long and involved journeyings (p. ix).

Because Wittgenstein could not cast his philosophy in linear-hierarchical form, it had to remain a journey through a network of interrelated topics. He often despaired of ever finishing his book (Baker & Hacker, 1980, p. 23). At one point he wrote: "The only presentation of which I am still capable is to connect [my] remarks by a network of numbers which will make evident their extremely complicated connections" (p. 24). Baker and Hacker believed that he actually intended to publish his *Philosophical Investigations* as an interconnected network of entries. That is, he intended to number each entry and to indicate after each the numbers of other entries to which it was related (pp. 25–26). When the book was finally published, the entries were numbered, but Wittgenstein had abandoned the scheme of adding what we would now call the links. (In writing their commentary on the *Philosophical Investigations*, however, Baker and Hacker constructed diagrams to mark connections that they perceived.) At least for a time, then, Wittgenstein had conceived of the *Philosophical Investigations* as a true hypertext. Unlike Barthes, however, Wittgenstein was a prose innovator in spite of himself. His notion of a book was still determined by the old model, and he wanted very much to find a perfect order for his ideas. So both Wittgenstein and Barthes rejected linear argument, but not the physical form, the "look and feel," of the printed book. The reader picks up their books, opens to the first page, and reads in the conventional way. Some poststructuralist writers extended their attack to the typography of the book itself, creating antibooks that disrupted the traditional notion of how a book should look and behave.

Derrida's *Glas* (1974, 1976a) was such an antibook. Each page of *Glas* was divided into two columns: the left offered passages from Hegel with comments, and the right was a commentary on the French novelist Genet. Paragraphs set in and around other paragraphs and variable sizes and styles of type gave the page an almost medieval appearance. There was no linear argument that spanned the columns, yet the reader's eye was drawn across, down, and around the page looking for visual and verbal connections. And the connections seemed to be there, as words and sentence fragments referred the reader back and forth between Hegel and Genet. Thus, an isolated passage in the right column of the first page seemed to be referring both to the text and to the reader's response: "Two unequal columns, they say, each of which—envelops or encloses, incalculably reverses, returns, replaces, marks again, cross-links the other" (Derrida, 1974, p. 7). In *Glas* Derrida laid down a textual space and challenged his reader to find a path through it. Whatever else he was doing, Derrida was certainly writing topographically, as if for a medium as fluid as the electronic. Seven years earlier, in *Of Grammatology* (1976b), Derrida was already drawing a contrast between linear and nonlinear writing. He argued that linear writing was "rooted in a past of nonlinear writing, ... a writing that spells its symbols pluri-dimensionally; there the meaning is not subjected to successivity, to the order of a logical time, or to the irreversible temporality of sound" (Derrida, 1976b, p. 85; see also Neel, 1988, pp. 105–107). Nonlinear writing had been suppressed, although never eradicated, by linear writing. Nonlinear writing resurfaced in the literature of the 20th century, when it seemed that the modern experience could not be recorded in the linear way. Derrida concluded that a new form of nonlinear writing was possible, and this new writing would entail a new reading of earlier texts: " ... beginning to write without the line, one begins also to reread past writing according to a different organization of space. If today the problem of reading occupies the forefront of science, it is because of this suspense between two ages of writing. Because we are beginning to write, to write differently, we must reread differently" (Derrida, 1976b, pp. 86–87). Derrida suggested that "[t]he end of linear writing is indeed the end of the book" (p. 86).

Another possibility, however, is that digital media might refashion the book in a way that enhances the possibilities of multiple presentation without eliminating the book's cultural significance. In the printed *Glas* the network of relationships that normally remain hidden beneath the page has emerged and overwhelmed the orderly presentation we expect in a printed book. In the World Wide Web, on the other hand, the many relationships among textual elements simply float to the surface. An antibook like *Glas* would no longer be an antibook in an electronic edition, because it would appear to work with, rather than against, the grain of our expectations of the medium. The dialogic structure of hypertext might also enable us, as Derrida put it, to "reread past writing according to a different organization of space." Texts that were originally written for print or manuscript can be not only transferred to machine-readable form, but also translated into hypertextual structures.

In some cases the translation would refashion texts into a form closer to their original, conversational tone. Many of the texts of Aristotle, for example, are notes and excerpts from lectures that the philosopher delivered over many years; they were put together either by Aristotle himself or by ancient editors. Since the 19th century, scholars have been trying to sort out the pieces. Printed editions make each text into a single, monumental treatise, but an electronic edition of Aristotle could record and present all the various chronological and thematic orders that scholars have proposed. This might be the best way for readers to approach the carefully interwoven philosophy of Aristotle, because following the electronic links would allow readers to sample from various texts and move progressively deeper into the problems that each text poses. This moving back and forth is the way that scholars reread and study Aristotle even now. The computer would therefore make explicit the implicit act of deeply informed reading, which is itself a dialogue with the text.

Digital technology might be, indeed is being, used to give earlier texts a new "typography." A text always undergoes typographical changes as it moves from one writing space to another. Greek literature, for example, has moved from the papyrus roll, to codex, and finally to the printed book. When we read a paperback edition in English of Plato's dialogues or Greek tragedies, we are aware of the translation from ancient Greek to a modern language. But we should also remember that the original text was without book or scene divisions, paragraphing, indices, punctuation, or even word division. All these conventions of modern printing are significant organizational intrusions into the original work. They make it easier to read Sophocles, but they change the Sophocles that we read. We would find it difficult to read an English manuscript of the 14th century, or even an early printed book, because of the visual conventions. Transferring earlier texts to digital form will be just another in the series of such transitions. On the other hand, these early texts now belong to a relatively small audience of scholarly readers, and whether they ever undergo a thorough remediation will depend on the decisions of that audience.

THE HYPERTEXTUAL ESSAY?

J. Hillis Miller (1991) noted that:

> "*Glas* and the personal computer appeared at more or less the same time. Both work self-consciously and deliberately to make obsolete the traditional codex linear book and to replace it with the new multilinear multimedia hypertext that is rapidly become the characteristic mode of expression both in culture and in the study of cultural forms" (pp. 20–21).

It seems, however, that the mode of expression is changing more rapidly in popular culture than in the study of cultural forms. Although, in the 1990s, the World Wide Web has become one of the most popular and economically favored forms of communication, the traditional academic essay *as a form* has not changed much, if at all. Research essays in true hypertextual format remain uncommon even on the Web.

As cultural studies along with various versions of feminist or postfeminist theory have come to dominate humanistic discourse, the study of popular media forms, including new media in general and the Web in particular, has become correspondingly important. Yet such studies still take the form of the traditional essay, published in a journal or anthology. Academics are not publishing their most valued thoughts about new media—the ones for which they hope to obtain tenure or promotion—in new media. Although there is more experimentation than ever before, only the most consciously avant-garde among scholars are producing hypertextual "essays." Even the fully electronic journal *Postmodern Culture* (jefferson.village.virginia.edu/pmc July 9, 1999), which publishes only online, nevertheless presents linear articles. Rather than refashioning their arguments as hypertext, scholars are more inclined simply to use multimedia to illustrate their presentations and publications. A CD-ROM or DVD that contains a database of art reproductions would be an obvious asset to an essay on art history, without challenging the basic form of argument characteristic of the printed monograph. On the other hand, hyperlinking could alter the form of the argument, and scholars have been reluctant to remediate the essay to that extent.

It is significant that even the debate over the meaning and value of hypertext itself has been conducted in print. Not only the opponents of the new form (Birkerts 1994; Miller, 1998; Slouka, 1995; and so on), but also the proponents (Douglas, 1991, 2000; Joyce 1995, 2000; Landow 1994, 1997; Moulthrop 1991a, 1994, 1997; and so on) have all published in printed journals, anthologies, or monographs. Although these proponents have also produced CD-ROM or Web versions of their texts, they realize that they can only reach a traditional academic audience by resorting to traditional media forms. In the late age of print, scholars in the humanities continue to regard print forms as authoritative.

Poststructuralist theory may challenge the notion that a text speaks with a single voice, yet few academics, even those who have pursued poststructuralist or postmodern theory, have been willing to challenge the voice of the text by experimenting with hypertextual form. In scholarly essays destined for print publication, the writer still speaks apparently in his own voice and is still expected to take responsibility for a text that will go out to hundreds or thousands of readers under his name. Publishing is fundamentally serious and permanent; a scholar or scientist cannot even retract his own previously published argument without embarrassment. A dialogue, on the other hand, speaks with more than one voice and therefore shares or postpones responsibility. It proceeds by apparent indirection and may gradually zero in on its target. A hypertextual essay in the computer could in fact be fashioned as a dialogue between the writer and her readers, and the reader could be asked to share the responsibility for the outcome. Instead of one linear argument, the hypertext could present many, possibly conflicting arguments. Hypertext could therefore redefine scholarship in a way that reveals what Sontag has called the "impossibility or irrelevance of producing a continuous, systematic argument." This redefinition applies to all academic disciplines, in which scholarship is now understood as the producing of systematic argument for publication. Traditional scholars—and in this sense even radical postmodern scholars are traditional—have resisted such a redefinition, apparently believing that the fixed quality of print is necessary to legitimize their arguments.

The resistance may go even deeper. If hypertext could remediate the voice of the text, it might suggest a return to oral forms, such as the dialogue. In this sense Derrida and other poststructuralists might recognize and even approve of hypertext as a refashioner of our culture's deep commitment to the power of the word, or logos, especially in its spoken form (= > p. 161). On the other hand, the remediations of digital forms also extend to visual media (= > p. 47). The success of the World Wide Web derives from the ways in which it borrows from and reforms not only print, but also graphics design, photography, film, and television. Although we do not seem to regard the Web as a place for a new kind of essay, we do think of it as a space for a multimediated writing with high visual appeal. This very appeal tends to devalue the Web for many scholars in the humanities, especially those influenced by French theory with its tendency to distrust visual representation—what Martin Jay (1993) has labeled the "anti-ocularist" tradition. The field of cultural studies examines the popular iconography of television and magazine ads, and film studies and art history take as their objects of study visual or audiovisual media. Yet even these disciplines produce essays and monographs. Although scholars are aware that popular culture is using new media to renegotiate the relationship between the verbal and the audiovisual, they continue to write about this renegotiation in printed essays, often without images.

Thus, neither the dialogue between print and electronic forms of verbal writing nor the dialogue between the verbal and the visual has so far found expression in a new form of scholarly research essay. The remediating potentials of hypertext and the Web *are* being explored, but in teaching rather than in research.

EDUCATIONAL DIALOGUE

If humanists as researchers remain committed to the linear essay (whether published in print or stored on a Web site to be printed on demand), as teachers they have been quicker to exploit digital technologies. Teachers of writing and reading in particular have been willing to redefine the genres and the practices into which they initiate their students (see, for example, Hawisher, Leblanc, Moran, & Selfe, 1996; Hawisher & Selfe, 1999; Johnson-Eilola, 1997; Kaplan & Moulthrop, 1994; Slatin, 1999; VanHoosier-Carey, 1997; Wysocki, Grimm, & Cooper, 1998; and so on). The printed journal *Computers and Composition* and its online version (www.hu.mtu.edu/~candc July 9, 1999) are devoted to the refashioning of writing in digital media. The online *Kairos: A Journal for Teachers of Writing in Webbed Environments* (http://129.118.38.138/kairos/default.htm July 6, 1999) claims on its home page that:

In hypertextual environments, writers are ... learning to weave a writing space that is more personal than the standard sheet of paper. We are writing differently; we are reading differently; we are learning differently; we are teaching differently.

Many have even come to regard the networked classroom as a means for social or political change, as they combine digital writing with various strategies of cultural critique. Although they may not by any means approve of all the ideological implications of the new technology, they nevertheless seek out ways in which the technology can reinforce, rather than contradict, the perspectives of cultural studies, feminism, postfeminism, or postcolonialism. So for example three educators (Myers, Hammett, & McKillop, 1998) can write:

We define *critical literacy* as the intentional subversion of meanings in order to critique the underlying ideologies and relations of power that support particular interpretations of a text ... Hypermedia is a particularly powerful environment for this critical literacy practice ... [H]ypermedia authoring can support the emancipation of one's self and others through the authoring and publication of critical texts that by questioning representations of the self, expand the possibilities for the self in future actions as a member of a community (pp. 64–65).

In this spirit, educators in a variety of disciplines have devised forms that incorporate hypertext and hypermedia. The forms range from the purely verbal (MOOs and chat rooms) to the highly visual (Web sites and stand-alone hypermedia applications). Although many of these forms still depend on assumptions about good writing for print, educators are prepared to modify those assumptions to achieve what they regard as a greater degree of authenticity or immediacy.

Teachers of writing, who remain committed to the power of the spoken and written word, have looked first for computer applications that will refashion the voice of the text and reform the dialogue that goes on inside and outside of the classroom. MOOs and such chat programs as Daedalus refashion class discussion by relocating it to an electronic space, a virtual room (Haynes & Holmevik, 1998). Students seated at computers, sometimes together in their physical classroom, sometimes alone in their dorm rooms or elsewhere, type in their contributions, which are then displayed so that other students in the same virtual room can read and reply. These keyboard exercises are meant to complement rather than replace face-to-face discussion in the classroom. The discussion may be carried on across time as well as space—through e-mail and various Web-based applications, such as WebCrossing (Fig. 6.1). In such a system, the teacher can define discussion areas or threads, and students can sign in at any time, read previous entries, and contribute their own. The entries are typically shorter and less elaborately structured than a conventional essay, although they are more rhetorically considered than the brief and immediate exchanges of MOOs and chat rooms (=> p. 74).

These forms of digital dialogue make claims of immediacy or authenticity against the traditional essay. Unlike the traditional essay, they allow students to participate in an apparently immediate exchange of ideas and feelings that our culture associates with conversation. Educators have argued that MOOs, chat rooms, and threaded discussion groups offer students an opportunity for authentic exchange despite or even because of the fact that the student must type her messages at a keyboard and read them on the computer screen:

FIG. 6.1.   A Web page from WebCrossing, a program for asynchronous discussion by teachers and students.

> The CMC [computer-mediated communication] technology creates a distinctly unique social context in which participants are actively employing reading and writing strategies required for participation in the exchange ... [P]articipants are receiving immediate written reactions to their messages that they can read and reflect on (Beach & Lundell, 1998, p. 95).

Although this technology can mediate discussions on topics in traditional literary history or other disciplines, many teachers of writing like to use it to examine the politics of identity through the lenses of race, gender, and class. MOOs and chat rooms seem well-suited to exploring the issue of postmodern identity, perhaps because the student must construct her identity solely through her words. (= > p. 198) Beth Kolko writes that "[t]he MOOs power lies in our ability as educators to make students aware of how the characteristics of their situated selves inform their virtual decisions ... [I]t is by using MOOs to examine the reified relations of identity and power in real space ... that the educational use of MOO as an object lesson in politics becomes most articulated.... Ultimately the MOO with its lessons in play, partiality, and situatedness holds a particular power to teach us about our bodies, our place, and our politics" (Kolko, 1998, pp. 259, 260, 263).

In addition to environments for synchronous and asynchronous discussion, educators have developed hypertextual applications to remediate such forms as the anthology, commentary, and textbook. One of the best examples is *The Victorian Web* (www.stg.brown.edu/projects/hypertext/landow/victorian/victov.html July 1, 1999), a hypermedia textbook, created by George Landow, who has pioneered the use of hypertext to "reconfigure" education in English literature (Landow, 1997, pp. 219–266). Now offered as a Web site, *The Victorian Web* has grown out of materials developed since the 1980s on a variety of networked systems. It is an archive of primary sources, essays on primary sources, and images—a database to which students as well as Landow himself and other experts have contributed texts and links. It is the capacity of hypertext for collective writing and growth that grounds the claim of *The Victorian Web* to an immediacy not available in most printed textbooks. In reflecting the concerns and insights of many contributors, including the students who use it, this Web site ushers students into the kind of exchange that professional scholars conduct when they share ideas at conferences and through journal papers. The same advantage is offered by Landow's *Postcolonial Literature Web* (www.stg.brown.edu/projects/hypertext/landow/post/misc/postov.html July 1, 1999) and other pedagogical sites. Such sites constitute hypertextual writing as a cooperative effort, which is designed to overcome the barriers of authority that separate professors from students in the traditional classroom.

When we write for the Web, cultural expectations invite and ultimately demand that we use multimedia. Although primarily textual, *The Victorian Web* includes numerous images in its archive: for example, images of women in Pre-Raphaelite painting and a gallery of paintings by John William Waterhouse. This form of hypertextbook therefore also distinguishes itself from the traditional essay by renegotiating the relationship between textual and visual representation. A decade or two ago, it was both difficult—and generally thought unnecessary—for students to include images or illustrations with their essays. Now, student Web pages frequently combine text and images. Educational applications for CD-ROM and DVD or the Web often adopt the design aesthetics of commercial and entertainment multimedia, so that their educational content is incorporated into a "windowed" and "buttoned" style radically different from the style of a traditional printed textbook. An example of this new visual sophistication is Gunnar Liestol's *Kontiki Interactive*, which explores the expeditions of Thor Heyerdahl through sound, animation, and graphics as well as text (Landow, 1997, 163–166; Liestol 1996).

Many educational theorists have examined the effectiveness of hypertext and hypermedia as new dialogic forms (Reinking, McKenna, Labbo, & Kieffer, 1998; Rouet, Levonen, Dillon, & Spiro, 1996). In particular, cognitive scientists such as Rand Spiro have argued that hypertext is the mode of presentation best suited to "ill-structured" domains, such as the knowledge required for medical diagnosis. Spiro's hypertextual materials for diagnosis are designed to promote a "cognitive flexibility" that, he argues, is not encouraged by the linear printed monograph (Spiro, Feltovich, Jacobson, & Coulson, 1991). Such research and such applications show how educators have chosen to pursue the remediating possibilities of hypertext and hypermedia. They are seeking to supplement or to bypass altogether the traditional essay or monograph for their students, even though, as the citations above indicate, they continue to present their own results as traditional conference papers and published articles.

MULTIPLE DIALOGUES

We have seen that three dialogues are simultaneously refashioned in electronic writing: the dialogue between the writer and reader, the dialogue between verbal and audiovisual modes of representation, and the dialogue among various new and old media forms (such as the Web page, the essay, and the textbook). We have also seen that the academic community is reluctant to participate fully in some of these refashionings. Although scholars are prepared to study and critique new media forms and genres, they are less likely to change their own forms of expression. Popular culture at large has had the opposite reaction. For various ideological reasons, the business world, the entertainment industry, and most users of the World Wide Web have shown little interest in a serious critique of digital media, but they are all eager to use digital technology to extend and remake forms of representation and communication.

Since 1993, a number of remediated genres have appeared on the World Wide Web. Although the hypertextual essay is rare, traditional linear essays made available either as Web pages or in other file formats (such as Adobe's Portable Document Format) are abundant on the Web. The commercialization of the Web has also meant the transfer and transformation of advertising forms. Graphic design for advertising in magazines and on billboards has been transformed into Web advertising, in particular the so-called Web "banner," a static or animated graphic. Entertainment forms include Web sites associated with first-release films, record company and jukebox sites, official sites for television programs, book club sites, and even Web soap operas. Meanwhile, large corporations have invented a Web genre that combines and remediates a number of forms, including the promotional ad or brochure, the stockholder's report, and marketing and sales materials. Colleges and universities have created sites that combine promotional materials with the traditional catalog; they often promote their site as a virtual campus with access to the online catalog of the library, to syllabi and courses notes, and to special facilities, such as campus museums.

It is no accident that the Web relies heavily on the principles of graphic design for print (= > p. 68). Graphic design developed in close association with mass advertising in the early part of the 20th century and was directed toward popular forms, such as magazines and posters, rather than the elite form of the book. So today, the Web is not as concerned to refashion the book itself as to remake these ancillary forms. In this respect, the sensibilities of the late age of print and of the late age of capitalism have coincided.

The Web has also occasioned a set of new, "grassroots" forms that would seem to affirm the democratizing thrust of digital technology. These forms are, or represent themselves as, expressions of the typical Internet user, who can establish her own presence in cyberspace through a tool as simple as a Web editor. The individual home page, of which there must now be millions, is an act of self-expression and self-promotion that recalls several earlier forms, including the greeting card, the resumé, and the photograph album. On a "fan" page, a digital version of the earlier, photocopied fanzine, an individual designer reports facts and gossip and posts pictures of her favorite celebrity. The fan page is subgenre of the "gift" page or site, through which an individual gives something back to her perceived community on the Web. The gift may be a page that collects links on baseball, space exploration, or AIDS; it may be a Web site with photographs of the designer's cat or her favorite riddles. In each case the designer is working in the collaborative spirit of the "old" Internet (of the 1980s), making a uncoerced contribution just as she benefits from the contributions of others—all without any organized economic exchange. Gift sites are utterly eclectic and may follow any design paradigm. Both the home page and the gift site depend for their rhetorical effect on the cultural belief in the democratization of the Web: that the Web allows individuals not only to represent themselves in words and images, but also to publish these representations to an audience of millions at almost no expense. By contrast, access to the printing press is controlled by publishers, who pride themselves on their "gate-keeping" role, eliminating unworthy, uninteresting, and unprofitable submissions (= > p. 208). The rhetoric of Web publishing is certainly not that of the extended literary or persuasive essay; gifts sites are usually descriptive, and there is usually no recognizable argument at all.

The individual voice of these popular Web forms is both more and less insistent than the voice of the essay. It is more insistent in the sense that these pages "stand for" their author: they stake out a bit of cyberspace for her and often speak ostensibly and naively in her voice. Less formal than a printed or typed resumé, a home page may include the author's personal history—hobbies, likes and dislikes, links to favorite Web sites, and even lovers and friends. On the other hand, the author's representation on the Web may depend as much on the look of the site as on its verbal content. The author presents herself in images and through the layout itself so that the rhetoric is visual as well as verbal (Fig. 6.2). We understand a printed essay as an author's engagement with other texts as well as with the reader himself. Similarly, highly designed pages of the Web (those that are not mere repositories for printed materials) constitute an implicit dialogue with earlier media forms, as well as an interplay between words and images in the windowed space of the screen.

Thus, designers on the Web are not only remediating the voice of the text, but also challenging the ideal of purely verbal communication that

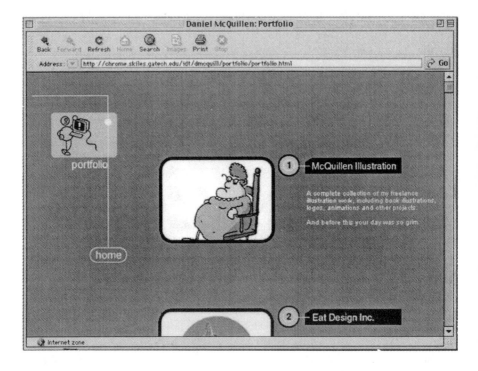

FIG. 6.2.   The visual rhetoric of the Web: The home page of Daniel McQuillen, a student of Web design.

went largely unquestioned during hundreds of years in which printing was our dominant technology. Because scholars are still unwilling to confront that challenge, they have not refashioned the essay itself into a hypertextual form. Some writers of fiction, however, have taken up the challenge posed by hypertext and hypermedia and have created new forms of "interactive fiction."

7

Interactive Fiction

Bibliographic databases and technical documents have long been regarded as legitimate texts for the computer: novels, short stories, and poems have not. Although many, perhaps most, novelists now use word processors to prepare manuscripts for publication as printed books, our literate culture still believes fiction belongs in the space defined by printing. Relatively few authors have attempted to write fiction to be read in the electronic space—that is, nonlinear fiction that invites the reader to interact with the text. Yet that relatively few now amounts to several dozen innovative writers, who in the late 1980s and the 1990s have created a significant body of work. In fact, hypertext fiction has become the most convincing (and to some disturbing) expression of the idea of hypertext. Whereas the hypertext nonfiction essay hardly exists as a genre (other than for teaching purposes), we can already distinguish several, overlapping genres and forms of interactive fiction, including hypertext novels or short fictions, hypermedia narrative forms that refashion film or television, hypermediated digital performances, and interactive or kinetic poetry. A publishing house (Eastgate under the direction of Mark Bernstein) has devoted itself primarily to hypertext fiction.

It makes sense that creative writers should lead the way in developing the possibilities of electronic hypertext. Throughout the 20th century, modern and postmodern fiction and art in general have been by definition open to experiment, and being open and open ended are qualities that we now associate with networked digital communication as well. The World Wide Web is an open, experimental structure. Our culture has come to expect experimentation in new media—with the usual failure and occasional wild success. The experimentation that gains widespread attention has often been commercial: the cultural rhetoric, at least in North America, has been to

121

praise the "visionary" entrepreneurial spirit that led to such Internet successes as Yahoo! (www.yahoo.com) or Amazon (www.amazon.com). Experiments in interactive fiction, both on and off the Web, have received much less attention, but they too are expressions of our belief that electronic space is a place in which to locate new forms. The creators of hypertext fiction have been assigned, both by supporters and detractors, the now traditional role of the avant-garde—traditional since the Romantic Revolution at the beginning of the 19th century and especially since the early modern period at the beginning of the 20th. The electronic literary forms constitute perhaps the most important and visible avant-garde in our contemporary, and otherwise conservative, literary culture.

The novelist Robert Coover has become an articulate champion of hypertext fiction—teaching classes and providing the impetus for an online manifestation called the Hypertext Hotel. In a series of articles in the *New York Times Book Review* under provocative titles such as "The End of Books," "HyperFiction: Novels for the Computer," "And Hypertext is Only the Beginning. Watch Out!" (Coover, 1992, 1993a, 1993b), Coover has argued that hypertext is a legitimate and even innovative form of literary expression. The reaction by the traditionalists is exactly what we expect from those responding to an avant-garde: that hypertext writers have abandoned the essence of the art. In this case, the essence consisted in the authoritative voice of the author in perfect control of the text. We recall Laura Miller's words published as a belated response to Coover: "[r]eaders like me stubbornly resist hyperfiction's efforts to free them from what Coover calls 'domination by the author'.... [The] surrender ... and the intimacy to be had in allowing a beloved author's voice into the sanctums of our minds, are what the common reader craves." (Miller, 1998, p. 43) (=> p. 44). The traditionalists attack hypertext as both insignificant and unreadable, exactly the kinds of claims that were made against modernists, who sought to expand or break what they perceived as the bounds of traditional forms.

Interactive fiction is indeed about the breakdown or rather the refashioning of traditional forms. It challenges our understanding of fictional forms that have flourished in print as well as forms from other media besides print. In its role as avant-garde expression, hypertext makes a claim to an authenticity different from the authenticity of print: it offers the reader a new literary experience in which she can share control of the text with the author. Whereas a printed novel presents its episodes in one order, the electronic writing space removes that restriction. Instead of a single string of paragraphs, the author may lay out a two- or even three-dimensional textual space within which her fiction operates. The reader may join in actively constructing the text by selecting a particular order of episodes at the time of reading and by otherwise intervening in the text. The reader's experience of the fiction depends on these interventions.

In its simplest form, interactive fiction requires only those two elements that we have already identified for electronic writing: episodes (topics) and decision points (links) between episodes. The episodes may be paragraphs of prose or poetry, they may include bit-mapped graphics or other media as well, and they may be of any length. Their length will establish the rhythm of the story—how long the reader remains a conventional reader before he or she is called on to participate in the selection of the next episode. The author also inserts a set of links to other episodes together with a procedure for choosing which link to follow. Each link may require a different response from the reader or a different condition in the computer system. The reader may answer a question posed in the text; the computer can also keep track of the previous episodes readers have visited, so that they may be barred from visiting one episode before they visit another. Many other tests are possible, but even with the simple matching technique and the tracking of previously visited episodes, the author can create a fictional space of great flexibility. Readers may be allowed to examine a story in chronological order, in reverse chronology, or in a complicated sequence of flashbacks and returns. They may follow one character through the story, and then return to follow another. A reader might play the role of the detective trying to solve a murder, a role familiar from the computerized adventure games. A reader might be asked to influence events in a novel by choosing episodes that promise to bring two characters together or to punish an evil character for his or her deeds: each choice would define a new course for the story.

Such multiple plots, however, are only one possibility—and not the most promising. The electronic writing space can accommodate other literary strategies. It can offer the reader several different perspectives on a fixed set of events, in which case the reader would not be able to affect the course of the story, but she could switch back and forth among narrators, each with his or her own point of view. An electronic text can also establish relationships among episodes that are not narrative at all: for example, a poet could define multiple reading orders for an anthology of poems according to theme, image, or other criteria under the poet's or the reader's control, as hypertext poets William Dickey, Robert Kendall, Deena Larsen, and others have done.

Electronic fiction in this sense need not be automatic or "computer-generated" fiction. The computer does not create the verbal text: it presents that text to the reader according to the author's preconditions. The locus of creativity remains with the author and the reader, although the balance between the two has shifted. Nor is electronic fiction necessarily random. The author may put any number of restrictions on the reading order. The extent of the reader's choices and therefore the reader's freedom in examining the literary space depends on the links that the author creates between episodes. The reader may have to choose from among a few alternatives or may range widely through the work. Each author can relinquish as much or as little control as she chooses; she simply has another literary dimension with which to work.

AFTERNOON

One of the earliest of the interactive fictions remains one of the most compelling: *afternoon, a story* by Michael Joyce. (Like many other standalone interactive fictions, *afternoon* was written using the hypertext editing system Storyspace, created by Bolter, Joyce, and Smith [1990–1996].) *afternoon* combines the literary sophistication that we have associated with printed fiction with the immediacy of an interactive adventure game. It is a fiction and a game at the same time, and yet its visual structure is very simple. The reader confronts a window on the computer screen: episodes of *afternoon*, containing from one to a few hundred words, will appear successively in the window. At the bottom of the screen is a small bar, where the reader types replies in order to move to the next episode; she may also initiate movement by selecting a word from the current episode in the window. All the text of the episodes was written by Joyce, but the particular order in which the episodes are visited is determined at the time of reading.

afternoon begins:

I try to recall winter. 'As if it were yesterday?' she says, but I do not signify one way or another.

By five the sun sets and the afternoon melt freezes again across the blacktop into crystal octopi and palms of ice—rivers and continents beset by fear, and we walk out to the car, the snow moaning beneath our boots and the oaks exploding in series along the fenceline on the horizon, the shrapnel settling like relics, the echoing thundering off far ice.

This was the essence of wood, these fragments say. And this darkness is air. 'Poetry' she says, without emotion, one way or another.

Do you want to hear about it?

If the reader types yes, then a link will flash another episode on the screen, whose first sentences are:

> She had been a client of Wert's wife for some time. Nothing serious, nothing awful, merely general unhappiness and the need of a woman so strong to have friends....

If the reader types no, another episode will appear beginning:

> I understand how you feel. Nothing is more empty than heat. Seen so starkly the world holds wonder only in the expanses of clover where the bees work....

afternoon does not accept no as the reader's last word: instead, it moves the reader along a different path. But the reader has other choices as well: she can select a particular word directly from the text (such as "poetry," "winter," or "yesterday" in the first episode). Certain words in each window will "yield" and branch to another episode. If the reader defaults by hitting the Return key, then yet another link will be followed. Many different responses will cause the text to move, but until the reader responds with some action of the keyboard or the mouse, the text of an episode remains on the screen, conventional prose (occasionally poetry) to be read in the conventional way.

One voice in a later episode in *afternoon* describes the reading experience this way:

> In my mind the story, as it has formed, takes on margins. Each margin will yield to the impatient, or wary, reader. You can answer yes at the beginning and page through on a wave of Returns, or page through directly—again using Returns—without that first interaction. These are not versions, but the story itself in long lines. Otherwise, however, the center is all—Thoreau or Brer Rabbit, each preferred the bramble. I've discovered more there too, and the real interaction, if that is possible, is in pursuit of texture ...

This is the great difference between *afternoon* and a fiction written on and for paper. There is no single story of which each reading is a version, because each reading determines the story as it goes. We could say that there is no story at all; there are only readings. Or if we say that the story of *afternoon* is the sum of all its readings, then we must understand the story as a structure that can embrace contradictory emotional and perhaps factual outcomes. Each reading is a different turning within a universe of paths, often full of "bramble," set up by the author. Reading *afternoon* several times is like exploring a vast house or castle. Although the reader may proceed often down the same corridors and through familiar rooms, she may also come upon a new hallway not previously explored or find a previously locked door suddenly giving way to the touch. Gradually, she pushes back the margins of this electronic space—as in a computer game in which the descent down a stairway reveals a whole new level of the dungeon. *afternoon* is constructed to remind the reader of the affinities between electronic fiction and computer adventure games.

afternoon is metaphorically related to computer video games as well. It is like a video game in which the player pilots a spaceship around planetary obstacles that each exert a gravitational force. Readers of *afternoon* move along paths with their own inertia, while at the same time experiencing the attraction of various parts of the fiction as they move by. It is easy to fall into an orbit around one set of episodes, one focus of the story. Readers may find themselves returning to the same episodes again and again, trying to break free by giving different answers and therefore choosing different paths. When it succeeds, this strategy may then push the reader into another orbit.

The planets in *afternoon*'s solar system are its characters: a poet named Peter, who is working as a technical writer for a software company; his employer Wert, Wert's wife Lolly, and another employee in the company with the unlikely classical name of Nausicaa. Peter's is the narrative voice in most of the episodes, but the reader may follow paths in which each of the two women also narrate. Various paths concern the history of these characters, and the reader can find herself parked in an orbit around one of them. The events in *afternoon* may be significant in the traditional narrative sense: one is an automobile accident that may have killed Peter's former wife and his son. But one of the most gravitationally powerful events is commonplace: Peter has lunch with his employer. What makes the event important is that it is a structural crossroad: the intersection of many narrative paths. Peter's lunch may be the occasion for him to think about Wert's wife, or about his own affair with Nausicaa, or about the crazy computer project on which he is engaged. As Jane Douglas points out in her reading of *afternoon*, the significance of the lunch episode depends on where the reader has been before and where she goes next (Douglas, 2000, p. 99–100). In some readings *afternoon* is a picaresque novel in which the characters seem to stay put while the reader wanders.

Sometimes there is only one path leading from a given episode; sometimes there are several. The author's control of the narrative is inversely proportional to the number of paths and the kinds of responses expected of the reader. A single path gives the author the same degree of control as a printed book—in fact, even more control, because the reader cannot flip pages or turn to the back of the book, but must simply hit Return and go on. An episode with many paths offers the reader the opportunity to head in any of several directions, although she may only be aware of this freedom after she has returned to the episode many times. And even after visiting all the episodes, the reader has still not exhausted the writing space, because the significance of the episodes changes depending on the order of reading. At one point several characters are invited to tell about themselves. If they do this early in the reading, then their subsequent words and deeds will be measured against this history. Nausicaa, for example, who seems a benign presence, turns out to have been a drug addict and prostitute. If the reader comes upon the self-revelatory episodes late in the reading, then these episodes must be read as explanation and justification of what went before. In either case, we find ourselves invoking familiar literary structures in the effort to understand this electronic fiction. The difference is that both contradictory structures coexist in the same electronic space, and, at least after several readings, the reader becomes aware of this double presence and reflects on the difference between the two possible readings.

The presence or absence of paths changes the feel of a particular part of the fiction. Wherever the choices narrow to a single path, *afternoon* becomes a traditional story: it imitates the space of the printed book before broadening again into its multidimensional, electronic space. The capacity to imitate the printed book is one important way in which *afternoon* makes its comment on the nature of reading. *afternoon* suggests to us that it can reform the act of reading by freeing us from the constraints of print and that it can therefore offer a more authentic narrative form than the forms we have come to associate with print. This hyperfiction's claim to greater authenticity is that it can do justice to the truth and sanctity of human recollection. At one point Lolly says: "I have dedicated my life to a certainty that recollection is somehow sacred, without sanction, blameless, and liberating." Memory is not univocal, and the multiple narrative paths of this fiction are offered to us as a means of capturing the authentic multiplicity of memory. Joyce has in fact continued to explore the relationship between memory and narrative form in subsequent electronic works, *WOE-or a Memory of What Will Be* (1991), *Twilight* (Joyce, 1996a), and *Twelve Blue* (Joyce, 1996b).

Each of the many paths in *afternoon* seems to be a mixture of the accidental and the inexorable. A path can have a sense of the inevitable, as when Peter tries to find out whether his wife and son have been in an automobile accident. Following this trajectory makes the story quite linear, as Peter fights his way through various telephone calls, in an effort to get information, at the same time reticent to make the most direct call, that is, to take the most direct path to the information he anticipates. As readers we must do the same: we must be careful about our answers at the end of each episode in order to stay with this narrative strand. A wrong answer will shunt us to another path from which it may be difficult to return to Peter's frantic calls. In this way we see how electronic fiction can take into itself and redefine the experience of reading. When the reader's struggle with the story mirrors the struggle that the character goes through, *afternoon* becomes an allegory of the act of reading. This struggle for meaning is enacted by the characters in this hypertext. The struggle for meaning, a paradigmatic theme of modernist literature, is renewed and reformed in *afternoon*, because it is also enacted by the reader as she reads. *afternoon* becomes the reader's story in this remarkable way, for the reader's desire to make the story happen and to make sense of what happens is inevitably inscribed in the story itself.

THE RHETORIC OF THE MULTILINEAR

We noted that *afternoon* is about the problem of its own reading. In its attempt to redefine the act of reading, *afternoon* has served as a paradigm for much of the early hypertext fiction (see Landow, 1997, pp. 192–197). Its redefinition of reading, however, is not simply a rejection of our experience as readers of print. *afternoon* depends on the rhythms and expectations of printed fiction, multiplying and refracting those expectations in order to achieve its effects. As many have pointed out, hypertext is not nonlinear, but multilinear. Each reading of a hypertext must be a linear experience, because the reader must move from episode to episode, activating links and reading the text that is presented. The problem that hypertext poses for the reader is the problem of understanding the multiple lines she must travel in traversing the web of the text—lines that may ignore or contradict one another. *afternoon* has shown how a multilinear text can play with the reader's notions of cause and effect, making the words and actions of the characters radically ambiguous. Jane Douglas has explored the ambiguities of *afternoon* and *WOE* in her meticulous (and multiple) readings of the texts (Douglas, 2000, pp. 97–120).

Hypertext can adopt organizing principles that we associate with modern printed fiction, such as the stream of consciousness of one character or the point of view of several characters. A hypertext can narrate the same events from different points of view, a technique familiar from Faulkner's *The Sound and the Fury* and Durrell's *Alexandria Quartet*. It can speak with multiple authorial voices, as does Judy Malloy's and Cathy Marshall's *Forward Anywhere* (1995), in which each of the two authors addresses us apparently in her own voice. Through these and other techniques, hypertext authors have set about refashioning the rhetoric of the linear plot, calling into question the notion that fiction should narrate events in a single, clear order. For hypertext writers and their readers, the single narrative line is no longer adequate to capture the reality that they wish to pursue—in Joyce's case, for example, the reality of memory with its confusions and multiple versions. Early hypertext fictions by Joyce and others have worked to subvert the ideals of clarity and propriety in narrative. Their rhetoric, different from the rhetoric that has defined printed prose fiction (and nonfiction), relies heavily on the violation of the expected and conventional order.

Such violations of clarity and causality seem to be defining qualities of all hypertexts that permit the reader to make significant choices in the order of presentation. If there is a narrative structure that extends across several episodes, it must sometimes happen that the reader will choose paths in which the episodes are presented out of their temporal or causal order. In some of these works, the episodes are written so that there no single well-defined chronology, so that the reader's choices always seem to be out of their "natural" order. Hypertexts sometimes explicitly challenge our assumptions about narrative flow, as does Jane Douglas' hyperfiction *I Have Said Nothing* (1994).

It might seem that chronological order is the "natural" way to represent a story in any technology of writing or communicating. Even oral poets, however, sometimes used more complex strategies: the *Odyssey*, for example, contains a long flashback lasting thousands of lines, as well as many digressions. There is a classical rhetorical term for the violation of expected order, *hyperbaton*. In fact, ancient rhetoricians and their Renaissance followers cultivated a sensitivity to classes of such violations of expected sound or sense. Most, if not all, of their figures concern displacement or departure from what is thought of as natural or clear exposition (see Lanham's

Handlist of Rhetorical Terms, 1991, p. 86). Hyperbaton was the name given in particular to the departure from conventional word order in a sentence, but we can also think of the displaced order of episodes in a hypertext as hyperbaton. This displacement is perhaps what most troubles new readers of interactive fiction. The technique requires suspension: the reader must hold the displaced unit in mind while waiting for the rest of the syntax. Hyperbaton calls on the reader to make a special effort at understanding and indeed threatens her faith that there is any conventional meaning to be gotten out of the text. The suspensions required by hypertext threaten never to be resolved.

From ancient times to the present, any technology flexible enough to meet a culture's writing needs could surely accommodate multiple narrative modes. Print certainly did not require chronological storytelling. The 19th-century novelists in what we have called the industrial age of print found many ways to complicate the simple narrative line: e.g. multiple narrators or stories within stories. In the 20th century, modernist writers continued and expanded these techniques. The point is that techniques of digression or inversion were understood as unusual, as violations of the reader's expectations, and for that very reason fiction writers explored them. Our culture in the age of print has always regarded the chronological narration of events as the natural way to tell a story. Hypertext refashions and revalues techniques of displacement, such as the flashback, that had already developed in printed fiction. Because hypertext fiction is still understood as the remediation of printed fiction, the constant violations of order are read as attempts to undermine the method of storytelling that the tradition of print appears to sanction.

DISPLACEMENT AND REPETITION IN *VICTORY GARDEN*

Victory Garden by Stuart Moulthrop (1991), another of the most important early hypertexts, is a network of about 990 episodes and 2,800 links. Most of the narrative takes place on the night the bombing began in the Persian Gulf War, January 17, 1991, and most of the scenes occur in a mythical town that is and is not Austin, Texas, home to an institution called the University of Tara. The characters are academics, students, professors, or administrators, all of whose problems, professional and psychosexual, are connected in some way with the war. They constantly allude to the bombing in conversation, and above all they watch it on television—in a bar, at a party, or in their bedrooms.

Television is an obsessive theme and at the same time the narrative engine for *Victory Garden*. It is not only that the characters watch television; the reader also comes across quotations from Dan Rather or Peter Jennings, descriptions of the live coverage, passages from books on the impact of television, and musings by one or more authorial voices on the TV coverage of the war. In *Victory Garden* the ubiquity of the televised reports and the fact that so much is happening more or less simultaneously on this night serve to relieve some of the reader's uneasiness with disruptions of the narrative. Wherever the reader branches in *Victory Garden*, the television is on, offering its version of the war. This helps to locate the reader in the narrative world and to combat the feeling of being uprooted by the displacements of the fiction. Metaphorically, television provides a continuous visual background against which the action occurs.

Victory Garden offers the reader a second way to visualize the narrative. With hundreds of episodes and thousands of interconnections, this hypertext constitutes a labyrinth of possible reading paths. Appropriately it begins with a map (Fig. 7.1). What the reader sees is a garden of intersecting paths and at each intersection the name of an episode. The garden serves as a visual symbol for the whole fiction; it is also an allusion to Borges' story "The Garden of Forking Paths." What is most important is that the diagram functions operationally as well as metaphorically to control and organize the space of the fiction. The named intersections are linked to various epi-

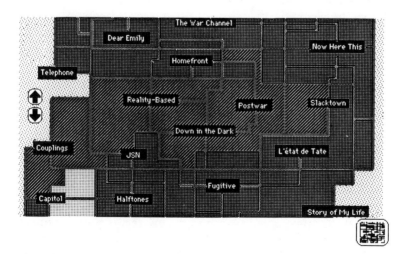

FIG. 7.1.   The middle map from Stuart Moulthrop's *Victory Garden*. (Reprinted with permission of the author.)

sodes: by moving the cursor over a name and clicking twice with the mouse, the reader branches to that episode. Thus, the map is not ancillary, as maps and diagrams usually are in printed text: it is a part of the symbolic structure of *Victory Garden*. It functions both as a picture of the garden and as a set of symbols woven into the fabric of the text. Hypertexts with such linked graphics remind us of medieval manuscripts, in which the illuminated letters work simultaneously as abstract or figural art and as verbal elements in the text (= > p. 65).

Because the map of the garden is too large to fit on one screen, it is divided into three parts: north, central, and south. As a reader, I might begin in the central part and click on the rectangle labeled "L'état de Tate." I will find myself thrust into a series of scenes involving characters named Tate, Madden, and Urquhart. Who are these people and what are their relationships? I glean something from the episodes as I proceed, but there is much more that I can learn only later, if and when I return to this area of the garden after having visited others. On my return, I know that Urquhart is an unstable computer scientist and has just been chased across town by Madden, who is an FBI agent. The suspension of meaning, the hyperbaton, has to some degree been resolved. When I first visit the scene, I may be impatient to discover who Tate and Urquhart are and what brings them together. It is an apprehension that a reader may also feel with conventional literature: that the text is proceeding in a direction that will never satisfy a question that the reader has. In a conventional text, however, the promise of closure is more likely to be kept. The printed book has a final page, which the reader can be sure of reaching. In a hypertext, the reader may never reach an episode that resolves the hyperbaton.

There are other traditional devices that help to give coherence to the narrative: among them, allusions to Borges' *Garden of Forking Paths*. The title *Victory Garden* is an explicit reference, and the text includes quotations from Borges. There are also numerous allusions: the scene in which Urquhart visits Tate in his tower alludes to the scene in which Yu Tsun visits the Sinologist Stephen Albert. Just as Yu Tsun has come to kill Albert, so Urquhart says at one point that he has come to kill Tate. Urquhart has also come to get "the answer," whereas Yu Tsun receives from Albert the unexpected answer to the mystery of the Chinese manuscript. In *Victory Garden*, Tate also reads to Urquhart from a lost oriental work. The reader who notices these allusions may also wonder whether Boris' action may be semiotic in the way that Yu Tsun's is. Could the killing of Tate be taken as a sign, and indeed does Urquhart kill Tate?

The allusive dialogue between *Victory Garden* and *Garden of Forking Paths* is a device whose familiarity helps to convince us that there is meaning and intentionality in *Victory Garden*. There is, in fact, a tension between the hyperbaton and these devices of familiarization. If such devices give the reader a sense of place, the hyperbaton keeps pulling the reader out of place. In one sense, to read is to find one's place: this is certainly true of conventional reading of conventional linear fiction, where the voice of the text defines a perspective for the reader, a place from which to examine the events narrated. Hyperbaton in hypertext, its discontinuities and branches, keeps wrenching us out of a comfortable or familiar perspective and putting us down somewhere else. After each branch, the reader must ask: from what perspective am I to understand what happens next?

Victory Garden is not without conventional narrative coherence. There are relatively long narrative strands (of four or five episodes) that do appear in chronological order. The reader enters one of these strands and may then continue in a linear fashion. But the reader can also branch willingly or inadvertently into another strand. Strands cross and recross, so that there is no certainty that one will continue. It is very seldom that a strand will continue to a decisive closure.

Displacements in a hypertext disrupt conventional meaning by presenting one episode beside another, without allowing the reader to assume a simple or single relationship between the two. There is a particularly effective series of such displacements in *Victory Garden*. When the reader comes upon a quotation from Neil Postman's *Amusing Ourselves to Death*, the relationship of this quotation to the rest of *Victory Garden* is problematic. It seems to be a gloss on the story:

> *It is conceivable to use television as a lamp, a surface for texts, a bookcase, even as radio. But it has not been so used and will not be so used, at least in America.*
> — *Amusing Ourselves to Death*

By clicking on the appropriate word or phrase in this quotation, the reader can call up any one of a number of different episodes. As it turns out, each branch forces the reader into a different relationship with the original Postman quotation.

Clicking on the word "lamp" leads to an episode that begins:

> Thea turned the TV to the wall, watching the auroras of living color that leaked from the edges of the tube and played across the wallpaper. She felt hollow, disconnected, almost viscerally shocked. She wanted another cigarette and she needed a drink....

This branch takes us back into the story, and the narrative immediately contradicts Postman's assertion: Thea does use the television as a lamp, turning the TV to the wall so that it serves only to light the room. The party itself is part of the larger fabric of the narrative, into which the reader again enters.

Clicking on a "surface for texts" produces:

> *Constructive hypertexts require a capability to act: to create, to change, and to recover particular encounters within the developing body of knowledge. These encounters … are versions of what they are becoming, a structure for what does not yet exist.… A constructive hypertext should be a tool for inventing, discovering, viewing, and testing multiple, alternative, organizational structures.…*
>
> *There is no simple way to say this.*
>
> — Michael Joyce, "Siren Shapes"

This phrase "surface for texts" is read as inviting a comment on hypertext: we branch not back into the story, but to a observation on hypertext by Michael Joyce. This episode again contradicts the Postman quotation—in practice as well as in theory. For at this moment, the reader's computer screen has become a surface for texts. *Victory Garden* is itself a text that plays across the surface of a videoscreen, as only hypertext can.

Clicking on "radio" presents an episode that includes the following passage:

> … "I don't believe it," Veronica insisted. "What are we seeing? The same pictures over and over. Some suits talking. A lot of slick graphics, like this is some kind of warm-up for the Superbowl. We might as well be getting this on the radio, like that *War of the Worlds* that fooled everybody in the fifties."
>
> "That was 1938, dear. Way before my time of course."
>
> "Whatever. It still seems wrong to me. Some kind of big show."

Again we are taken back into the story, and the war is compared to the radio broadcast of *The War of the Worlds*. Elsewhere, *Victory Garden* offers further comments on the reduction of television to radio in the war. Television did indeed become radio when CNN and other networks put the voices of their reporters on the air when they lacked video. So again this branch serves to contradict Postman's argument; television can be used as radio.

The words "bookcase" and "America" open other narrative lines. What might be called a "solipsistic narrator" intrudes. He sounds as if he were the author, and he talks about himself. He is truly a solipsist, for in one thread leading from this episode he writes: "All that is really happening is happening to me … " This authorial intrusion also provides several entry points back into the fiction.

All the preceding branches can be regarded in some sense as hyperbaton. Beginning in the Postman quotation, each branch thrusts the reader into a different place in the narrative or the essay on media that *Victory Garden* sometimes seems to be. With each branch the reader has the opportunity to expand Postman's list in a different way. The original list, which seems to offer a way to encapsulate and to bring under control much of the story, serves as a set of launching points and may send the reader on a variety of trajectories. These examples of displacement can also be analyzed under the larger category of substitution or metonymy, and Richard Lanham (1991) has noted that figures of metonymy are instances of changes of scale (p. 102). All these branches substitute one verbal gesture for another: a different episode for the original Postman quotation, and each involves a change in scale. The act of branching expands each of these elements into a narrative of indefinite size.

The Postman quotation was arrived at by clicking through several other quotations about media or descriptions of or excerpts from newscasters. From the perspective of the fiction in *Victory Garden* (the story of Thea, Boris, and the others), the Postman material seems to be a digression. In traditional fiction, the narrative is the center, and whatever takes the reader away from the narrative is marginal and digressive. As we travel back and forth through the Postman material, however, the priorities can be reversed. The whole of *Victory Garden* can be read as an analysis of the American media and the Persian Gulf War. The narrative can be read as a fictional digression on the reality of the war, as reflected in the prose excerpts, or we can call it a fictional reaction to or explanation of the prose excerpts. What then displaces what? What comes first, the media or the story—the televised war as offered to us as reality on CBS or Moulthrop's fictional account? The ambiguity works both ways: Postman and Rather threaten to become characters in the fiction, no more real than Thea or Emily. And in this way the rhetorical device of hyperbaton seems to deconstruct itself. The device of displacement is itself displaced. This double displacement is what we would expect: that hypertext would use the device until it "used it up" and end as a critique of the received rhetorical division between the center and the digression.

When we have followed the figure of hyperbaton into its own dissolution, we can start over with another rhetorical device: repetition. The technique of repetition is one of the most compelling ways in which hypertext refashions and reforms print. Anyone who reads such hypertexts as *WOE* (Joyce, 1991) or *Victory Garden* notices the repetitions. The reader often cycles around to the same place—either intentionally or inadvertently in an effort to get somewhere else in the text. In *Victory Garden*, for example, one can move in a circle sometimes simply by pressing the Return key repeatedly. The Postman example contains no immediate cycles, although there may be long-term ones. But the reader can always press the back icon on the control bar to create her own cycles.

Consider again what happens when I branch on the word "lamp" in the Postman episode. I find first that the Postman quotation is being used to introduce and at the same time to contextualize the story. I also find that the story serves to contradict the quotation. If I branch back, I read the Postman quotation differently. The quotation seems both more encompassing and more questionable. We have just considered the possibility that the quotation provides a frame for the story. Yet the story also refuses to be encompassed by the frame: it spills out beyond the frame and (in a thoroughly postmodern fashion) threatens to encompass the quotation and make it a part of the story. If I try each of the other words in the list, branching forward and then back in each case, then at each return my reading of the Postman quotation changes again.

Thus, if repetition is a common feature of hypertexts like *Victory Garden*, it is repetition with a difference. The reader understands the repeated episode differently precisely because of the path she has traveled to get to that repetition. The same is true of the experience of repetition in print, but hypertexts exploit repetition to a far greater degree than conventional printed fiction—both because the text is divided into smaller units, which the reader is likely to encounter more than once, and because the repetition can be programmed into the link structure of the hypertext. Jane Douglas (2000) has explored repetition in hypertext in her readings of *afternoon*, *WOE*, and other works. She has shown, for example, how in Michael Joyce's *WOE*, repetition with a difference is perhaps the dominant trope, because the narrative voice repeatedly seeks to revisit memories and repeatedly fails.

As readers, we may perceive hypertextual repetition as an attempt to improve on a previous version. Hypertextual fiction often seems to attempt to take back what has been said and replace it with something better. This quality may be due to the experimental nature of the early hypertexts, but it is also a claim about the nature of electronic writing. Our understanding of print is that it is hard, indeed impossible, to erase and correct the published expression of an idea. In electronic writing, we may interpret everything as a palinode; the hard task is to achieve fixity.

DISRUPTING THE LINEAR

We have been considering the ways in which hypertext disrupts the ostensibly simple "linear" experience of reading. Even in the industrial age of print, that experience only existed in the ideal, but it was important as a norm against which the deviations and elaborations of fiction were measured. Like earlier printed fiction, hypertexts must contend with our desire for the linear. Although this desire may be more or less powerful in various cultures and at various times, it is certainly still powerful here in North America in the late age of print, where truly popular fiction, the bestsellers, are plot driven and often quite linear. With bestsellers today, as with much fiction of the 19th century, displacement works as an ornament because it successfully plays with the reader's expectation of and desire for the linear. The difficulty with hypertext is that it does not offer alternative orders as mere ornamentation—that is, as exceptions to the "normal" practice of linear development. For hypertext, displacement becomes the customary rhetorical strategy, whereas consecutive, chronological order is the exception. Hypertext reverses the relative values of ornamented and "clear" narrative. When we read a hypertext, we expect to jump around from one place and time to others. In *Victory Garden* it almost comes as a surprise how easily we can move along narrative threads in five or six screens. In hypertext, clear narrative itself becomes ornamental, and, because the turning of clarity into ornamentation is never likely to appeal to a large audience, literary hypertext may never become a popular genre.

One reason why literary hypertext may remain esoteric is that the technique of displacement thwarts the reader's desire to be left alone with the story. The traditional and still popular view is that prose should be transparent: on analogy with illusionistic painting, the reader of a fiction should be able to believe that he is looking through a window onto a fictional world. Ornamentation threatens to interrupt the reader's gaze, making him aware of the text as a structure of verbal elements. The reader is suddenly looking *at* the prose rather than looking *through* it. Richard Lanham (1993) has argued that modern (and postmodern) art constantly plays with the distinction between "looking at" and "looking through" (pp. 14, 45ff) (=> p. 184). Hypertextual fiction does the same. In exploring a hypertext, the reader oscillates between looking through the prose of each episode and looking at the junctures or links between episodes. Whenever the reader comes to a link and is forced to make a choice, the illusion of an imagined world must break down, at least momentarily, as the reader recalls the technical circumstances of the electronic medium. It may be possible for the reader to ignore these circumstances, if only a click is required to bring the next chronological episode onto the screen. After all, in a printed book the reader can turn pages without much conscious effort. Usually, however, interactive fictions are calculated to make the reader aware of their links, their technical circumstances. In most of the interactive fictions of the past decade, rhetorical displacement draws attention to itself and therefore away from any simple illusion the narrative might create.

THE TRADITION OF EXPERIMENT

In its pervasive use of displacement, interactive fiction shows how it can be both innovative and traditional. In remediating printed forms, interactive fiction must both rely on the tradition of print and yet somehow surpass or reform that tradition. It must be both new and old (= > p. 7). It is certainly new to automate and animate the presentation of text, so that the reader's decisions are automatically registered and cause other words to appear. However, in disrupting the stability of the text, interactive fiction belongs in a "tradition" of experimental literature that has marked the 20th century—the era of modernism, futurism, Dada, surrealism, letterism, the nouveau roman, concrete poetry, and other movements of greater or lesser influence (see Douglas, 2000, p. 55–62; Lanham, 1989; 1993, pp. 31–52). The experiments of Dada, for example, were aimed at breaking down all structures of established art and literature, and in that breakdown the Dadists worked in the same spirit as writers now work in the electronic medium. Jean Arp wrote that in his poems: "I tore apart sentences, words, syllables. I tried to break down the language into atoms, in order to approach the creative" (Grossman, 1971, p. 136). Tristan Tzara proposed a poetics of destruction, when he gave this recipe for creating a Dada poem: "To make a dadist poem. Take a newspaper. Take a pair of scissors. Choose an article as long as you are planning to make your poem. Cut out the article. Then cut out each of the words that make up this article and put them in a bag. Shake it gently. Then take out the scraps one after the other in the order in which they left the bag. Copy conscientiously. The poem will be like you.... " (Grossman, 1971, pp. 124–125).

Dada was an early and influential example of the modernist will to exper-iment. The modernist attack was often aimed at the conventions of the re-alist novel that was supposed to tell its story with a clear and cogent rhythm of events. In the course of their attack, modern authors found themselves straining at the limitations of the printed page. Because the linear presenta-tion of the printed book was so well suited to the conventions of plot and characters of the realist novel, to attack the form of the novel was also to question the technology of print. The French led the way with the nouveau roman and Philip Sollers and the Tel Quel group. From France and else-where, we have had programmed novels and aleatory novels, all of which were instances of subversion: they worked from within, attempting to un-dercut the conventions of printed literature while themselves remaining printed books. The notion of literature as subversion unites modern and postmodern literature and art. Postmodern authors (that is, those often characterized as postmodern, from Thomas Pynchon to Robert Coover and Italo Calvino) have also called into question premodern traditions of narra-tive organization, the stability of narrative identity, and so on. Both modern and postmodern writers set out to refashion printed fiction from within.

Much of the literature of the 20th century has been accused of subver-sion. In that sense, avant-garde movements like Dada were extending or perhaps caricaturing the mainstream. Joyce, Virginia Woolf, Pound, Eliot, and others all participated in the breakdown of traditions of narrative prose and poetry, because breaking with such traditions was the definition of be-ing modern. Pound and Eliot set out to replace the narrative element in po-etry with fragmented anecdotes and classical allusions. Joyce and Woolf devised new ways of structuring their works based on stream of conscious-ness or on multiple layers of topical and mythical organization. All of these writers were trying to establish new relationships between the mo-ment-by-moment experience of reading a text and our perception of the text's organizing and controlling structures. Our culture understands the authors of literary hypertext in the same way: that they are experimenting with our perception of the text. Just as modern and postmodern authors were refashioning the tradition of printed fiction from within, hypertext au-thors have remediated that tradition from the perspective provided by a new technology of writing.

On the other hand, experimentation with and fragmentation of the form of the novel is certainly older than modernism: it dates back at least to the 18th century. That whole tradition of experimentation needs now to be re-considered in the light of the new technology, because each previous experiment in print suggests ways in which electronic writing may now refashion print altogether. In printed fiction there is always a tension between the linear flow of the narrative and the associative trains of thought touched off by the narrative. The electronic medium provides a new set of techniques for mediating that tension. From the perspective of hypertext fiction, works by authors from Laurence Sterne to Jorge Luis Borges are not only explorations of the limits of the printed page but also possible models for electronic writing. Some of their works could be transferred to the new writing space and playfully remediated there, and in fact at least one has been. On the other hand, experimental fictions written in the age of print depend for their significance on their adversarial relationship with their own medium. They need to be read as unusual, even "failed," printed books in order to refashion from within what hypertext now remediates from without.

STERNE AND THE NOVEL AS CONVERSATION

Readers have long recognized Sterne's *Tristram Shandy* as an assault on the form of the novel and its conventions of narration. The Russian formalist Victor Shklovsky pointed out more than 50 years ago that "[b]y violating the form [of the novel], [Sterne] forces us to attend to it; and, for him, this awareness of the form through its violation constitutes the content of the novel" (Shklovsky, "Sterne's Tristram Shandy: Stylistic Commentary," 1965, pp. 30–31; see also Rabkin, 1981). Shklovsky saw Tristram Shandy as an example of the way in which a novelist dislocates or distorts the order of events in a simple story in order to create a complex plot. Any reading of Sterne's novel is necessarily a catalogue of the digressions from and dislocations of the events of Tristram's uneventful life. Tristram as narrator seldom lets us alone with the story: he is always breaking in to remind us that he is in fact writing his life story and to point out when he is digressing, omitting, or delaying. He does his best to remove us from the action. There are stories within stories, and characters often read aloud from books and papers. Tristram explains that " … when a man is telling a story in the strange way I do mine, he is obliged continually to be going backwards and forwards to keep all tight together in the reader's fancy … " (Sterne, 1965, Book 6, Chapter 33, p. 351). In fact, the jumps do not keep all tight in the reader's fancy. The wandering style of narration is reflected in Book 7 in the storyline, when Tristram sets out on a hasty trip through France in his effort to avoid death, in a journey as filled with delays and indirection as the narrative itself. Yet, despite all the obstacles he seems to impose, Tristram is not hostile to his readers. He claims to establish a relationship of equality, to overcome the formal and one-sided relationship between author and reader assumed by the conventional novel:

> Writing, when properly managed (as you may be sure I think mine is) is but a different name for conversation: As no one, who knows what he is about in good company, would venture to talk all;—so no author, who understands the just boundaries of decorum and good breeding, would presume to think all: The truest respect which you can pay to a reader's understanding, is to halve this matter amicably, and leave him something to imagine, in his turn, as well as yourself. For my own part, I am eternally paying him compliments of this kind, and do all that lies in my power to keep his imagination as busy as my own (Book 2, Chapter 11, p. 83).

As narrator, then, Tristram pays readers the compliment of expecting them to help construct the novel as they read. The more the narrator digresses and distances us from the story, the closer we feel to the narrator himself, as if we were conversing and not simply reading. Tristram Shandy is not only an attack on the conventions of the novel as a coherent narrative of events; it is also an assault on the conventions of presentation, on the technologies of writing and printing. Sometimes the assault on the book is physical. Chapter 24 of Book 4 is missing: Tristram claims he has torn it out and proceeds in Chapter 25 to tell us what was lost. The pages are misnumbered to indicate the loss. Other characters go further in their mistreatment of the printed page. One learned doctor recommends wrapping a burn in a "soft sheet of paper just come off the press" (Book 4, Chapter 28, p. 246). Later Tristram loses his "remarks" (his manuscript) by leaving them in a carriage that he has sold. He returns to discover that a woman is using the papers to curl her hair, and so his remarks are twisted this way and that.... "[A]nd when they are published ... ," Tristram adds, "[t]hey will be worse twisted still" (Book 7, Chapter 38, p. 405). Tristram involves his reader not only in the construing of the narrative, but in the very making of the book. Omissions in the text are indicated by asterisks, and Tristram turns the omissions into games. Sometimes he leaves one asterisk for each letter and so creates a code for the reader to decipher. Occasionally he leaves a blank space where the reader may add his own words. He challenges the reader to do precisely what a reader can never succeed in doing—to write in the printed text.

It has long been pointed out that *Tristram Shandy* seems to anticipate the work of 20th century writers who have brought the novel to its end. We can now add that *Tristram Shandy* anticipates electronic writing in important ways. Sterne is a topographic writer, whose achievement is more remarkable because he works in the intractable medium of print. By insisting on a conversation with his reader, Sterne is contravening the "natural" use of print. In a playful way, he is inviting the reader to give up his safe status as reader and to share responsibility for the narrative. Electronic writing puts its reader in a similar position. But if Sterne can only pretend to offer the reader a chance to participate in the construction of the text, electronic writing can demand that the reader participate, for, as we have noted, no text may be given until the reader calls it forth. For our current cultural moment, electronic writing seems to come close to the conversation between author and reader that Tristram imagines. The reason is not that the computer is itself a human partner, but rather that it seems to give a greater presence to the author than does the printed page. The author is present in the electronic network of episodes that she creates and through which the reader moves along associative paths. Tristram Shandy's conversation too proceeds by association. As Shklovsky puts it:

> [the novel's] diverse material, which is augmented by extensive excerpts from the works of various pedants, would undoubtedly tear the novel to bits were it not drawn together by crisscrossing motifs. A stated motif is never fully developed, never actually realized, but is only recalled from time to time; its fulfillment is continually put off to a more and more remote time. Yet its very presence in all the dimensions of the novel ties the episodes together (Shklovsky, 1965, p. 40).

Already a large conceptual network, *Tristram Shandy* could in fact be represented as a structure in the computer's writing space, in which each chapter was a topic and in which chapters or runs of chapters were linked according to their several motifs. The reader could then examine the effect of Sterne's digressions by taking alternative routes through the text. The result would be a critical demonstration of the power of association to organize across the linear dimension imposed by the paged book. The network could serve as a critical tool for understanding the novel in a new way. Such a network would not, however, be *Tristram Shandy*, which depends for its effect on the pleasurable annoyance of reading the many digressions on the printed page.

JAMES JOYCE AS HYPERTEXT

If in all modern fiction there is a tension between the linear experience of reading and the structure of allusion and reference, critics have recognized that this tension is particularly strong in the later works of James Joyce. Michael Groden has explained how *Ulysses* embodies two different conceptions of fiction. The book is a novel, the story of a day in Dublin and the meeting of Stephen Daedalus and Leopold Bloom; it is also a "symbolistic" poem, a pattern of allusions to previous literary and cultural texts. The narrative carries us forward from one incident to the next in that eventful day of June 16, 1904, while the references and allusions pull us away from the narrative flow. According to Groden, Joyce first conceived of *Ulysses* as a more conventional novel, although with an unusual style including both third-person narration and first-person monologue, a style that would focus on the minds of Bloom and Stephen Daedalus. Later Joyce began to complicate his text and to expand the style to include the thoughts of other persons as well as omniscient narrative comments. In the final sections of *Ulysses*, Joyce was in fact developing the encyclopedic technique that he would use in *Finnegans Wake*. As Joyce was finishing the last and most allusive episodes, he returned to the first sections and added allusions there too. But he did not completely eliminate the earlier style. He left portions of the earlier novel, perhaps because he wanted the reader to experience not only the finished work but its entire genesis as well. "He only partly reworked the episodes, however, as if to present *Ulysses* as a palimpsest involving all three stages" (Groden, 1977, p. 4).

The word "palimpsest" brings us back to the technology of writing. A palimpsest is a medieval manuscript in which the pages have been whitened and reused, so that one text sits on top of another. In a medieval palimpsest, one text replaces another; the reader is not supposed to see the earlier text. But in *Ulysses* Joyce has written a second text over the first without bothering to white it out: we see and are meant to see both. Moreover, in *Ulysses* it is not clear to the reader which writing is the overlay. Groden can distinguish older and newer layers of text because he has studied Joyce's drafts and letters. The final printed edition is seamless; it may be showing us its entire development, but we cannot necessarily read that development.

What the reader finds is a self-referential text. Even without the work of disentangling the genesis, the reader must still move back and forth through the book in order to appreciate the complex relationships of its parts. *Ulysses* is not a book that can be understood by reading straight through or by *listening* to a sensitive reading. Hugh Kenner has argued that Joyce was aware of the technology at his disposal and that *Ulysses* was designed to be read in print: … the text of *Ulysses* is not organized in memory and unfolded in time, but both organized and unfolded in what we may call technological space: on printed pages for which it was designed from the beginning. The reader explores its discontinuities at whatever pace he likes; he makes marginal notes; he turns back whenever he chooses to an earlier page, without destroying the continuity of something that does not press on, but will wait until he resumes (Kenner, 1962, p. 35).

Kenner is saying that Joyce's writing is topographic and that topographic writing requires a technology that permits the reader to move freely through the text. This is an important insight, although Kenner is too generous in his judgment of print as that technology. Print technology was all that Joyce had available. Joyce, Kenner adds, is careful "to reproduce in his text the very quality of print, its reduction of language to a finite number of interchangeable and permutable parts" (p. 36). However, the interchangeable parts of print technology are merely letters, and they are interchangeable only during the production of the text, not during its reading. In print, production is separate from reading. Joyce's topical units range in size from words to whole sections, and the permutations of these units are part of the reader's moment-by-moment experience of the text. How easy is it for the reader to find a reference in a printed edition of *Ulysses*? How can one find all the references to Troy or Tolstoy or Hermes Trismegistus? Flipping through the numbered, standardized pages of the edition is certainly easier than making one's way through a manuscript or a papyrus roll, but it is still a matter of labor and chance. The reader is bound to miss many of the references that Joyce worked into the fabric of his text. Furthermore, there was no convenient way in a printed edition for Joyce to represent to his reader the genetic development of his text, which Groden discovered by insightful scholarship.

The question of genesis becomes even more important in *Finnegans Wake*. In its final form, this text is so thick with linguistic distortions and allusions that the novel seems completely lost in the poem. Often we seem to be reading sentences that have a conventional narrative sense, but we cannot see what that sense is. Scholars have been able to chip away layer upon layer of revision and discover that much of *Finnegans Wake* does have a storyline. Joyce started at least some sections with a kind of prose paraphrase, to which he kept adding greater complexity. Moving backwards through the drafts (as we can do for example, for the Anna Livia Plurabelle section; see Joyce, 1960) gives us the uncanny experience of watching the text resolve itself into a conventional meaning. But the reader who has only the final printed version cannot imagine this genesis. He is forced to read *Finnegans Wake* along the final temporal layer and then try to work his way down through the layers of allusion.

Joyce places this enormous burden on his reader. The superstructure of the final text alone is taxing; the layers of genesis are even more so. For that reason it is not quite right to claim that Joyce is seeking to reproduce in his text the quality of print. It is true that Joyce employs most every technique available in the repertory of print: like Sterne before him, he experiments with the layout of text, or recapitulates the history of those techniques, by using footnotes, side notes, various styles of type, and even by including musical notation in his text. But Joyce's narrative strategy is too complex and too dynamic for the medium of print.

Joyce could not have anticipated the electronic medium, but his works would be a rich source of experimentation for writers in that medium. Students of Joyce could, for example, begin to map the network of references in a chapter of *Ulysses* or *Finnegans Wake*. Michael Groden is himself creating an electronic companion to *Ulysses*, a multimedia work that includes maps, images, and sound as well as textual hyperlinks (www.nyu.edu/acf/ humanities/seminars/groden.html January 22, 2000). Working one's way through such a hypertextual or hypermediated presentation is clearly not the same experience as reading a printed edition of Joyce. It may instead be regarded as a reading of readings—both watching and becoming the ideal reader of Joyce in the act of reading, a literary and a literary-critical experience at the same time.

BORGES AND EXHAUSTION IN PRINT

Jorge Luis Borges' most famous short piece is perhaps the "Library of Babel" from his *Ficciones*. It is a fantasy in which the human race lives in a gigantic library composed of an indefinite number of cubicles connected by stairs—something like a drawing by M. C. Escher. The shelves of each cubicle are lined with books that, as the narrator, himself an inhabitant of the Library, explains:

> … contain all the possible combinations of the twenty-odd orthographic symbols (whose number, though vast, is not infinite); that is, everything which can be expressed, in all languages. Everything is there: the minute history of the future, the autobiographies of the archangels, the faithful catalogue of the Library, thousands and thousands of false catalogues, a demonstration of the fallacy of these catalogues, a demonstration of the fallacy of the true catalogue, … , the veridical account of your death, a version of each book in all languages, the interpolations of every book in all books (Borges, 1962, p. 83).

The narrator goes on to describe the crazy and often desperate reactions of the inhabitants as they come to realize the implications of living in a universal library of random typography. What is this library, after all, but the exhaustion of human symbolic thought? All of the combinations of Gutenberg's letters have been realized and now sit on the shelves waiting for readers. There is nothing left to be written, only discovered, but discovery is impossible because of the crushing number of nonsense books that overwhelm those that are supposed to have meaning. The inhabitants of this world, whom Borges calls "librarians," wander about the cubicles looking for sensible books, but they are helpless before the logic of permutation. Their library is the ultimate static text; the frozen technique of the printed word has become the universe. The exhaustion of writing also means that time has stopped for these readers. The librarians exist in an eschatological moment in which there is nothing left to wait for, because nothing new can be described.

In his other *Ficciones* too, Borges explores worlds of exhausted possibilities or extreme conditions. John Barth (1967) characterized Borges' work itself as the "literature of exhaustion." The *Ficciones* are tiny pieces without much plot or characterization, pieces that are utterly insignificant by the standards of the 19th-century novel. With Borges we have the sense that a long literary tradition is breaking down, that the novel and perhaps the monograph too are used up. Borges suggests that our culture can no longer produce novels and offers instead anemic book reports and brief descriptions of freakish characters and fantastic worlds. The theme of exhaustion applies not only to literary form, but also to the human condition, precisely because Borges treats reading and writing as synonymous with life itself. Borges is intrigued by the fact that a frozen text cannot change to reflect possibilities that unfold in time. "An Examination of the Work of Herbert Quain" is the literary obituary of a writer who tried to liberate his texts from linear reading and static interpretation. Quain's novel *April March* is nothing less than an interactive fiction. It consists of thirteen chapters or sections representing nine permutations of the events of three evenings. The novel is therefore nine novels in one, each with a different tone. Borges tells us the work is a game, adding that "[w]hoever reads the sections in chronological order ... will lose the peculiar savor of this strange book" (Borges, 1962, p. 76). He even gives us a tree diagram of the novel's structure.

The longer and more elaborate "Garden of Forking Paths" is a detective story. At its center the story contains a description of a Chinese novel, a novel that seeks to explain and in its way to defy time. It was thought that the author Ts'ui Pên had retired from public life with two objects: to write a book and to build a labyrinthine garden, but the Sinologist Stephen Albert has discovered that these two goals were really one: that the book *was* the garden. The manuscript Ts'ui Pên left behind was not, as it seemed, "a shapeless mass of contradictory rough drafts" (p. 96), but instead a ramifying tree of all possible events. Albert explains:

> In all fiction, when a man is faced with alternatives he chooses one at the expense of the others. In the almost unfathomable [work of] Ts'ui Pên, he chooses—simultaneously—all of them. He thus creates various futures, various times which start others that will in their turn branch out and bifurcate in other times. This is the cause of the contradictions in the novel (p. 98).

Albert goes on to explain that "[t]he Garden of Forking Paths is an enormous game, or parable, in which the subject is time" (p. 99). Ts'ui Pên " believed in an infinite series of times, in a dizzily growing, ever spreading network of diverging, converging and parallel times" (p. 100).

Although Albert does not make clear to us how these multiple versions were organized in manuscript, the metaphor of the garden suggests a luxuriant growth of textual possibilities. Both that suggestion and the story itself are closed off as Albert himself is murdered by the narrator of the story. The abrupt ending stands in contrast with the novel as Albert describes it—a novel that refuses to close off its bifurcating paths and come to a single definite end. "The Garden of Forking Paths" thus suggests that the end of a text is always arbitrary or tentative. As Stuart Moulthrop put it, "[t]he story could turn out otherwise, and in a sense does—but that sense cannot be realized in a fiction committed to conclusive definition and singular seriality" (see Moulthrop, 1988, p. 7–8; see also *Reading for the Plot* by Peter Brooks, 1984, pp. 317–319). Moulthrop himself has written a hypertext fiction based on "The Garden of Fork Paths" and has alluded to this story extensively in *Victory Garden* (= > p. 132).

For Borges literature is exhausted because it is committed to a conclusive ending, to a single storyline and denouement. To renew literature one would have to write multiply, in a way that embraced possibilities rather than closed them off. Borges can imagine such a fiction, but he cannot produce it. The *Ficciones* are themselves conventional pieces of prose, meant to be read page by page. Yet the works he describes, the novels of Herbert Quain or "The Garden of Forking Paths," belong in another writing space altogether. Borges himself never had available an electronic space, in which the text can comprise a network of diverging, converging, and parallel times. The metaphor of exhaustion is appropriate to the cultural space of print, while the electronic writing space seems anything but exhausted. A hypertext fiction, such as *Victory Garden*, gives the impression of endless growth, as if, like a true library of Babel, it could never be exhausted.

COMPOSITION NO. 1

There have been so many experimental novels and novelists in the past few decades that any choice among them is arbitrary. The will to experiment even extends to children's fiction: books in the series entitled "Choose Your Own Adventure" or "Find Your Fate" offer young readers an experience something like that of the computerized adventure game. Each book contains a garden of forking paths, from among which the reader must choose. At the bottom of page 18, one may read: "If you choose to risk the curse, turn to page 29. If you press on down the tunnel, turn to page 42" (Wenk, 1984, p. 18). Thus, the book sacrifices the linear order of pages to allow for multiple reading. Some programmed novels are even intended for adult readers. The novel *Rayuela*, or *Hopscotch*, by Julio Cortázar offers two possible reading orders: one a linear narrative and the other a satirical comment on that narrative. Other writers who have experimented with fragmented narrative include Raymond Queneau, Italo Calvino, Robert Coover, and Michael Butor. (On Queneau and Calvino as forerunners of electronic writing, see Paulson, 1989, pp. 296-299. On Michel Butor see Grant, 1973, pp. 27-32.)

One such experiment is Marc Saporta's *Composition No. 1*, a work consisting of about 150 unnumbered pages, published in France in 1962 and in English translation in 1963 (see Sharon Spencer's analysis in *Space, Time, and Structure in the Modern Novel*, 1971, pp. 85–87, 209–211). This fiction consists of loose sheets of paper, each containing one or a few paragraphs printed on one side. The sheets (at least in the English version) are somewhat larger than octavo, larger than a deck of playing cards, to which the author compares them. In the introduction, which is printed on the box and also appears as one of the pages, the author explains:

> The reader is requested to shuffle these pages like a deck of cards, to cut, if he likes, with his left hand, as at a fortune teller's. The order the pages then assume will orient X's fate. For time and the order of events control a man's life more than the nature of such events.... A life is composed of many elements. But the number of possible compositions is infinite (Saporta, 1963).

Composition No. 1 consists of passages in the story of X, a character we learn about only through his reflection in the events and other characters of the narrative. X, an unsavory figure, is married to Marianne, has a mistress named Dagmar, and also rapes a girl named Helga. He apparently steals to support the compulsions of his neurotic wife, and he possibly dies in an automobile accident. By way of redemption, he seems to have played some role in the French resistance, although this strand in the story is the most obscure.

It is Saporta's tour de force that the reader is able to figure out this much from the experience of reading the pages one at a time, when each page offers necessarily only a vignette. Even for a contemporary reader, accustomed to fragmentation and suspension, the natural impulse is to turn the page in order to find out what happens next. But here the next page bears no immediate relation to the previous one. This fiction is not static: on most pages there is action or at least dialogue that promises to advance our knowledge of the characters. We do get the impression that we are reading pages torn from a conventional novel, and we find ourselves searching for their "proper" order—that is, for an order that makes chronological and causal sense. We become literary detectives. The pieces in this puzzle are topical elements in a written text, and connecting these topics reminds us of papyrology or other scholarly detective work with the fragmentary remains of ancient writings. It is always the papyrologist's hope that newly found fragments will turn out to be part of a known or, better still, unknown, but identifiable ancient work—that both the text and its context will be revealed. We feel that hope as we read Saporta. Indeed, to call the work "fragmented" is to assume that it was originally whole, that the fragments belong in one order.

As readers of 20th-century fiction, we may be prepared for radical shifts in focus, but we still want to find reasons for such shifts. Each time we shuffle the pages, some intriguing juxtapositions happen by chance. It is a characteristic of our literary imagination that we can so often provide an interpretation for these juxtapositions. Whatever order falls out becomes a lesson in the nature of reading, and we become active readers, fashioning texts as we shuffle pages. Saporta's trick makes us uniquely aware of the effect of narrative order on the reading experience, as we see in practice what we are always told in theory. There is not one possible order for the episodes, but a broad class of acceptable orders, each producing its own literary effect. Some orders are better than a simple chronological story, and many are worse. The number of reading orders for Saporta's composition is not infinite, as the author claims. If there are 150 pages in the set, then the number of possible presentations is 150!—a number with 263 digits, but still finite. *Composition No. 1* has necessary limits: as Sharon Spencer (1971) points out, in every possible rearrangement of its pages we will still have a portrait of X, the silent, second character in each fragmentary scene (p. 211).

Composition No. 1 is an exercise in choice within a large but still limited fictional universe; indeed, it is a tiny universe in comparison to Borges' Library. Saporta's universe is one of French existential romanticism, fascinated by the interplay of chance and fate. Moreover, Saporta seems to be working in a different direction from the one we have been considering for topographic writing in the computer. The author of *Composition No. 1* apparently disavows responsibility for the structure of his work. In seeming to deny form, he displaces the formal responsibility onto his reader.

Saporta's experiment in chance fiction seems to position his work as an inevitable, final step in the exhaustion of printed literature. When all the other methods of fragmenting the novel have been tried, what remains but to tear the pages out of the book one by one and hand them to the reader? From the ideal of perfect structural control, Saporta brings us to the apparent abdication of control. But we can also see in Saporta's experiment, and in others like it, not only the end of printed fiction, but also a bridge to the electronic medium. In that sense *Composition No. 1* seems emblematic of the late age of print.

Composition No. 1 brings us back to interactive fictions such as *afternoon*, because we can regard Saporta's work as an interactive fiction operating under the limitations that print imposes. Each page of *Composition No. 1* is a topographic unit, like an episode of *afternoon* as it appears on the screen. In both cases, the burden of constructing the text is thrown back upon the reader. And in both cases the reader works to make narrative sense of the episodes as they present themselves: to construct from these disordered episodes a story in which characters act with reasonable and explicit motives. In *Composition No. 1* we may resort to stacking the pages in piles. In *afternoon* the medium itself resists that solution, because we cannot get at the episodes except by typing responses, and even then the episodes appear only one at a time.

MULTIPLE READING AND WRITING

Earlier experiments in print from Sterne to *Composition No. 1*, and especially the work of 20th-century modern and postmodern writers, define themselves by subverting current assumptions about how fiction should operate. The 20th-century works in particular are subtly or blatantly works in revolt. Their sense of revolt is borrowed and remediated by hypertext fiction. In this late age of print, our literary culture treats hypertext fiction as avant-garde—in either a good or bad sense, depending on one's literary allegiances, and without regard to the wishes of the hypertext authors. In re-fashioning printed fiction, hypertext makes claims about the nature of the storytelling and the power of the print medium to represent reality. The printed "forerunners" of hypertext seem to be making similar claims, al-though of course the works of Sterne, James Joyce, or Calvino only seem to be forerunners of hypertexts now that computers are available for creating electronic hypertexts. Electronic hyperfictions necessarily affect us as read-ers somewhat differently, because they come to us in a different media form.

Both hypertext and their "forerunners" seem to define a new kind of reading. Both *Composition No. 1* and *afternoon* encourage us to read "multi-ply," as Stuart Moulthrop described it (Moulthrop, 1988). Both revolt against the assumption of our literate culture that we should read and write linearly. To read multiply would be to resist our desire to close off possible courses of action; it would be to keep open multiple explanations for the same event or character. Yet *Composition No. 1* also shows that it is a difficult task for the reader to remain open in a medium as perfected as that of print. Saporta must tear his novel apart in order to resist the perfection of print, and still our first impulse is to try to put the novel back together. *afternoon*, on the other hand, seems to do easily what experimental writers in print could do only with great difficulty, offering us a narrative that encompasses contradictory possibilities. In *afternoon* an automobile accident both does and does not occur; the narrator does and does not lose his son; he does and does not have a love affair. The story itself does and does not end:

> Closure is, as in any fiction, a suspect quality, although here it is made manifest. When the story no longer progresses, or when it cycles, or when you tire of the paths, the experience of reading it ends. Even so, there are likely to be more opportunities than you think there are at first. A word which doesn't yield the first time you read a section may take you elsewhere if you choose it when you encounter the section again; and sometimes what seems a loop, like memory, heads off again in another direction.
>
> There is no simple way to say this.

What *afternoon* and other hyperfictions are suggesting is that there is no simple way to say this in the linear writing of print, that what is difficult in print is simplified in and through electronic media, and that it will soon no longer need saying at all because it can be shown.

In keeping with their role as experimenters, topographic writers in print (James Joyce, Borges, Saporta) are "difficult" writers because they challenge the reader to read multiply. They call to the reader's attention the contrast between the temporal flow of narrated events and the interruptions and reversals that the act of writing imposes on those events. All their works are self-consciously concerned with the problems of their own writing and reading, a concern shown by the difficult relationship between the narrator and text, between the text and its reader, or both. The difficulty in writing and therefore in reading appears with Tristram Shandy, who is always getting further behind his own lived experience as he writes, and again and again in the 20th century. Saporta and Cortázar must give special instructions to their readers, while *Finnegans Wake* may well be the most demanding book that has ever been published and critically received. In each case, the printed fiction must work against its medium in order to be topographic. There is a conflict between the printed volume as a frame and the text that is framed, and the frame is not adequate to contain and delimit the text, which is constantly threatening to spill out of its container.

By contrast, the computer provides a frame that gives way whenever the text strains against it; the stubbornness of the printed book seems to disappear. In *afternoon*, in a technique pioneered by Michael Joyce, the margins "yield" to the reader. The elements of the text are no longer fragments of a prior whole, but instead form a space of shifting possibilities. In this shifting electronic space, writers seem to need a new concept of structure. In place of a closed and unitary form, they need to conceive of their text as a structure of possible structures, and they must practice a second order of writing, creating coherent lines for the reader to discover without seeming to close off the possibilities prematurely or arbitrarily.

Interactive fiction thus promises (or threatens) to refashion writing as well as reading, and in this refashioning hypertexts written expressly for computers seem to go beyond their printed forerunners. The computer gives the reader the opportunity to intervene in the text itself, an intervention not possible in print, where the text lies on a plane inaccessible to the reader. Readers of a printed book can write over or deface the text, but they cannot write in it. When in *Tristram Shandy* Sterne offers his readers the opportunity to finish writing a chapter, he is setting an impossible task. In the electronic medium, however, readers cannot avoid writing the text itself, because every choice they make is an act of writing. The author of *afternoon* wrote the prose for each episode and fashioned electronic structures of expectation and fulfillment on analogy with the static structures of printed fiction. When he gave the reader a role in realizing those structures, he also ceded some of his traditional responsibility as author. That ceding of responsibility is a both challenge and a tacit assertion that this electronic form of reading–writing is more authentic than the participation that a traditional printed novel affords its readers. In some hyperfictions, the reader may be invited to alter existing episodes and links and add new ones. Deena Larsen's *Marble Springs* (1994), for example, invites the reader to revise and extend the text (Douglas, 2000, p. 141). In this way the reader becomes a second author, who can then hand the changed text over to other readers for the same treatment. Electronic fiction can operate anywhere along the spectrum from tight control by the author to full collaboration between author and reader. The promise of this new media form is to explore all the ways in which the reader can participate in the making of the text. Stuart Moulthrop (1988) argued that the reader should be " … invited not just to enter a garden of forking paths, but to expand and revise the ground plan at will. This would cause a substantial shift in the balance of authority, one with enormous implications for the idea of literature itself; but it would nonetheless be a logical development of writing in the electronic medium" (p. 16); (see also Joyce, 1988; 1995, pp. 39–59).

DIGITAL POETRY AND PERFORMATIVE TEXTS

Larsen's *Marble Springs* (1994), a collection of poems, also shows that electronic text is not limited to narrative prose. Nor is it limited to the conventional display of prose or poetry: even the typography of an electronic text can be altered to give it a new visual meaning. Such changes too have been prefigured by writers, especially poets, in print. Mallarmé with his spatial poem "Coup de dès" and Apollinaire with his *calligrammes* were followed by the Dadaists, by LeMaître, and more recently by the writers of "concrete" poetry, who deployed letters and words in defiance of the conventions of lines and strophes (Solt, 1970, p. 8; see also Seaman, 1981; Winspur, 1985). Experiments in typography (by the Russian constructivists and others) as well as the making of art books were expressions of a growing dissatisfaction with the conventional forms of print (see Johanna Drucker's *The Visible Word*, 1994, and *The Century of Artists' Books*, 1995). But again concrete poetry and these earlier movements expressed that dissatisfaction from *within* the technology of the printed page; they stood as a critique of the conventions of the medium.

Breaking the conventions of typography from the perspective of the new electronic medium began as early as the 1980s, when William Dickey (1991) created his first interactive poems. In "Heresy: A Hyperpoem," words, images, and icons compete on the screen for the reader's attention.

The poem is a network of many screens, and the reader moves from one screen to others by activating one of the snowflake-shaped icons. Each screen, a different arrangement of verbal text and image, vigorously asserts its visual identity. The typography of this hypertext encourages the reader to examine and savor each screen before activating an icon to move on. Sometimes the verbal text penetrates the graphic image, as it does in Fig. 7.2. Sometimes the spatial arrangement of text against the white background reminds us of the experiments of Mallarmé or LeMaître. In "Heresy," as in Michael Joyce's *afternoon*, each textual unit is static; the reader sets the hypertext in motion by moving between fixed units. The same is true of Robert Kendall's hypertext collection *A Life Set for Two* (Kendall, 1996a; 1996b; Landow, 1997, pp. 217–218), Stephanie Strickland's meditations on the nature of navigation, *True North* (1997), and John Cayley's hypertextual version of Yang Lian's poem *Where the Sea Still Stands* (illumin.co.uk/ica/wsss/ July 29, 1999).

A number of poets have also explored the computer as a space for a truly kinetic poetry that shifts and changes under their or their reader's control. Jim Rosenberg has fashioned a number of electronic poems, including his *Intergrams* (see www.well.com/user/jer/inter_works.html July 30, 1999). These pieces begin as a tangle of words on the screen, lines colliding with

We were left hesitant and orphaned when the skies dissolved. Nothing in our experience had prepared us for the need to establish ourselves in writing.

FIG. 7.2.   A screen from "Heresy: A Hyperpoem" by William Dickey. (Reprinted with permission of the author.)

other lines in a hypertrophy of typography and meaning. As the reader passes her cursor over hotspots, however, some of the tangles disappear to reveal legible strophes (Fig. 7.3). In this case reading is played out as the visual, almost physical, untangling of strands to reveal meaning.

John Cayley has written and written about what he calls "machine modulated poetry" (www.demon.co.uk/eastfield/in/ July 29, 1999). His works merge hypertext with installation and performance art, and invite the reader to participate in the performance. In *Book Unbound*, for example, the reader gets the following instructions:

> When you open the book unbound, you will change it. New collocations of phases generated from its hidden given text—a short piece of prose by the work's initiator—will be displayed. After the screen fills, you will be invited to select a phrase from the generated text by clicking on the first and the last words of a string of language which appeals to you. Your selections will be collected on the page of this book named Leaf, where you will be able to copy or edit them as you wish (www.demon.co.uk/eastfield/in/incat.html#BUNB July 29, 1999).

In *Book Unbound* the order and appearance of the words themselves are determined by the interaction of the reader with a program created by the original programmer–poet. The reader thus fashions a book of poems as she reads.

Such works as *Intergrams* and *Book Unbound* explore a typography based on the electronic animation of letters and words. The reader interacts with the text not by determining episodes in a narrative, but rather by manipulating the appearance, movement, and significance of individual verbal elements. She participates in the reordering of the ultimate constituents of writing—letters and words. For these kinetic poets the reordering of such symbols is both reading and writing at the same time.

HYPERMEDIA: POPULAR AND AVANT-GARDE

The hypertextual works that we have been examining have limited themselves mainly to verbal representation, to remediations of the printed word. Our culture, however, regards the computer and new media in general as eclectic forms that combine verbal, visual, and sound presentations. Already poets Cayley and Rosenberg have used the computer to arrange letters and words for their visual effect, conceiving of their electronic texts as

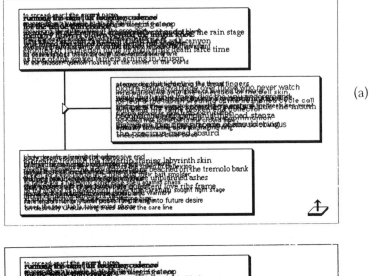

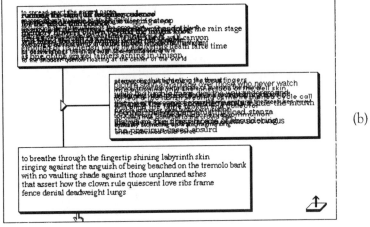

FIG. 7.3.   A screen from Jim Rosenberg's Intergram: The reader passes the cursor over the knots (a) to reveal portions of the underlying text (b) (Reprinted with permission of the author.)

visual objects with which the reader interacts. Their works are new versions of the art book that dates back to William Blake, to Renaissance emblem poetry, and ultimately to the medieval illuminated manuscript. Neverthe-less, Cayley's and Rosenberg's image poems are still composed of alphabetic symbols. Other hypertext writers have taken another course, introducing nonalphabetic images into their works to serve as maps, presenting the reader with a visualization of possible reading orders. The images are often clickable—in Web fictions, they are called "imagemaps"—so that the reader can branch directly from the map to different episodes in the space.

A pioneer example was Moulthrop's *Victory Garden* (=> p. 130). Another early example was the structure map presented to the reader when she launched Michael Joyce's (1991) *WOE* (Fig. 7.4). The boxes represent episodes and the arrows possible paths through the episodes. *WOE*'s principal schema is the mandala, which is also the name of the central episode. The "mandala" episode serves as a hub connected to sets of episodes on the rim of the wheel. The reader starts in the center, travels out to the rim, and then returns to the center. But each return gives the central episode a different significance, precisely because the reader is returning from a different episode on the rim. Repeated visits to and from the rim cause the reader's possibilities to narrow; eventually, if read often enough, *WOE* resolves itself into a single linear narrative. That is, the hypertext is arranged so that after repeated readings its possible branches close down until the reader has only one choice leading from each episode. This kind of manipulation (narrowing or broadening) of the reader's choices, which can occur metaphorically in print, can be realized operationally in presentation on the computer. (For a thorough reading of *WOE*, see Douglas, 2000, pp. 106–120; see also Bolter, "The Shapes of WOE", 1991.)

In another fiction, *Twelve Blue* (1996b), written for the World Wide Web, Joyce again presents his structure to the reader as part of the reading experience. The Web page includes a frame with an imagemap consisting of twelve light-colored strands against a dark blue background. These strands become part of the apparatus for reading the separate, but sometimes intersecting narrative lines. As Douglas (2000) notes, the microplots represented by each strand function like the interwoven strands in Robert Altman's films *Nashville* and *Short Cuts* (p. 157). Many other hypertext fictions, including John McDaid's *Uncle Buddy's Phantom Funhouse* (1991), Deena Larsen's *Marble Springs* (1994), and Shelley Jackson's *Patchwork Girl* (1995), have incorporated visual representations of structure into the text that they present to the reader. *Patchwork Girl* is remarkable for the way in which its structure map—the image of the female Frankenstein—is simultaneously dissected and "stitched," as the author puts it, into the fabric of the narrative (Fig. 7.5). *Patchwork Girl* is both a visual and a verbal collage (Landow, 1997, pp. 198–205).

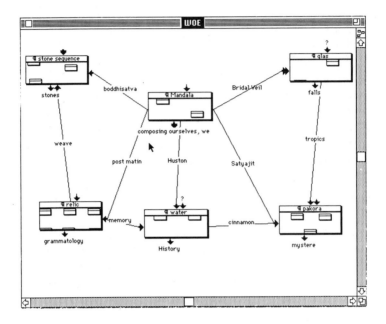

FIG. 7.4.   The mandala figure from Michael Joyce's WOE. (Reprinted with permission of the author.)

Even in *Patchwork Girl*, however, the clickable images remain symbolic and operate in a space that is essentially verbal. As computer graphics and audio have improved, hypertexts have become hypermedia, using sounds as well as still and moving images for their own presentational effect, not as enhancements or complements to the verbal text. For our culture today, the computer is not only a new kind of book, but also a site for the refashioning of film, television, and photography (= > p. 24). Hyperfiction authors have responded to this cultural imperative by renegotiating the relationship between word and image in their work. John McDaid's multimedia piece *Uncle Buddy's Phantom Funhouse* (1991) was a pioneer in incorporating multiple media, including recorded songs, into an eclectic media package. Michael Joyce's *afternoon* (1990) and *WOE* (1991) were almost wholly verbal, but *Twilight* (Joyce, 1996a) and *Twelve Blue* (Joyce, 1996b) began to incorporate both images and sounds. *On the birthday of the stranger* (1999) is a refashioned emblem book or photographic anthology with captions. Stuart Moulthrop has followed a similar trajectory, but gone even further in exploiting new visual forms. *Forking Paths* was wholly verbal, and *Victory Garden* (1991b) and

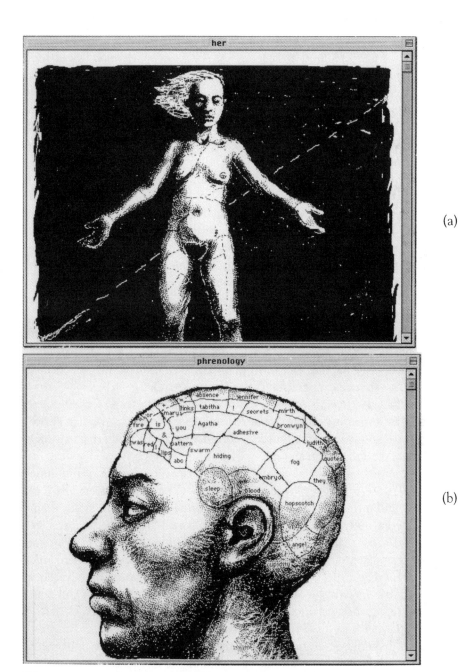

(a)

(b)

FIG. 7.5.   Two clickable imagemaps from Shelley Jackson's *Patchwork Girl*: (a) the creature (b) the creature's phrenology, in which clicking on each labeled area leads to a different episode. (Reprinted with permission of the author.)

Hegirascope (1997) almost completely so. *The Color of Television* (Moulthrop & Cohen, 1996) already made greater use of images, and in *Reagan's Library* Moulthrop has begun to exploit a 360-degree graphic technique (Quicktime VR) to give the reader so-called "desktop virtual reality." Although M. de Coverly (Luesebrink, 2000) calls her work *Califia* "a hypertext novel," she in fact refashions the novel into a multimedia structure that combines words, images, and music.

Some hypertext authors or designers have set out expressly to define an interactive (or hypertextual) version of film: examples include *Hypercafe* by Nitin Sawhney, David Balcom, and Ian Smith (1996), and John Tolva's hypertextual remediation of the Robert Altman film *Short Cuts*. Their experiments come close to a form of popular entertainment, the video or computer game. Meanwhile, dozens of films and television shows, such as *The X-Files*, *Star Wars*, and *Star Trek*, have been repurposed as computer games. *Doom*, *Quake*, and many other video and computer games are busy remediating the genre of the action-adventure film. These computer games all have some hypertextual qualities. Although purely verbal hypertexts will probably continue to appeal to a relatively small audiences, popular hypermedia, perhaps in the form of interactive dramas, may eventually reach an audience that considers itself mainstream.

Finally, some hypermedia works are closely related to performance art; indeed, hypermedia becomes a way to remediate the tradition of live performance art. Many hypertext authors conduct public readings of their work, and these readings, even more than those of conventional novelists, take on the character of a performance, when the author often invites the audience to participate by suggesting links to follow. The kinetic poetry of John Cayley and others is meant to be performed as well as read. Some hypermedia authors, like Shelley Jackson and Mark Amerika, are also themselves performance artists. Mark Amerika's *Grammatron* (www.grammatron.com January 6, 2000), exhibited at the Ars Electronica festival for digital art, combines aspects of live performance, particularly in its soundtrack, with the qualities of concrete or kinetic poetry. And many virtual reality performance or installation pieces, beginning with Jeffrey Shaw's *Legible City* (1988–1991), make claims of remediation similar to those of hypermedia fiction. Works that combine electronic multimedia with live performance remind us yet again of the connection between the hypertext movement and the avant-garde tradition.

8

Critical Theory in a New Writing Space

In the 1960s and 1970s there began an earnest and seemingly endless debate in the academic community over the nature and uses of literature. Traditional readers and critics have had to confront the theories first of the poststructuralists and then of a variety of others, including postmodernists, neoMarxists, feminists and postfeminists, and postcolonialists. Until recently, electronic writing played a very small role in this debate. Academics generally ignored hypertext itself and addressed electronic media forms simply by including them in their critique of the ideologically driven mass media—at least until the global hypertext of the World Wide Web caught their attention. Those academics working in hypertext and hypermedia, however, have taken part in the debate and have tried to associate this new form of writing with the various critical theories. It would seem to be a natural alliance. Just as electronic writing can be interpreted as a radical departure from traditional writing, the many poststructuralist and postmodern theories have also identified themselves as radical departures from traditional ways of understanding literary texts. George Landow has made the authoritative case for what he calls a "convergence" between hypertext and poststructural critical theory (Landow, 1997).

Because electronic writing technology is so malleable, however, it can in fact support a variety of forms of representation and can be understood according to a variety of critical theories. Although electronic writing seems to possess qualities that grow out of the material characteristics of computer technology, these characteristics cannot fully determine the character of electronic writing (= > p. 19). The forms and genres of electronic writing are in this sense underdetermined, so that they can develop and indeed

161

have developed in ways that depend on the desires of their users. Both the computer as a writing technology and the forms of electronic writing can be allied to almost any theoretical position, including the most traditional. After all, the computer is now used to prepare most printed books for publication: as a tool for photocomposition, it reinforces the stability and fixity associated with print, the traditional views of the nature of authorship, and finally the economic dominance of major publishers and distributors. But traditionalists have generally regarded electronic technology as a threat to, rather than an extension of, their literary values. Landow's position that hypertext is ultimately poststructural in its orientation has prevailed among many opponents as well as proponents. Those who want to legitimize hypertext as a radical literary form have turned to Derrida, Barthes, and others as the theorists who can help us to understand how electronic writing redefines the critical object (the text) and the act of reading itself.

WRITING TECHNOLOGIES
AND THE LITERARY CRITICAL TRADITION

Prior to the advent of electronic writing, tradition assigned to good literature the qualities of stability, monumentality, and authority. Works of literature were monuments, and the author who created monuments was, as the etymology suggests, an authority. If a text was regarded as mimetic, the author deserved credit for the ability to represent nature faithfully. Thus, Homer and Shakespeare showed us what people were and are "really like"—qualities of human nature that have not changed from their day to ours. If a text was regarded as an emotional expression, then the author deserved praise for his depth of feeling, his "lively sensibility," as Wordsworth put it. These traditional literary values, still widely held today, constitute a status quo from which radical theories of literature diverge. It is important to remember, however, that the values of stability, monumentality, and authority are themselves not entirely stable: they have always been interpreted in terms of the contemporary technology of handwriting or printing.

As early as the 5th and 4th centuries B.C., Greek poets and historians stressed the power of writing to fix ideas, to extend human memory. The history of Herodotus would prevent the wars between the Greeks and Persians from being forgotten; a written epic poem would preserve the glorious deeds of Alexander the Great. (Alexander lamented the fact that there was no poet of Homer's authority to tell his story.) The text was regarded as a monument to the deeds and actors it described. And if the Greeks were concerned about the immortality of the subject, the Roman poets seem to have been just as concerned about the immortality of the author. It was Horace who said he had erected a monument more lasting than bronze. Horace's claim was a motif in Latin poetry, and we have embarrassing examples of the claim of immortality made for works that did not survive. Catullus made this claim for the poem of his colleague Cinna: not only has Cinna's work perished, but Catullus himself barely survived the neglect of the Middle Ages. Catullus and Horace trusted rolls of papyrus to preserve their poems, and even this technology showed that text could be preserved indefinitely, although not with complete accuracy, by recopying rolls that had deteriorated.

The Latin language is responsible for the words "author" and "authority." Certainly in the 1st century A.D. and later, the Romans regarded their traditional authors (Virgil, Cicero, Livy) with nostalgia and reverence—authorities to be studied, excerpted, and imitated. The appeal to written authority was perhaps even stronger in the Middle Ages with the somewhat more durable technology of parchment, particularly of course the appeal to the Bible and the Church fathers. But the monument could not be perfectly fixed: scribal errors tended to alter the text over centuries. Serious consideration of the transmission of texts began in the Renaissance with scholars like Lorenzo Valla, who were trying to restore authoritative texts of the ancients by separating out interpolations and false ascriptions.

The printing press preserved texts with greater accuracy than before—both ancient texts, as restored by Renaissance scholars, and texts by contemporary authors. European and North American literary culture has also used the press to strengthen the author's claim to authority, as the technology and economics of printing widened the gulf between the author and his readers. Because printing a book is a costly and laborious task, relatively few readers have the opportunity to become published authors. An author is a person whose words are faithfully copied and sent around the literary world, whereas readers are merely the audience for those words. The distinction meant less in the age of manuscripts, when "publication" was less of an event and when the reader's own notes and glosses had the same status as the text itself. Any fully literate reader could decide to cross over and become an author: one simply sat down and wrote a treatise or put one's notes in a form for others to read. Once the treatise was written, there was no difference between it and the works of other "published" writers, except that more prestigious works existed in more copies. However, there was a great material and conceptual difference between a manuscript and a printed edition of that manuscript. For most kinds of writing, the printed copy had more authority because of its visual simplicity, regularity, and reproducibility. As the author in print became more distant, and less accessible to the reader, the author's words became harder to dismiss. In the later Renaissance, scientific writers in print called old authorities into question, and they did so by setting themselves up as new authorities. They published works meant to replace the outdated works of their predecessors: Vesalius sought to be the new Galen, Copernicus to replace Ptolemy (see Eisenstein, 1979, pp. 566–574, 585).

The audiences for popular and "elite" literature both expanded gradually in the first 300 years of printing, and then rapidly in the past two centuries. This expansion, together with the abolition of patronage, has further enhanced the authority of the author. Martha Woodmansee (1984, 1992) argued that the notion of creativity grew in the 18th century as the author increased his intellectual and economic power through the rise of the royalty system of publication (see also Kernan, 1990; Woodmansee & Jaszi, 1994). Today, a successful author's readers are dispersed throughout his or her country or indeed throughout the world and so have a variety of cultural backgrounds. At least since the 18th century, successful authors have been celebrities, whom we honor not simply for their power to entertain, but also for their presumed insight into the human condition. It is a curious notion, but one that we still take for granted today: an American novelist is allowed, indeed expected, to pronounce on, say, race relations in her country; a German on the dangers of a right wing extremists in his; a Latin American author on repressive governments in that region. Part of the explanation is perhaps that 19th-century critics believed that poets had special visionary powers. That belief carried over into our times, and the poet's vision is now supposed apply to important social and political questions. The authority that we ascribe to print publication still helps to sanction this belief. Well-known writers can get their opinions on almost any topic into print, and the act of printing itself makes those opinions worthy of our consideration.

The precision of printed technology has suited the view of the poem as a monument and of the poet as an authority. In the first half of the 20th century, the influential New Criticism conceived of a poem in terms appropriate to a printed text: self-sufficient, perfect, and untouchable. In a good poem, not a word or comma should be out of place, just as a good typographer insisted that a page be perfect before it is printed. What the New Criticism made explicit was an implicit assumption of most writing in the age of printing. Through the technology of printing, the author and the editor could exercise absolute control over the text: nothing they did could be undone after publication. Because everything on the page was part of the author's design, it was natural to assume that even the smallest details were part of the poem's meaning.

THE END OF AUTHORITY

These traditional views of literature and authorship have been undermined not only by the work of academic theorists but also by the uses to which both popular culture and the academic community are putting new electronic technologies of communication. Most (postmodern and cultural studies) theorists have rejected the distinction between elite literature and popular texts; for them, the authority accorded to established authors is an expression of power relationships and dominant ideologies. Meanwhile, our popular culture has welcomed the World Wide Web as a new space for communication and representation along with books, television, and film. Our culture seems to have accepted and endorsed the transient, casual, and generally unauthoritative nature of Web sites. Although there have been calls (in the United States, at least) for censoring the sexual content of the Web, there has been no widespread support for requiring sites to be vetted for the accuracy of their content. Subversive Web sites and corporate Web sites have been allowed to exist side by side; sites by medical authorities and institutions are balanced and often contradicted by sites by activist groups (AIDS activists, for example) or simply by individuals who wish to promote their views on particular diseases and conditions. An "authoritative Web site" is an oxymoron. Meanwhile, those theorists specifically working on hypertext, both on and off the Web, have succeeded in portraying electronic writing as a medium that questions authority and fixity. For them, electronic writing reforms print by replacing the qualities of authority and fixity with the flexibility and responsiveness that we have seen in the literary hypertexts by Joyce, Moulthrop, Jackson, and dozens of others.

There has remained of course a traditional literary establishment, associated with the technology of printed publication. There remain conservative social groups who view literature as an ally in what they still regard as the "culture wars." Throughout the 1980s these groups took part in the debate over the literary canon. It was, and to some extent still is, common to believe in the "timeless" quality of great works of literature, which define our cultural ideals, and therefore to argue in a favor of a canon of such works. Meanwhile, literary theorists and historians had been examining how canons had formed in the past few hundred years of Western culture and why certain works and authors had been included or excluded. In general, these theorists disliked the idea of a canon, and they particularly disliked recent Western canons because of the bias against minority and third-world writers (see, for example, the special issue of *Critical Inquiry* edited by von Hallberg, 1983). Traditionalists defended the canon as containing the best work of a tradition with which every educated reader should be familiar: authors in the canon were central to our culture, whereas other authors were relegated to the margins. What they approved of was exactly what the critics decried: that the canon told us whom we must read and whom we could read for pleasure or omit altogether.

This debate over the canon was really a debate over the purpose and nature of reading. In 1984, William Bennett, then Chairman of the National Endowment for the Humanities, defended the idea of grounding education in the reading of works sanctioned by tradition and offered a rather exclusive list of texts that should form a core for teaching in the humanities: works by Homer, Dante, Shakespeare, Dickens, the predictable American authors, and so on. "Why these particular books and these particular authors?" Bennett asked. "Because an important part of education is learning to read, and the highest purpose of reading is to be in the company of great souls ... " (Bennett, 1984, p. 11). Bennett's notion of reading as communion with great souls was in fact borrowed from the theory and practice of the romantics, who ultimately fashioned a religion of art to supplement or replace the truths of revealed religion (either consciously as in the case of Matthew Arnold or more tentatively as with Schlegel, Coleridge, or Shelley). Some compared poets to prophets and indeed even to God in their creative powers. Some began to treat literature as biography, reading Shakespeare and even Homer in order to peer into the souls of these great artists. Carlyle was a good example, whom M. H. Abrams calls "king among those who read an author not for what he made, but for what he was" (see Abrams, 1953, pp. 248–249; also for Keble's reading of Homer, pp. 256–262). But how could an ordinary reader hope to hold a conversation with a great soul? The more the romantics and their recent followers like Bennett emphasized the greatness and uniqueness of the authors of the canon, the less accessible these authors became. Critical reading became more difficult, criticism necessarily muted. The conversation became a kind of worship.

On the other side were those who disagreed with the claim of universality. Robert Scholes (1986) wrote in reply to Bennett that:

The purpose of humanistic study is to learn what it has meant to be human in other times and places, what it means now, and to speculate about what it ought to mean and what it might mean in the human future. The best texts for this purpose should be determined locally, by local conditions, limited and facilitated by local wisdom. Above all, they should not be imposed and regulated by a central power (p. 116).

This reply too had roots in romanticism, for it suggested the romantic revolt against authority and tradition. In fact Scholes did not merely distrust centralization; he denied the idea of a center or a mainstream, which necessarily pushed some texts and authors to the margins. No text should be "outside the bounds of humanistic study" (p. 116). At the same time Scholes attacked Bennett's proposal for worshipful reading, reading as a respectful approach to the monuments: "[t]his soulful rhetoric is guaranteed to drain the life out of the texts studied, because it permits only worship and forbids all criticism" (p. 114). Scholes called into question the whole complex of assumptions of Bennett and the traditionalists: the belief that there was a center to our culture, that great works were unchanging in their message and importance, and that great authors were authorities.

In the late age of print, these traditional views of the canon and of reading, which Scholes criticized, seem appropriate to the technology of printing. If handwriting already suggested the goal of fixing the text, printing achieved a greater cultural fixity, allowing texts to survive unchanged for centuries. The idea of declaring authors canonical is certainly much older than print. Greek scholars of the Alexandrian period, for example, compiled their canons of epic, lyric, and tragic poets. Our modern notion of canon has as its paradigm the Christian canon of sacred writings, which developed in late antiquity, a relatively sophisticated age of handwriting. The New Testament canon apparently formed in association with the technological breakthrough of the codex. But throughout antiquity and the Middle Ages, copying by hand continued to expose canonical texts to errors. In printing, Western culture developed a technology that could foster the ideal of a single canon of great authors, whose works would be distributed in thousands of identical copies to readers throughout the world. And in the industrial age of printing, scholars became obsessed with assigning authorship and verifying texts. Such scholarship, called "textual criticism," began in the Renaissance, but reached its zenith in the 19th century. The goal of this exacting scholarship was to determine letter by letter what Plato, Euripides, or the Church fathers "really" wrote: to apply the standards of printed accuracy to the manuscript tradition of ancient and medieval authors. Textual criticism set out to establish a little canon for each author—a definitive list of works and a definitive edition of each work in which all scribal deviations were relegated to the footnotes. Print also provided dignity and distance for works of the canon, placing authors in a writing space not available to other literate men and women. By ensuring that the reader cannot enter into the space that the text occupies, printing still remains the appropriate technology for those who wish to encourage worshipful reading.

Hypertext writers have shown how the electronic medium can accommodate a different relationship between author and reader. No longer an intimidating figure, an electronic author assumes the role of a craftsperson, working with prescribed materials and goals. She works within the limitations of a computer system, and she imposes further limitations upon her readers. Within those limits, however, her reader is free to move. If in print the subjectivity of the author was expressed at the expense of that of the reader, in electronic hypertext two subjectivities, the author's and reader's, encounter one another on more nearly equal terms. The reader may well become the author's adversary, seeking to make the text over in a direction that the author did not anticipate.

Adversarial reading is not new. One of the advantages that writing in any medium has over oral communication is that readers can stop, reflect on a passage, and disagree. They can deliberately misread the text in the sense of imposing their own constructions that forcefully contradict the text. In *The Anxiety of Influence* (1973), Harold Bloom claimed famously that misreading was an essential part of the poetic tradition: that each poet must misread his or her predecessors in order to create a new text under their otherwise crushing influence. In the hands of certain hypertext authors, the computer can make concrete the act of reading (or misreading) as interpretation and can therefore challenge the reader to engage the author for control of the writing space. This engagement is apparent in *afternoon*, where the reader must make an effort to find and stay on the path she wishes to travel. In *afternoon*, as in other hyperfictions, the control of the presentation of text becomes part of the text itself, because the text consists not only of the words the author has written but also of the structure of decisions that the author creates and the reader explores (=> p. 124).

The computer can therefore make visible the contest between author and reader that in previous technologies has gone on out of sight, "behind" the page. The author had always before had the upper hand, although, in developing previous technologies of writing, literate cultures allowed for a different kind and degree of control. With the purely linear presentation of the papyrus roll, neither author nor reader had many choices. Because there were very few visual cues, the author had to build all textual structure into the words themselves; the reader could hardly move back or forward without losing his or her place in the structure. Gradually the structure became externalized through the development of the paged book, marginal notes, use of various scripts, and other techniques culminating in modern printed typography. Although it is still linear in the ideal, the printed book is sophisticated in its visible structure of chapters, sections, and paragraphs and, for nonfiction, indices—all available to the author to delimit the reader's experience of the text. Yet that same structure makes it possible for the reader to exert some control. There is no convenient way for the author to prevent the reader from skipping over one chapter or turning to the back and reading the last page first; authors in the age of print have had to exert their authority in subtler ways. As it has been used so far, the electronic medium has challenged all such attempts to circumscribe the reader's participation.

The traditional view of literature as mimesis, or imitation, is also troubled by electronic writing and for the same reason, the active participation of the reader. Because the text may change with each reading, the electronic author cannot be simply capturing a replica of nature in her text and offering that replica to the reader. The relationship between the author, the text, and the world represented is made more complicated by the addition of the reader as an active participant. Rather than envisioning an electronic text as a reflection of our world, we might think of it as a self-contained world, a heterocosm—a notion that dates back to the 18th century and can also be found in romantics like Shelley, for whom the poet "creates anew the universe" (Abrams, 1953, pp. 272–285; see also Culler, 1981, p. 156).

If it is a world, however, an electronic text is a world in constant motion. Electronic writing is as animated as the famous shield of Achilles in the *Iliad*. In Homer's description, the shield is remarkable for its impossible movement: figures embossed on the shield talk and fight and dance in scenes that could not possibly be captured in a frozen image. Such ekphrastic movement is appropriate for the oral poet Homer, for whom poetry was a spontaneous performance, not a fixed text. There is an obvious comparison to be made with Keat's famous description of figures on a Grecian urn. For Keats the paradox was that the urn depicts figures whose actions are frozen and therefore immortal. And Keats was writing in the industrial age of print, when poems too were frozen texts, no matter how active they were in metaphor.

Thus, traditional belief in the fixity of the text does not seem to be surviving the shift to electronic writing. A computer text, whether a hyperfiction or simply a web page, is neither stable nor detached from the changing contexts that readers bring to it. Regarding the text as heterocosm only enhances the authority of the author, who serves as a kind of a deity for this world, and it suggests a passive reader who "loses himself" in the world of the story. Today, losing oneself in a fictional world is still construed as the goal of the naive reader or one who reads for entertainment. It is sometimes disparaged as a feature of genre fiction, such as romance and science fiction. The capacity of electronic text ironically to comment on itself keeps the reader from falling too far or too long into passivity. The reader of *afternoon* is required at every turn to reflect on the experience of reading. An electronic text like *afternoon* does not close itself off as a heterocosm; instead, it reaches out to other texts and invites the reader to participate in its own construction. This hypertext in particular seems to care little about its own closure and tells it reader: "When the story no longer progresses, or when it cycles, or when you tire of the paths, the experience of reading it ends." The margins of *afternoon* yield in a way that the secure white space surrounding a traditional printed poem cannot yield.

HYPERTEXT AND POSTSTRUCTURALISM

We see that the traditional views of the author as authority and of literature as expression or as mimesis do not seem to correspond to the experience of reading hyperfiction. The tradition helps us mainly by providing a negative measure for electronic texts, because like any avant-garde, hypertextual authors are using the computer to negate those qualities of literature that the tradition regards most highly. Hypertext authors and theorists have encouraged us to look elsewhere than traditional (still largely romantic) criticism to find a paradigm for electronic reading and writing. They have encouraged us to look first at the work of the poststructuralists (including reader-response theory, semiotics, and deconstruction) published in the 1960s through the 1980s, just before the appearance of the first hyperfictions. We may use the term "poststructuralist" to refer somewhat arbitrarily to the writers of this period whose primary concern was with the making or unmaking of meaning in literary and other discourse. It is poststructuralist theory that has seemed most relevant to hypertext. Later we will consider other groups of theorists, such as postmodernists and those engaged in cultural studies, who may have begun in the same era but whose work continues to be treated as contemporary rather than historical. Just as hyperfictions were necessarily read as an avant-garde response to literature in print, poststructuralist theories were read as a revolt against earlier critical traditions. Even today, when theoretical interest has largely gone elsewhere, it remains striking how well the poststructuralists did seem to be anticipating electronic writing.

At least two theorists had been early in noticing the relationship between poststructuralism and electronic technologies (although not hypertext itself). In *Teletheory* (1989), Gregory Ulmer applied Derrida's work to electronic communication in the form of television. (Ulmer goes on to address electronic hypermedia in *Heuretics*, [1994].) In *The Mode of Information* (1990) Mark Poster argued that electronic communication constituted a new mode of symbolic exchange, which could best be understood by applying the methods of poststructuralism. Specifically, Poster choose Derrida to help understand electronic writing, although by electronic writing Poster meant word processing and electronic messaging, not hypertext itself. It was George Landow in *Hypertext* (1992) and again in *Hypertext 2.0* (1997) who identified hypertext as the manifestation of electronic writing that "converged" with poststructural theory. Although the work of the poststructuralists is no longer the dominant critical discourse, it is worthwhile to review the relationship between poststructuralism and hypertext. For it is not only that poststructuralism clarifies the cultural significance of hypertext; the reverse is also true. Hypertext also helps us to see how poststructuralism belonged to a moment in the late age of print.

READER RESPONSE
AND THE ARCHITECTURE OF HYPERTEXT

Some literary theorists in the 1970s and 1980s emphasized the role of the reader, who had in some ways been neglected ever since the romantic revolution—first in favor of the poet and then of the poem itself. The reader, they pointed out, responds actively to the words on the page, and this response determines the text, which exists from moment to moment in the act of reading. The task of the literary criticism, then, was not to examine the text in isolation, but rather to understand the text through its effect on the reader—a technique called reader-response criticism. Wolfgang Iser explained how the reader must participate in the literary act by realizing the author's text:

... the literary work cannot be completely identical with the text, or with the realization of the text, but in fact must lie halfway between the two. The work is more than the text, for the text only takes on life when it is realized, and furthermore the realization is by no means independent of the individual disposition of the reader.... The convergence of the text and the reader brings the literary work into existence.... (Iser, 1980, p. 50).

The work therefore has a dynamic nature, changing from reading to reading. Indeed the text itself is "an arena in which reader and author participate in a game of the imagination" (pp. 51–52). The words on the page constitute the rules or parameters by which the game is played: "the written text imposes certain limits on its unwritten implications.... " But these limits still leave the reader room to exercise his own imagination. Indeed, every text leaves gaps for the reader to complete:

[o]ne text is potentially capable of several different realizations, and no reading can ever exhaust the full potential, for each individual reader will fill in the gaps in his own way, thereby excluding the various other possibilities; as he reads, he will make his own decision as to how the gap is to be filled (p. 55).

Filling in the gaps is a different temporal experience with each act of reading:

... In every text there is a potential time sequence which the reader must inevitably realize, as it is impossible to absorb even a short text in a single moment. Thus the reading process always involves viewing the text through a perspective that is continually on the move, linking up the different phases.... [W]hen we have finished the text, and read it again, clearly our extra knowledge will result in a different time sequence; we shall tend to establish connections by referring to our awareness of what is to come, and so certain aspects of the text will assume a significance we did not attach to them on a first reading.... (p. 56).

Although Iser was referring to printed texts, his description characterizes the reading of hyperfiction too; all of the qualities that he described would follow from the way in which hyperfiction authors freed the text from its embodiment as a set of bound, paper pages. (On reader response in electronic text, see Ziegfeld, 1989, pp. 364–366. Douglas, 2000, reinvigorates reader-response criticism in her readings of hyperfiction.) Stanley Fish (1980) also emphasized the paradox of the physical (we would say printed) text:

The objectivity of the text is an illusion, and moreover, a dangerous illusion, because it is so physically convincing. The illusion is one of self-sufficiency and completeness. A line of print or a page or a book is so obviously there—it can be handled, photographed, or put away—that it seems to be the sole repository of whatever value and meaning we associate with it (p. 82).

Yet the text is not complete until it is experienced by the reader.

The pages of a printed book exist prior to and apart from any reader, and the text as a sequence of words on the page is entirely determined by authors and printers. What the reader fashions is the text as a structure of sounds, images, or ideas in her own mind. This figurative text was for Fish, Iser, and others the only text worth studying, perhaps the only text available for study, because one could not know the words on the printed page except by reading them and calling forth such a mental structure. Electronic hypertext, however, seems to realize the metaphor of reader response, as the reader participates in the making of the text as a sequence of words. This participation is true of hyperfiction and even of conventional pages on the World Wide Web. In both cases, if the author has written all the words and chosen all the images, the reader must still call them up and determine the order of presentation by the choices made and links followed. The author writes a set of potential texts, from which the reader chooses, and there is no single univocal text apart from the reader.

The role of the reader in electronic fiction therefore lies halfway between the customary roles of author and reader in the medium of print. These two roles are most clearly delineated in the traditional novel or essay, in which a silent reader absorbs and reflects upon the words of the author. There are other kinds of texts that define different roles. In drama, for example, a special class of readers, the actors, interpret the text before an audience. Dramatic texts are like musical scores, in the sense that the words on the page direct the actors in their effort to bring the drama into existence as sound and image. The written text could never be a complete record of the experience of the play; it has always to be filled out and therefore interpreted. Even if the playwright is also directing, he is in a sense interpreting his own work. This role of performer or interpreter now extends to all forms of hypertextual writings, so that in the electronic writing space all texts are like dramas or musical scores. The reader performs the text, perhaps only for herself, perhaps for another reader, who may then choose to perform the first reader's text for others. In this way electronic writing can serve to define new levels of creativity that fall between the apparent originality of the romantic artist and apparent passivity of the traditional reader.

An electronic text may be open to performance by the reader, its structure or architecture realized in time as the reader reads, but the quality of performance also belonged to texts in manuscript and in print. What we have traditionally called the structure of the text is the relationship between the linear experience of reading and the network of allusions among elements that are separated in the physical space of the book and the temporal dimension of its reading. The fluid architecture of the text has been a particular concern of modernist critics, because modern literature has made such radical and obvious efforts to distort the space and so to manipulate the reader's time. In modern prose as well as poetry, the narrative is often purposely fragmented. The step-by-step development of the story is ignored; causal relationships among events may also be omitted. Here modern prose and hypertext come together again, and this convergence should not be surprising. Hypertext as the remediation of print has relied on the techniques that were pioneered in the modernist literary revolt. As we see, then, theorists who helped us read modern authors could also help us read hypertextual authors.

Joseph Frank was one of the first critics to discuss these qualities of modernism, and he coined the term "spatial form" to describe the architecture of a text that works against "strict causal-chronological order ... " (Frank, 1981, p. 235; see also Douglas, 2000, pp. 108–112). Of the modern poets Eliot and Pound, he wrote that they "undermine[d] the inherent consecutiveness of language, frustrating the reader's normal expectation of a sequence and forcing him to perceive the elements of the poem as juxtaposed in space rather than unrolling in time" (Frank, 1963, p. 10). Joyce's extraordinary structure of allusion and reference in *Ulysses* and *Finnegans Wake* makes him the best example of the assault on the chronological order of the text. Joyce expects that the reader of *Ulysses* will have to work his way back and forth through the pages of the book in order to perceive the references: the reader will have to abandon the linear experience of the story (= > p. 142). *Ulysses* and much of *Finnegans Wake* have a simple storyline, but the story is buried beneath several layers of allusions and neologisms. In Joyce's case the archaeology of these layers is far more rewarding than the story itself. As Frank put it, " ... Joyce cannot be read—he can only be reread" (Frank, 1963, p. 19). And Frank's characterization of James Joyce remains appropriate for the hyperfictions of Michael Joyce.

While 20th-century novelists have often been straining with progressively greater violence against the conventions of the novel, their critics have been arguing that we must therefore reconsider the nature of narrative and indeed of writing itself. That reconsideration continued with the poststructuralists. Gérard Genette wrote:

One has long considered writing ... as a simple means for the notation of speech. Today, we are beginning to understand that it is a bit more than that, and Mallarmé already had said that 'to think, is to write without flourishes.' Because of the specific spatiality to which we have referred, language (and thus thought) is already a kind of writing, or, if one prefers, the manifest spatiality of writing may be taken as a symbol for the profound spatiality of language.... Since Mallarmé, we have learned to recognize (to re-cognize) the so-called visual resources of script and of typographical arrangement, and of the existence of the Book as a kind of total object; and this change of perspective has made us more attentive to the spatiality of writing, to the atemporal disposition of signs, words, phrases, and discourse in the simultaneity of what is called a text (taken from "La littérature et l'espace" in *Figures III*, cited by Frank, 1981, p. 242).

If these are indeed the lessons offered by the poets since Mallarmé, hyperfiction would seem to give the fullest expression yet to the spatiality of writing. The electronic reader is encouraged to think of the text as a collection of interrelated units floating in a space of at least two dimensions. Her movement among units does not require flipping pages or consulting the table of contents; instead, she passes instantly and effortlessly from one place to another. It is a key element in hypertext's remediation of print that references and allusions should work more easily in this new medium.

The electronic author can make her references more precise and more numerous. This facility in making references is true for Web pages (with their numerous link anchors underlined in blue) as well as for literary hypertexts. Far from abandoning control of the text, the electronic author can, if she chooses, exercise greater control over the process of cross-reference. In printed fiction, not all the readers, perhaps very few, will register any particular reference, and the author cannot know which reader will find which references. He cannot predict how the reader will move through the fictional space. In *Finnegans Wake*, there are no doubt still many references that no one has noticed. Joyce could perhaps envision an ideal reader of *Finnegans Wake* who recognizes all the allusions and references, but he could not know how closely any flesh-and-blood reader would approach that ideal. In the electronic reading space, the author can make the process of reference contingent upon the reader's response or insist that the reader follow a particular path of references before following another. The electronic author can manipulate her reader's time at one remove—not only through the words on the pages, like all previous authors, but also by determining the presentation of the electronic pages themselves. The traditional printed novel molds time as a static sculpture molds the space it occupies, creating a complex but unchanging form. The electronic text manipulates time as a piece of kinetic sculpture manipulates space.

ELECTRONIC SIGNS

Semiotics was a theoretical discourse that developed throughout the 20th century, but it acquired through the work of Umberto Eco and others a particular resonance for literary theory in the 1970s and 1980s. The fact that electronic writing seems to illustrate semiotic views of language and communication is again hardly surprising, because semiotics itself grew in the same cultural matrix that produced the computer. The computer was constructed as a machine for creating and manipulating signs, which could themselves be mathematical, verbal, or pictorial. Computer programming and indeed all kinds of electronic writing and reading by computer are exercises in applied semiotics. The first lesson any programmer must learn is the difference between a sign and its reference, between the address of a location in the computer's memory and the value stored at that address. This dichotomy characterizes the machine at all levels, and it is at the essence of hypertext. The process of semiosis, the movement from one sign to another in the act of reference, is embodied in the computer.

We have seen that, in accordance with reader-response theory, the reader can take an active role in the making of an electronic text—that the text can become a contested ground between author and reader. There is a third player in this game, the electronic space itself. The computer can be seen as doubling the author for the reader, just as it doubles the reader for the author, interpreting and misinterpreting each to the other. Once the author has set up the text as a delicate balance of signs, the computer can be made to perform operations on individual signs or on the whole structure without the direct and continuing intervention of author or reader. The author may fashion the text so that it changes permanently when readers traverse a certain path—so that readers burn their links behind them. Readers may search the text for the occurrence of various words and form new paths based on that search. The computer could even be programmed to rearrange its structure overnight in response to a dozen different variables—or mischievously in response to a computer virus. The use of webcrawlers and other software agents on the World Wide Web has become common, and these agents act precisely as the reader's double. In collecting a library of printed books, we can be sure that our texts will be the same in the morning as they were the night before. For an electronic library, or simply for our collection of bookmarked Web pages, we have no such assurance, as the texts may age, mature, and degenerate to reflect the time that we have been away. On the World Wide Web, pages and sites do often disappear without warning, leaving us with dangling links, signifiers without signifieds.

In semiotic theory, a sign is not a static thing, but rather a function, a relation between the signified and the signifier: it is this sign function that relates expression to contents. As Umberto Eco (1976) explained it, "the classical notion of a 'sign' dissolves itself into a highly complex network of changing relationships. Semiotics suggests a sort of molecular landscape in which what we are accustomed to recognize as everyday forms turn out to be the result of transitory chemical aggregations and so-called 'things' are only the surface appearance assumed by an underlying network of more elementary units" (pp. 48ff). Signification is activity, like the pulsing world of molecules as they form and dissolve bonds. Eco's appeal was to a metaphor from chemistry, but the "network of changing relationships" also perfectly describes the World Wide Web and hypertext. Electronic writing allows us to display and manipulate our network of relationships with far greater facility than chemists can control the molecular landscape. The electronic writing space seems to be not a metaphor for signification, but rather a technology of signification. Signs in the computer do precisely what students of semiotics have been claiming for their signs for more than a century, as they generate text automatically.

Text as texture, as a weaving together of signs, *is* a metaphor, one that dates from the Middle Ages. The signs in a text mingle and interrelate, as points in a space whose coordinates are determined, as Eco (1976) argued, by the intersection of many codes (pp. 57ff). Both the written page and the printed page are fields in which codes can intersect, but the computer as hypertext claims to offer a more appropriate space for these intersections. A text in the computer, a Web site or a hyperfiction, is a dynamic network of relationships, and each path through the network defines an order, interpretation, and meaning for the text according to a certain code. The sum of all connections becomes all possible interpretations of the text. All the interpretive meaning of an electronic text is embodied in the ramifying structure of its connections. In the computer we can see, as students of semiotics have long maintained, that a text is never anything more than a structure of relations. By changing the relations, as we do when we make and break connections, we change the meaning of the text. Saussure and his followers showed that sounds in a language have only relative meaning defined by the distinctions that we make among them. Students of semiotics have extended this principle to all codes: meaning lies in the systems of differences among their elements. As Jonathan Culler put it: " ... elements of a text do not have intrinsic meaning as autonomous entities but derive their significance from oppositions which are in turn related to other oppositions in a process of theoretically infinite semiosis" (Culler, 1981, p. 29). Electronic writing seems to make those differences operative for every level of topical writing. The differences are seen and manipulated as a set of connections that hold topics in tension, both binding topics together and keeping them apart. The reader uses the computer to move along these lines of force, and this movement is the meaning of the text.

Intertextuality, on the other hand, is a facet of poststructural theory that the computer both endorses and subtly undermines. Jonathan Culler explained that " ... literary works are to be considered not as autonomous entities, 'organic wholes,' but as intertextual constructs: sequences which have meaning in relation to other texts which they take up, cite, parody, refute, or generally transform. A text can be read only in relation to other texts, and it is made possible by the codes which animate the discursive space of a culture" (Culler, 1981, p. 38; see also Landow, 1989, pp. 184–188; 1997, pp. 35–36). In prior cultural moments, the printed book or written codex seemed to encourage the notion of a text as an organic whole—a unit of meaning physically separate from and therefore independent of all other texts. Stressing connections rather than textual independence, hyperfiction authors and Web designers are rewriting the possibilities of reference and allusion. Not only can one passage in an electronic text refer to another, but the text can bend so that any two passages touch, displaying themselves contiguously to the reader. Not only can one text allude to another, but the one text can penetrate the other and become a visual intertext before the reader's eyes. Intertextual relationships occur everywhere in print—in novels, gothic romances, popular magazines, encyclopedias, grammars, and dictionaries—yet the electronic space seems to refashion print technology to allow the reader to visualize and realize intertextuality (see Culler, 1981, p. 103).

Intertextuality is more than the references within a text and allusions between texts that are common in literature; it is the interrelation of all texts on the same topic, language, or culture. Some, like Roland Barthes, claimed that these interrelations cannot be mapped, because the text and indeed the reading subject himself depends on many anonymous codes that can never be set forth. Barthes wrote, for example, that "I is not an innocent subject, anterior to the text.... This 'I' which approaches the text is already itself a plurality of other texts, of codes which are infinite or, more precisely, lost (whose origins are lost)" (Barthes, 1974, p. 10; see also Culler, 1981, p. 102). But there is a great difference between the infinite and the inaccessible. Electronic writing with its graphical representations of structure encourages us to think that intertextual relations can be mapped out, made explicit—never fully, but with growing accuracy and completeness. Mapping in the electronic writing space can be a collective process: the writer creates some connections, which pass to the first reader, who may add new connections and pass the results on to another reader, and so on. This tradition, this passing on of the text from writer to reader, who then becomes a writer for other readers, is nothing new; it is the literal meaning of the word "tradition." Humanistic study carried on in manuscript and print was just such a tradition, in which scholars read and interpreted classical authors and then published their interpretations for a new generation of readers. Their work too was intertextual. We are now using the computer to simplify the technology of intertextuality so much that we seem to be refashioning the idea of tradition itself. In the computer, reading passes easily into writing, and the writing that the reader adds can have the same character as the rest of the text.

DECONSTRUCTION AND ELECTRONIC WRITING

Barthes was one of the French theorists from the 1960s through the 1980s, who along with Derrida and Foucault spoke a language that resonated uncannily with electronic writing (=> p. 107). In hindsight, how could we avoid seeing the computer in Roland Barthes's influential distinction between the work and the Text? "[T]he work," Barthes (1979) wrote, "is concrete, occupying a portion of book-space (in a library, for example); the Text, on the other hand, is a methodological field" (p. 74). "The Text is plural.... The Text is not coexistence of meanings, but passage, traversal" (p. 76). "The author is regarded as the father and the owner of his work; ... The Text, on the other hand, is read without the father's signature ... [N]o vital 'respect' is owed to the Text: it can be broken (this is exactly what the Middle Ages did with two authoritative texts, the Scriptures and Aristotle)" (p. 78). " ... The Text requires an attempt to abolish (or at least to lessen) the distance between writing and reading, not by intensifying the reader's projection into the work, but by linking the two together in a single signifying process" (p. 79). All that seemed left to say was that the paradigm for the work is a finely bound, printed volume, whereas the paradigm for the Text is a network in the computer's memory (see Ziegfield, 1989, pp. 364–365). Foucault's (1977) essay "What is an Author?" also suggested the difficulty of defining where the author's text ends and interpretation begins—the difficulty that hypertext seems to answer by showing how one author's texts can dissolve into an expanse of intertextual relationships (see also Grusin, 1996; Landow, 1997, pp. 92–93).

In this period, the deconstructionists, Derrida, deMan and many others, called forth perhaps the strongest reaction from traditionalist humanists because of their critique of important literary and philosophical texts. Jonathan Culler (1981) explained the task of deconstruction as " … reading the major texts of Western literature and philosophy as sites on the boundaries of logocentrism and showing, in the most subtle interpretations that scholarship has yet produced, how these texts are already riven by contradictions and indeterminacies that seem inherent in the exercise of language" (p. 43). The deconstructionists asserted that the meaning of any written text is radically unstable, a vain attempt to fix meaning, when all writing is condemned to drift in a space of possible meanings. Traditional critics, however, believed tacitly or explicitly in such hierarchies. For the traditional critic, a work such as "Hamlet" was obviously more important than a minor 20th-century novel. Tradition also asserted that each work of literature, central or marginal, has its own identity, that each work occupies a portion of "book-space." A work has predecessors, and it influences other works, but we can always identify and single out the text of "Hamlet" for study. We can always separate "Hamlet" from its influences and go back to the play itself.

The deconstructionists challenged those beliefs. Not only can the central become marginal and vice versa, but the very identity, the separateness, of the work was questioned. The text of "Hamlet" has no boundaries: it opens out in all directions and includes, for example, all the centuries of interpretation of the play. The play is not central and the interpretations marginal, as we would assume, for we cannot say where the play ends and interpretation begins. Derrida (1979) spoke of text as "a differential network, a fabric of traces referring endlessly to something other than itself, to other differential traces. Thus the text overruns all the limits assigned to it so far … " (p. 84).

Derrida's characterization of a text again sounded very much like text in the electronic writing space. And yet, when Derrida spoke of marginality or of the text as extending beyond its borders, he was in fact appealing to the earlier technologies of writing, to codices and printed books. The margins of a medieval manuscript often belonged to the scholarly reader: they were the reader's space for conducting a dialogue with the text. During generations of copying, text could also move from the margins into the center, as glosses from readers made their way into the text itself. In the age of print, marginal notes became truly marginal, part of the hierarchy of the text that the author himself defined and controlled: eventually they became footnotes and endnotes. Readers could still insert their own notes with a pen, where there was sufficient white space, but these handwritten notes could no longer have the same status as the text itself. When deconstructionists played on the dichotomy between the center and the margin, they were assuming a written or more probably a printed text that favored the center. In general, whenever the theorists set out to reverse a literary hierarchy, they were assuming the technology of print (or sometimes handwriting) that generated or enforced that hierarchy.

A text in electronic space seems to have no necessary margins, no fixed boundaries except for the ultimate limitations of the machine. In *afternoon* the margins yield to the reader, and this yielding serves as a safety valve to prevent the text from disintegrating under the force of a deconstructive reading (= > p. 124). The electronic writing space can support a network in which all elements have equal status and in which to be at the margin is itself only provisional. The author can extend and ramify this textual network limited only by the available memory, and the reader can follow paths through the space limited only by constraints established by the author. In some electronic fictions, the reader too may be allowed to change the structure of the text, to extend its borders in ways the author has not anticipated. Furthermore the connections can extend beyond one author's texts to many. An electronic library could include texts of all ages and subject matters, all organized into a reticulated network of topics: the World Wide Web is already a popular electronic library. In such a library the boundaries are fluid: pages dissolve into volumes or sites, which in turn may be organized into larger structures (= > p. 93).

If poststructuralist theories, and in particular deconstruction, seem to resonate with hypertext, it is important to remember that these theories developed among writers who were primarily working in and with earlier technologies. Deconstruction, for example, worked by reversal, by upsetting tradition, and perhaps the key tradition that it sought to upset was that of humanism in the age of print. To deconstruct a text, one used a vocabulary appropriate to the computer precisely because this vocabulary contradicted the assumptions of print. It was also a negative vocabulary because deconstruction had to negate what it was then: still the unquestioned paradigm for literary and indeed all "serious" writing—the printed page. Deconstruction and the other poststructuralist techniques, such as those of Barthes and the reader-response critics, aimed to refashion techniques associated with the printed book from within the technology. On the other hand, electronic writing remediates print itself—that is, it seeks to refashion print genres and forms from the perspective of a new technology.

Deconstruction thus assumed the fixed character of a text in its effort to undermine that text. The fixed text provided a fixed target; you could not say that a text contradicted itself unless the text appeared to make and defend claims worthy of contradiction. Because deconstructive critics sought to drive latent ambiguities in the text into the open, they often focused on problem texts, whose "message" was hard to decipher, such as Shelley's "Triumph of Life," James' "The Turn of the Screw," or Melville's *Billy Budd*. An electronic text, however, claims to be only a potential text, and as such even its ambiguities are only potential. It need not and probably will not present all of its claims, all of its ambiguities, to any reader. Because the text changes with each reading, it may not ever make a univocal statement that invites deconstruction. In one reading of *afternoon*, the narrator does not visit his lover's psychologist; in another he does. Which is the reading that needs to be subverted? The fact that the electronic space of *afternoon* contains both readings already recognizes the contradiction. Neither reading is the whole story, and yet unlike a printed work we cannot say that the two readings are embodied in the same narrative, for there are different narratives called forth by two different readers, or by the same reader at two different times.

Deconstruction itself was playful, but its playful attitude required a fundamental seriousness in its object. The hypertext authors since 1980s have in general created playful, allusive hypertexts that do not take themselves too seriously, as a printed text seems inevitably to do. Why would anyone want to deconstruct a work entitled *Uncle Buddy's Phantom Funhouse?* Such hypertexts are not hostile to criticism, but are instead self-referential and incorporate their own critique. *afternoon* includes critical comments as episodes that the reader may visit: for example, the comment on closure or a definition of hypertext. *Victory Garden* includes a complex and amusing web of allusions to itself and to other media forms, particularly television (= > p. 135). Joyce, Moulthrop, Douglas and many other authors have shown how hypertext can dissolve the distinction between writing and interpreting a text—a distinction that poststructuralist critics had worked so hard to negate for printed texts as well. The poststructuralists claimed that a text was no more important than its interpretations, because the text could not be separated from its interpretation. Now, in the electronic writing space, where every reading of a text is a realization or indeed a rewriting of the text, to read *is* to interpret. This insight turns out to be playful because the hypertext is fashioned with the expectation that it will be read in this critical fashion. When the author does not set out to exclude the reader from the process of making the text, she is not shocked to learn that her text is not inviolate. Electronic writing seems then to accept as strengths the very qualities—the play of signs, intertextuality, the lack of closure—that the poststructuralists posed as the ultimate limitations of literature and language.

NEW CONVERGENCES AND POPULAR FORMS

The poststructuralists wrote their most influential works before any hypertext fictions were created, and certainly before hypertext emerged as a cultural phenomenon in the form of the World Wide Web. As electronic communication—from hyperfiction to computer games and the Web—has actually developed in the 1990s, poststructural theory has seemed less adequate to describe its range of forms and genres. Digital technology has expanded its field of remediations from purely verbal text to audiovisual media (= > p. 24). The poststructuralists were often accused of wanting to discredit the monumental authors of Western culture, but it is clear that they simply wanted to reread these authors in a new way, not to stop reading them altogether. Poststructuralism focused on texts in print, which seem now to belong almost by definition to a cultural elite. Although poststructuralists were eager to open the canon to women or minority authors in print, they had less interest in other media. Although Barthes did important work on photography in *Camera Lucida* (1981), and Foucault on painting in *This is Not a Pipe* (1989), most poststructuralists were more interested in verbal representation. French theorists in general were often hostile to the power of the image and therefore to visual media (Jay, 1993). Perhaps for that reason, poststructural theory seemed most appropriate to describe the earliest hypertexts, which were almost exclusively verbal.

Although it is as old as poststructuralism, the broad field of cultural studies has emerged more recently as a dominant theoretical discourse in the United States. The field of cultural studies has been concerned as much with visual as with verbal communication, as it explores magazines, film, and television as well as books and newspapers for representations of and resistances to dominant ideologies (Grossberg, Nelson, & Treichler, 1992). Some researchers in cultural studies are now turning their attention to the World Wide Web, as another media form in which global capitalism is meeting forms of local resistance. The rise of multimedia authoring as well as viewing, especially on the World Wide Web, has resulted in a huge body of new popular material to be explored (millions of Web pages alone). Furthermore, like photography, but unlike film and television, multimedia is a form of visual expression in which millions of users can participate as creators. Multimedia and Web design are becoming truly popular cultural practices, pursued by digital artists, technical communicators, corporate information specialists, and amateur home page designers. Because of its close relationship to communications theory, the field of cultural studies has the resources to examine this wealth of new forms and genres produced on the Web, such as home pages, fan sites, and webcameras.

In addition to the cultural studies of new media, a growing number of critics and theorists are directing their attention specifically to hypertext. Many of them are exploring relationships between hyperfiction and more popular visual media forms. In *Cybertext: Perspectives on Ergodic Literature* (1997), Espen Aarseth argues that hypertext literature has important affinities to computer games, which he analyzes as instances of what he calls cybertext or "ergodic" literature in general. Silvio Gaggi (1998) works across media, analyzing the postmodern identity in popular film and the visual arts as well as printed fiction and hyperfiction. In *Hamlet on the Holodeck* (1997), Janet Murray has argued that the future of narrative belongs to a new immersive medium that combines audiovisual representation with interactivity; she does not distinguish between elite and popular narrative. All these works show that hypertext and hypermedia may now be giving rise to their own theoretical language and that that language will need to accommodate a variety of media forms.

LOOKING AT AND LOOKING THROUGH

The forging of a new critical language began with Richard Lanham's call, in an article in 1989 and again in his book *The Electronic Word* (1993), for a "new rhetoric of the arts, an unblushing and unfiltered attempt to plot all the ranges of formal expression now possible" (Lanham, 1989, p. 276; 1993, p. 14). Lanham claimed that electronic technology could help to break down the boundaries between literature and the other arts (1989, pp. 275–276; 1993, p. 13). The computer could textualize all the arts: that is, it could incorporate sound and images into hypertext as easily as words.

Lanham's new "digital" rhetoric would be inclusive and would make "no invidious distinctions between high and low culture, commercial and pure usage, talented or chance creation, visual or auditory stimulus, iconic or alphabetic information" (1989, p. 276; 1993, p. 14). It would compel us to reconsider the relationship between the text and the world to which the text refers.

In the age of print, the ideal was in general to make a text transparent, so that the reader looked through the text to the world beyond. This was the goal of realistic painting as well the traditional novel. In a digital rhetoric, transparency need not be the only virtue. The reader can be made to focus on the verbal patterns, on the text as a texture of elements. The text can be transparent or opaque, and it can oscillate between transparency and opacity, between asking the reader to look through the text to the "world beyond" and asking her to look at the text itself as a formal structure. This oscillation was already a characteristic of modern literature in print: it was manifested in the tension between the text as a story and the text as a structure of allusions. Here again, electronic writing seems to take the modern literary experience one step further. An electronic hypertext can make the structure visible, as its formal structure is embodied in the links between episodes. In reading an episode, the reader may succeed in looking through the text to the imagined world. But whenever she comes to a link, she must look at the text, as a series of possibilities that she as reader can activate. In *afternoon* we may get lost in Peter's compelling narrative of his search for his son, but the need to make choices keeps pulling us back to the fact that we as readers are participating in the making of a fiction. We are constantly critiquing the nature of these choices as we read. In *Victory Garden* the repetitions and displacements repeatedly remind us that we are reading a text with the capacity to refashion itself through our very act of reading. In *Patchwork Girl* the task of stitching parts together applies not only to the main character, but metaphorically to the text itself. In all these hypertexts, the links have the same status as the verbal episodes. It becomes therefore as appropriate for the reader to look at the formal arrangement of the text, as it is to get lost in the story.

Following on Lanham, Richard Grusin and I have suggested that the work of remediation in any medium relies on two apparently opposite strategies (= > p. 26). Sometimes the artist tries to erase the traces of the prior medium in her work and seeks to convince us that her work in the new medium represents the world directly. At other times, she accepts and even foregrounds the older medium. We call the first strategy "transparent immediacy" and the second "hypermediacy" (Bolter & Grusin, 1999, pp. 22–44).

In its remediation of print, hypertext adopts both of these strategies. When the author elects to leave the reader alone with an episode of conventional prose, she is relying on the power of traditional narrative prose to be transparent. When she emphasizes the reader's choices through the process of linking, she is evoking a strategy of hypermediacy. The same is true of hypermedia applications on the World Wide Web and elsewhere that remediate television, film, and photography as well as print. In such applications, graphics, sound, and digital video are often interpreted as transparent presentations of reality, while the buttons and hyperlinks remind the user that she is in control of a hypertextual computer program and is not looking through a transparent window onto the world.

Through a decade of experience with hypertext and hypermedia, we have come implicitly to regard the oscillation between looking at and looking through, between transparency and hypermediacy, as a defining characteristic of this new writing space. The "legibility" of texts in this new space depends on the character and the rate of this oscillation. Hypertext fictions tend to oscillate rapidly and abruptly, which more than anything else defines their status as avant-garde or "difficult." Conventional, commercial Web sites oscillate more slowly and in predictable ways, in order not to upset the visitors, who may be potential customers. Some rate of oscillation is inevitable: without it we would not define our experience of reading as hypertextual.

THE PRACTICE OF THEORY

In the last decade of the 20th century, the authors of hyperfictions have become some of the most important theorists: their theoretical work, often published in traditional print form, reflects the lessons they have learned as authors. In this sense theory and practice have converged in a way that was not true in the heyday of poststructuralism. In *Of Two Minds* (1995), Michael Joyce offered a compelling vocabulary for articulating the new writing space. He drew the distinction between exploratory and constructive hypertexts and offered the notion of "contours" to capture the reader's experience of making meaning as she moves along the linked paths in the hypertext. In *Othermindedness* (2000), Joyce is concerned in particular with the future of prose as a mode of representation in an era in which multimedia and the Web seem to pre-empt our culture's attention. The essays in both of these books were written in a form that Joyce (2000) himself characterizes as combining theory and narrative: "both a narrative of theory and a text theoretically at least a narrative" (p. 4). Stuart Moulthrop has interspersed his literary hypertexts with a series of articles that have explored the rhetoric and politics of electronic writing (for example, Moulthrop, 1991, 1994, 1997). Moulthrop has joined other fiction writers and theoreticians in exploring the theory of the rhizome of Deleuze and Guattari (Moulthrop, 1994). As he notes, Deleuze and Guattari presented their ideas in a book, *A Thousand Plateaus* (1987), that is a proto-hypertext and, although working in print, they envisioned writing as hypertextual network (see also Landow, 1997, pp. 38–42). Jane Yellowlees Douglas, the author of the literary hypertext *I Have Said Nothing*, has conducted intensive and extensive readings of other hypertexts, including *afternoon*, and provided definitive discussions of authorial intent and closure in these new literary forms (Douglas, 2000, pp. 89–148). Terry Harpold, himself a designer of multimedia and hypermedia systems, has offered subtle explanations of the hyperlink by applying the psychoanalytic theory of Lacan (Harpold, 1991a, 1991b, and forthcoming). The hypertext poet, Jim Rosenberg, has argued for a kind of reading in which the reader discovers "structure though activities provided by the hypertext" (Joyce, 2000, p. 112; Rosenberg, 1996, p. 22).

Beyond these printed works, we can point to a more intimate convergence: the way in which hypertext writers have explicitly incorporated theoretical insights into their hyperfictions or other electronic productions. Carolyn Guyer, author of *Quibbling* (1992), has identified hypertext as an intrinsically collaborative and feminist form of writing (Joyce, 1995, p. 89; see also Greco, 1996, p. 88; Landow, 1997, pp. 206–208). Her collaborative "High-Pitched Voices" was an attempt to define a feminist form of electronic writing through the practice of a community of women writers. The hyperfictions of Moulthrop, Joyce, and Jackson are all noted for their incorporation of theoretical texts as well as self-referential comments on the nature of the hypertext writing that they are practicing. John Cayley and Jim Rosenberg are electronic poets whose theoretical views on the nature of representation and the act of reading enter into and inform the electronic works they create.

In the age of modernism as indeed in earlier periods, literary practice and criticism were considered separate spheres, different genres with different rhetorical conventions, even though the same writer, for example, T. S. Eliot, might sometimes be successful in both spheres. Poststructuralists succeeded in "eliding" the distinction between literature and theory by insisting that all texts were interdependent or intertextual. They blurred the distinction in order to reverse the traditional relationship in which literature was considered primary and criticism secondary or even parasitic, with the result that traditionalists complained that students of poststructuralism often seemed to value their own theoretical writings above the literature itself. The insistence on the "triumph of theory" was again part of the oppositional strategy that poststructuralism adopted in order to challenge the assumptions of print culture. The practitioners of hyperfiction have been suggesting that this strategy may no longer be necessary. Their creative uses of hypertext have shown that theory can grow out of practice and return to practice: that is, hypertext writers—perhaps to an even greater extent than modernist print writers—can elucidate a theory through their writing. That theory yields for them a vocabulary by means of which they can articulate problems that they experience as authors. Because reading a hypertext is also a kind of writing, theoretical texts like Douglas' analyses of the experience of reading hypertexts are practical too. They guide us in the practice of reading these new media forms.

9

Writing the Self

If the technology of writing has always had a reflexive quality, allowing writers to see themselves in what they write, nevertheless each particular technology of writing (on papyrus, in codex, on the videoscreen) has been used to define a somewhat different relationship between the written word and the identity of the writer. The reflexive character of each technology permits writers to find themselves in the texts they create and therefore to know themselves in a new way. According to scholars such as Bruno Snell (1960) and Eric Havelock (1982), the ancient Greeks discovered the self during precisely those centuries in which writing was absorbed into their culture. It seems almost inevitable that literate people would come to regard their writing technologies as both a metaphor for and the principal embodiment of thought. The mind comes to be understood as a writing surface, and thinking as the activity of inscribing on that surface. This metaphorical use of writing is perhaps not a side effect, but rather a basic characteristic of the technology. It may be that cultures invent and refine writing technologies at least in part in order to refashion their definitions of mind and self.

Writing technologies, in particular electronic writing today, do not determine how we think or how we define ourselves. Rather, they participate in our ongoing cultural redefinitions of self, knowledge, and experience. Just as hypertext remediates print, hypertext and all other forms of electronic writing are participating in the refashioning of our notions of self in the late age of print. Because of their representational functions, media in general must always be among the most important metaphors that we have to express such changes. In the 20th century we have turned to (audio)visual media (radio, film, and television) in addition to print for the task of self-definition, and now we are turning to audiovisual digital media (graphics forms on the Web, virtual reality, computer games) along with electronic

189

writing. These new media depend on earlier definitions of self embodied in print and earlier visual media; the electronic self is a remediated version of the printed, filmic, or televisual self. For many, electronic writing is coming to be regarded as a more authentic or appropriate space for the inscription of the self than print.

In the past few decades, the metaphor of electronic writing has been applied to two very different views of mind and self. The earlier version of the metaphor treated hypertext as the inscription of rational, even Cartesian thought. The implicit claim was that hypertext could better represent or facilitate the associative processes of the rational mind. If print disguised these "natural" qualities of thought, hypertext made them transparent. The second, and now dominant version, is not concerned with electronic writing as a tool for rational thought, but rather as a reflection of a fragmented and constantly changing postmodern identity. The reflexive character of writing is emphasized: we write both to express, to discover, and to share who we are, and in a postmodern age our written identity is, like hypertext, dynamic, flexible, and contingent.

WRITING AS ANALYSIS

The earlier view—that the computer as a writing surface extends and amplifies the reasoning powers of the (Cartesian) mind—has its roots in the earliest attempts to deploy the computer as a cultural metaphor. It goes back to the work of the mathematician and computer pioneer Alan Turing and the artificial intelligence movement. In 1950 Alan Turing (1963) wrote a paper entitled "Computing Machinery and Intelligence," in which he proposed the following test of computer intelligence. A human tester would sit in one room and type questions at a keyboard, and a computer, located in another room, would try to give convincingly human answers; it would try to fool its human interrogator into thinking that he was talking to another human being. For decades, philosophers and computer scientists have debated whether a computer would ever pass the Turing test. In fact, no computer has passed the test. But it remains important to understand what kind of a test Turing proposed, what definition of intelligence or mind is presupposed by his test, for intelligence and the nature of mind are cultural definitions, subject to revision.

Turing's test is a measure of writing ability and reading comprehension. The computer reads the questions posed by the interrogator and writes responses. The machine is not asked to imitate the human sense of touch, taste, or smell; it does not have to demonstrate human dexterity and human corporeality. Its performance is judged entirely by the text that it produces. Turing defined intelligence as writing and reading, which he in turn understood as the kind of symbol manipulation that computers accomplish. This definition of intelligence underlay the artificial intelligence movement from the 1950s on. Working long before hypertext became practical with the invention of the personal computer in the 1980s, artificial intelligence specialists were in fact espousing a hypertextual view of mind. They set out to show that human thought could be explained as a network of interrelated symbols.

The metaphor of the mind as an (electronic) network of signs also fit with the semiotic view of language and thought in the tradition from C. S. Peirce to Umberto Eco. As Peirce put it, " ... thinking, too, is to connect signs together: 'each former thought suggests something to the thought which follows it, i.e. is the sign of something to this latter.' (5.284)" (Peirce cited by Eco, 1976, p. 166) (= > p. 176). Semiotic theory provided a larger philosophical perspective: it was not simply that the mind was a computer, as the artificial intelligence specialists proposed, but rather that the mind was a network of signs, of which the computer could be an implementation. To understand the mind as a network of signs was to understand the mind as a text. Semiotics was suggesting that we regard the mind as a writing space filled with interwoven signs. So all forms of writing could represent the process of thought.

In *Orality and Literacy* Walter Ong (1982) had made the McLuhanesque argument that writing was both a representation and a powerful extension of the natural process of thought. For him, writing was a transformative technology:

> Without writing, the literate mind would not and could not think as it does, not only when engaged in writing but normally even when it is composing its thoughts in oral form. More than any other single invention, writing has transformed human consciousness (p. 78).

Ong went on to list a series of characteristics that distinguished the oral from the literate mind. The literate mind was analytic; the oral mind was aggregative. The literate mind was objective; the oral mind was traditional and unable to detach itself from its context. Writing made it easier to see logical relationships and to subordinate one idea to another. Syllogistic reasoning, for example, was foreign to a culture without writing; the syllogism itself was first codified by Aristotle at a time when Greek culture had achieved a high level of literacy. Ong claims that "an oral culture simply does not deal in such items as geometrical figures, abstract categorization, formally logical reasoning processes, definition, or even comprehensive descriptions, or articulated self-analysis, all of which derive not simply from thought itself but from text-formed thought" (p. 55). (On literacy in the archaic and classical periods in Greece, see Lentz, 1989; Thomas, 1992).

Many criticized this strong claim that literacy is necessary for sophisticated, abstract reasoning, which was identified with a particular Western mode of thinking. Anthropologists and historians such as Brian Street in *Literacy in Theory and Practice* (1984) and Silvia Scribner and Michael Cole in *The Psychology of Literacy* (1981) argued that writing by itself does not enable or determine such modes of thinking (see also Olson, 1986; Thomas, 1992; Welch, 1999). Rather, it seems that different cultures and historical moments may choose to exploit writing technology for different purposes. Ancient and modern Western cultures have often constructed writing technology to enhance the power and status of abstract or technical discourse and thought, and it was this construction that Ong and others still espoused for the late age of print.

Under this construction, writing is seen to foster analysis and reflection—to bring forth such genres as the philosophic essay or treatise, the scientific or technical monograph, and the textbook. Ong and his followers appreciate the fact that various writing technologies permit the writer or reader to slow the insistent pace of spoken language, to control the rate at which he must produce or receive words. When an argument becomes a visible and therefore durable structure in two dimensions, the reader can take the time to examine both the soundness of the parts and their relation to the whole. Because the reader who can write may also take elements out of their original context for his own purposes, writing becomes a tool for reorganizing, for classifying, for developing and maintaining categories. The anthropologist Jack Goody argued for the importance in this respect of even the simplest written structure, the list:

> The list relies on discontinuity rather than continuity; it depends on physical placement, on location; it can be read in different directions, both sideways and downwards, up and down, as well as left and right; it has a clear-cut beginning and a precise end, that is, a boundary, an edge, like a piece of cloth. Most importantly it encourages the ordering of the items, by number, by initial sound, by category, etc. And the existence of boundaries, external and internal, brings greater visibility to categories, at the same time as making them more abstract. (Goody, 1977, p. 81).

For Goody and Ong, not only the making of lists, but all writing fosters categorical thinking and analysis, because analysis is built into the very act of writing. Writing in general becomes a technology for dividing the world into categories. What we might call the "Cartesian languages" of mathematics, symbolic logic, and computer programming are all primarily written rather than spoken, and they all rigorously and ruthlessly categorize. When a student sets out to learn a computer language, what he or she must learn by example and practice is the art of analyzing a problem into the operational categories provided by the language. Different languages provide somewhat different categories, but all require the programmer to find a discrete representation scheme and to break the task down into small, interrelated functional units. All languages require programmers to think analytically, where analysis is defined in the tradition of mathematical and symbolic logic since Descartes and Leibniz.

By emphasizing analysis, categorization, and method, the western construction of writing altered and, from Ong's point of view, improved our ability to reason. But it was not that writing gave its users a mental capacity that was unknown or impossible in an illiterate person, but rather that writing favored certain capacities at the expense of others. In Western culture as elsewhere, writing as a technological practice developed in association with other institutions and practices. Without schooling and other institutions, written texts could not permeate culture, and without writing, institutions (schools, the legal system, and modern bureaucracy) that accumulated around literacy could not exist in their current form.

WRITING THE CARTESIAN MIND

This construction of writing as a process of analytical reflection carries with it a definition of the human mind, and it leads to a definition of human identity by suggesting that what is important about us is our capacity for reasoned discourse, expressed in writing. In making verbal thoughts visible, writing can be used to fashion the mind as a personal and cultural metaphor. It is a metaphor in the strong sense—not simply a comparison between two disparate things (writing technology on one hand and mental states or capacities on the other) but rather an identification of the two. Memory and reason become a special and indeed privileged form of writing. The memory becomes a writing space, and the writer a homunculus who looks out at the world through our eyes and records what he sees. The homunculus translates perceptions into words and images and records them; he also puts down his inner thoughts and conclusions. To think is to write in the language of thought and to remember is to search the space of our memory until we find what is written there. This was exactly the view of artificial intelligence, which identified thought with the kind of symbol manipulation that the computer can do. The explicit definition of thought as the manipulation of symbols can be traced at least to the 17th-century thinkers who wanted to create a "universal character," a universal (written) language in which all ideas could be expressed unambiguously to all human beings. (For a discussion of the philosophical background, see Knowlson, 1975.) The universal character itself was another manifestation of the desire for a utopia of letters—like the medieval and modern encyclopedias and now the electronic library and artificial intelligence.

The association of the mind as a writing space goes back even further. It was common in ancient and modern Western literature, found in poets from Aeschylus ("remembering tablets of [the] mind" in *Prometheus Bound*) to Dante ("the book of memory") to Shakespeare ("the book and volume of my brain," *Hamlet*, Act 1, Scene 5), and beyond (see Curtius, 1973, pp. 302–347; also Paulson, 1989, pp. 291–293). Philosophers as early as Plato assumed that thinking and writing were inseparable. In the myth in the *Phaedrus*, Socrates invokes the metaphor of "writing in the mind" even as he seeks to deny it—when he says that the best argument is "that which is written with intelligence in the mind of the learner, which is able to defend itself and knows to whom it should speak and before whom to be silent" (Phaedrus 276A in Plato, 1919, p. 567); (= > p. 102). And in this respect, even modern psychology has not diverged from the line established by Plato. Cognitive psychology, under the influence of computer technology, is more than ever committed to the metaphor of writing. But so was Freud, who explicitly compared human memory to a child's toy, the magic writing pad. Derrida and his followers reminded us of Freud's dedication to the metaphor of writing: " ... Freud speculates that the very mansion of presence, the perceiving self, is shaped by ... writing" (G. C. Spivak, in the preface to *Of Grammatology* by Derrida, 1976b, p. xli). Indeed, the deconstructionists led the way in finding the paradigm of writing in all manifestations of Western culture.

If the technology of writing has been traditionally regarded as the creation of the human mind, possibly its greatest creation, we could also argue in the other direction: that the mind is the creation of writing. In *The Discovery of Mind: The Greek Origin of European Thought* (1960) the classicist

Bruno Snell showed how the Greek concept of mind developed slowly in the archaic period. "Homer," he pointed out, "had no one word to characterize the mind or the soul. Psyche, the word for soul in latter Greek, has no original connection with the thinking or feeling soul" (p. 8). A Homeric warrior did not have a mind: he had emotions, thoughts, plans, and preferences, but he did not unify all these mental states under a single name. He was not aware of himself as a unified thinking agent. The change came over centuries and can first be seen in the work of such lyric poets as Sappho and Alcaeus and finally in philosophers like Plato. "The early lyricists try to reproduce those moments in which the individual is all of a sudden snatched out of the broad stream of life.... Such are the moments which furnish man with his first glimpse of the soul" (p. 65). It is no coincidence that writing was working its way into Greek culture in exactly these centuries. Homer, living at the beginning of the Archaic period, was apparently illiterate, as was his audience. Sappho and the other lyric poets still recited their poems, but they could presumably write them down and perfect them in private. Sappho could see her writing as the product of her own mind and reflect on the person who produced that product.

The notion that writing unifies the mind was shared explicitly by the classicists and historians such Snell, Havelock, and Ong. For them, the reflexive character of writing allowed the writer to define his mind out of the confusion of thoughts and emotions that are experienced. These scholars were elaborating one version of a notion deeply ingrained in Western philosophy—the claim, associated with Descartes, that what makes each of us human is our ability to function as a reasoning agent. For the metaphor of the written mind lines up perfectly with the Cartesian ego. Descartes' reasoning agent can be understood as a writer who inscribes and therefore takes responsibility for his mental text. In the beginning of the *Meditations* (1960, originally published in 1641), Descartes takes leave of the world by doubting it all as the deception of evil spirit; that is, he questions the authority of his senses to report to him about the world. However, Descartes admits no doubt that his thoughts are his own: "[t]hought is an attribute that belongs to me; it alone is inseparable from my nature" (Second Meditation, p. 26). Descartes is saying that he is the author of his thoughts, his inner text. When Descartes claims "I think therefore I am," he is in effect claiming that the text validates him as author. Descartes as author then goes on to validate the text by reconstructing the world from his own "clear and distinct ideas." Cartesian philosophy provides a philosophical foundation for the classic age of printing, in which the author indeed both validates and is validated by the texts he publishes. But Cartesian philosophy was not limited to or determined by print technology.

HYPERTEXT AND THE CARTESIAN EGO

The Cartesian view of mind and of writing persisted in the late age of print, among those who, like Ong, emphasized the power of writing as a tool for rational analysis and the unified ego. It still persists among those computer specialists who define intelligence as symbol manipulation, whether done by machine or a human agent. In its classic form, artificial intelligence was an assertion that symbolic writing could completely encompass the key aspect of human nature, which was assumed to be the power to reason—the power that defined each human being as a unified and autonomous ego. On the other hand, the Cartesian construction of the ego has been challenged by philosophers throughout the 20th century—by Wittgenstein (Kenny, 1984, pp. 77ff), for example, who also chafed against the limitations of the medium of print (= > p. 108). More recently, many poststructuralists denied the Cartesian argument on precisely the grounds that the author has no special status in interpreting his own ideas, which are, after all, texts like any others. By denying the individual ego special powers as the author of its thoughts, the poststructuralists questioned the foundations of Cartesian philosophy.

Because, as Landow and others have shown, the poststructuralists also provided a theoretical foundation for hypertext, hypertext as writing technology can be aligned with the critique of the Cartesian ego (= > p. 170). Artificial intelligence specialists believed that the networks of symbols in their programs could constitute human intelligence as a process of Cartesian reason. Many hypertextual authors and theorists, however, have preferred to emphasize the deconstructive nature of the webs that they weave. For this group, if the mind is a network of signs, it is subject to the same process of infinite semiosis to which texts are liable. The ramifying network of signs spreads out beyond the individual mind to embrace other texts, both those that constitute other minds and those inscribed on conventional writing surfaces.

The idea of the mind as a symbolic text goes back at least to Pierce: "[the human mind] is a sign developing according to the laws of inference.... [T]he content of consciousness, the entire phenomenal manifestation of mind, is a sign resulting from inference" (Peirce, 1934, p. 188). People for Peirce were like words:

[t]he man-sign acquires information, and comes to mean more than he did before. But so do words. Does not electricity mean more now than it did in

the days of Franklin? ... In fact, therefore, men and words reciprocally edu-
cate each other; each increase of a man's information involves and is involved by, a corresponding increase of a word's information (pp. 188–189).

Pierce was no deconstructionist: he was not concerned with the ultimate
failure of meaning in the process of infinite semiosis. For the
poststructuralist, however, all texts wandered in their meaning, and the author had no way to stop the drift, no special warrant in determining the
meaning. This ultimate limitation would also affect the mind as a
hypertextual network of signs. So if the mind is a hypertext, then the same
arguments about instability and contingency apply to the mind as to literary
hypertexts. This version of the metaphor of electronic writing does not lead
to artificial intelligence, with its faith in the unified, Cartesian ego, but
rather to a fragmented and provisional identity, one that is often characterized as "postmodern."

ELECTRONIC WRITING AND THE POSTMODERN SELF

Hypertextual writing can be used to challenge the notion of the thought as a
transparent network of signs and the Cartesian ego as the author of that
network. Hypertext is not always transparent, but often confronts the
reader with its own opacity, its own presence as a system of representation.
So if the printed book was a good technology for embodying the transparent
Cartesian mind, then electronic hypertext offers to remediate and to
hypermediate the mind. Hypertext as a writing technology lines up with a
large and varied group of theorists, not only the poststructuralists, who have
criticized the Cartesian model. Theorists from Bourdieu to various feminists, such as Judith Butler, to sociologists, such as Kenneth Gergen, to the
now classic postmodernists, Lyotard and Baudrillard, have all denied the
Cartesian or Enlightenment notion of the autonomous, rational ego. They
have argued instead for notions of the self that are multiple, fragmented,
and in an important sense material. Some have also begun to argue for a relationship between these postmodern constructions of the self and new media technologies (see Bolter & Grusin, 1999, pp. 229–265). One of the most
influential theorists has been Donna Haraway (1991, 1997)—particularly
because of her notion of the cyborg as a postmodern hybrid of the natural
and the technological.
    A decade ago in the *Saturated Self*, Gergen (1991) noted that television
and radio:

… saturate us with the voices of humankind—both harmonious and alien … Social saturation furnishes us with a multiplicity of incoherent and unrelated languages of the self. For everything we "know to be true" about ourselves, other voices within respond with doubt and even derision. This fragmentation of self-conceptions corresponds to a multiplicity of incoherent and disconnected relationships. These relationships pull us in a myriad of directions, initiating us to play such a variety of roles that the very concept of an "authentic self" with knowable characteristics recedes from view (pp. 6–7).

If television and radio lead to saturations (and remediations) of the self, electronic writing forms (such as e-mail, newsgroups, chatrooms, and MOOs in addition to hypertext) can carry the process further. Unlike television and radio, these digital media allow the reader to write or to talk back and so to establish the reflexive relationship that also characterizes earlier writing technologies. Teachers of writing have discovered that these synchronous and asynchronous applications are ideal for the ongoing redefinition of the self (=> p. 114). Almost the sole purpose of chat rooms and MUDs and MOOs is the construction of and experimentation with the user's identity. Those who participate in these electronic environments are suggesting a new set of cultural uses for the computer and a new metaphor by which to understand this machine.

For decades after the computer's invention in the 1940s, our culture drew comparisons between the computer and the reasoning human mind. The discipline of artificial intelligence, which flourished from the 1950s through the 1980s, proceeded from the conviction that the human mind was in essence a program running on the "wetware" of the brain and could therefore be imitated and ultimately surpassed by software running on digital machines. MUDs, MOOs, and chat rooms, however, now change the terms of the metaphor. At least with their current interfaces, these electronic environments do not seem well-suited to complex or abstract discussion. Spontaneous, playful, and personal, these technologies seem to lend themselves more readily to the construction of the self as a social agent rather than as a reasoning machine. In writing about the cultural significance of these communications technologies, educators talk about the self rather than the mind.

In *Life on the Screen* (1995) Sherry Turkle examined how the regular participants in MOOs create and elaborate their identities. A MOO (or a MUD) is a collaborative, networked environment in which each participant assumes a name and provides a prose description of herself (=> p. 74). The MOO itself consists of a number of connected rooms or other spaces, each of which has its own associated description. Each participant can communicate with others in the same room by typing at her keyboard messages, which then appear on the screens for all the participants. The participants or characters are contributing to a collective play script or novel. A MOO is an electronic remediation of the printed novel, with its mixture of narrative and descriptive passages, and a chat room is the remediation of a play script, in which dialogue among the characters provides almost all of the text. The claim that these remediations make to heightened authenticity of experience is that they are collective and spontaneous. Each participant contributes the dialogue and third-person narrative for her character, as this extract from an online "wedding," the collective writing of three participants (Tarniwoof, Achilles, and Winterlight), indicates:

> Tarniwoof says, "At the engagement ceremony you gave one another an item which represents your love, respect and friendship for each other."
>
> Tarniwoof turns to you.
>
> Tarniwoof says, "Achilles, do you have any reason to give your item back to Winterlight?"
>
> Winterlight attends your answer nervously.
>
> You would not give up her gift for anything.
>
> Tarniwoof smiles happily at you.
>
> Winterlight smiles at you (Turkle, 1995, p. 195).

Like the traditional 19th- or 20th-century novel, the MOO is about the definition and maturation of character. On the other hand, the MOO magnifies the polyvocality of the printed novel. In reading a traditional novel by a single author, we know that all the characters really speak with one authorial voice, no matter how that voice may be modulated and disguised. When we join a MOO, however, we know that the polyvocality, and sometimes the cacophony, is real. Moreover, each participant in a MOO may choose to change her identity, by assuming a different name and providing a different description. Each networked user may also belong to several MOOs and chatrooms and have different identities in each. In the age of print, we have construed writing as a process of assuming multiple, somewhat different voices—one for personal letters, one for business communications, one for scholarly publications, and so on. Networked environments magnify the opportunities for identity assumption and at the same time greatly diminish the obstacles and the potential dangers of assuming false and conflicting identities. In a textual environment such as a MOO, no one can verify a participant's age or gender. In particular, women often assume male identities and the reverse (Bruckman, 1999). The combination of network connections, which allows participants to communicate in "real time," and the textual mode of communication have given our culture a perfect artifact with which to ring changes on the construction of postmodern identity. As Sherry Turkle (1995) puts it: "Internet experiences help us to develop models of psychological well-being that are in a meaningful sense postmodern: They admit multiplicity and flexibility. They acknowledge the constructed nature of reality, self, and other ... " (p. 263). Visual digital technologies, including visual MOOs, offer further and somewhat different opportunities for the construction of postmodern identity. Various applications for virtual or augmented reality also allow their users to explore multiple identities through interactive, point-of-view graphics (Bolter & Grusin, 1999, pp. 258–265).

In one sense a MOO is structured like a traditional hypertext with its predetermined nodes and links: the rooms of the MOO constitute the nodes that participants visit, and the doors or passageways between rooms constitute the links. Within each room, however, the dialogue is neither predetermined nor under the control of a single author, so that the MOO remediates the printed novel in a way different from the classic hypertexts by Michael Joyce and others. Nevertheless, the MOO remains hypertextual in its claims of flexibility and indeterminacy. Like the global hypertext of the World Wide Web, a MOO is laid down over the network that is the Internet, and communications links among the participants become the links of the MOO as hypertext. A MOO seeks to fulfill the promise of what Michael Joyce called "constructive hypertext," (Joyce, 1995, pp. 39–59), and in its remediation of the novel, the MOO offers participants a site for defining a networked self or indeed a whole series of networked selves.

THE MATERIALITY OF THE ELECTRONIC SELF

Whether they would call themselves postmodern or not, contemporary theorists have been unanimous in their rejection of the Cartesian division of mind and body. The assault on the mind–body dichotomy has been central to feminist theory as well. In *How We Became Posthuman* (1999), N. Katherine Hayles notes how theorists earlier in the 20th century had already denied the Cartesian dichotomy—Bourdieu, for example, with his notion of embodied knowledge, which:

> .... turn[s] Descartes upside down. The central premise is not that the cogitating mind can be certain only of its ability to be present to itself but rather that the body exists in space and time and that, through its interaction with the environment, it defines the parameters within which the cogitating mind can arrive at certainties.

Hayles shows how embodied philosophies such as Bourdieu's can be used to critique information technologies. As early as the 1950s, Claude Shannon, Norbert Weiner, and others had defined communication as the transfer of disembodied information (Hayles, 1999, pp. 50–83). In other words, they extended the Cartesian paradigm to the new field of cybernetics, just as Turing and the artificial intelligence movement were working within the same paradigm to define human intelligence as a program. The notion, Cartesian in spirit, that electronic technology can free human discourse and even human interaction from the body has continued into the late age of print. It is a theme that emerged repeatedly in cyberpunk science fiction, beginning with William Gibson's *Neuromancer* (1984), in which hackers express disdain for the "meat" of the human body in the real world and prefer to live in the networked environment of cyberspace. The theme of freedom from the body and from the constraints of society and culture in the embodied world also appears among enthusiasts for cyberspace, such as John Perry Barlow. In his "Declaration of Independence for Cyberspace," Barlow defined cyberspace as the home of "Mind," in which individuals are freed of the bodily markers—for example of gender and race—that characterize social order in the world of "flesh and steel" (www.eff.org/pub/Publications/John_Perry_Barlow/barlow_0296.declaration September 24, 1999). This popular but naive view has had its critics, such as Aluquere Rosanne Stone (1991), Lisa Nakamura (1999), and Beth Kolko (1998), who have argued that cultural and social constraints are indeed carried over into electronic environments. As early as 1991, Stone wrote that:

> ... (c)yberspace developers foresee a time when they will be able to forget about the body ... Forgetting about the body is an old Cartesian trick, one that has unpleasant consequences for those bodies whose speech is silenced by our act of forgetting; that is to say, those upon whose labor the act of forgetting the body is founded—usually women and minorities (p 113).

These critical voices have insisted on the relationship of the self, the body, and the cultural contexts in which we operate as embodied creatures. For them, there is an indissoluble connection between the human material condition and all cultural practices, which are inevitably grounded in the material world. Writing even in electronic environments remains a material practice (=> p. 17). Although some cyberenthusiasts have sought to re‑move electronic communication from the constraints of material culture, the critical voices of Hayles, Stone, and many others have come to domi‑nate the debate in the academic world. By insisting on the materiality of electronic writing, they have issued yet another challenge to the Cartesian paradigm. Our culture in the late age of print seems inclined to accept the materiality of writing not in spite of, but because of, our increasing use of electronic networked communication.

It becomes hard to imagine how the Cartesian paradigm could survive in a era of networked communication. Descartes asserted that he could guar‑antee his identity and agency separate from the vicissitudes of the world of the senses, and he grounded his assertion on a claim of authorship: that his thoughts constituted a text that belonged exclusively to him as their author. In making this claim, he was tacitly relying on a distinction of private and public writing that had grown up in Western European culture in the centu‑ries following the invention of the print press (Eisenstein, 1979, 230ff). There seemed to be an enormous and certain difference between printed publication (books, pamphlets, handbills) and private writing (notebooks, letters, etc.). Today in constructing electronic writing, our culture has cho‑sen to blur the distinction between the public and the private. Newsgroups, chat rooms, or MOOs are forms of electronic writing that often seem to be private, but are in fact broadcast instantly to hundreds or thousands of other, possibly anonymous readers. An electronic writer is seldom alone with her thoughts. She joins easily and repeatedly with others in the writing of an electronic dialogue—and breaks off just as easily. It is no coincidence that the participant in a MOO or a chat room assumes multiple identities in a thoroughly unCartesian way. Because the private and the public, the in‑ner self and the outer persona, are so closely connected, the writer is never isolated from the material and cultural matrix of her networked culture.

10

Writing Culture

THE NETWORK CULTURE

Just as we can claim to write our minds, we can also claim to write the culture in which we live. And just as we have used print technology in the past, so we are now turning to electronic technologies of writing to define our cultural relationships both metaphorically and operationally. If, as Sherry Turkle (1995) and others have argued, electronic communication corresponds to a postmodern sense of self, it may also correspond to a postmodern definition of affiliation and community. We exploit the World Wide Web, e-mail, and chat rooms to facilitate a culture of temporary allegiances and changing cultural positions—to fashion our "network culture." The Internet and particularly the Web become for us a metaphor for the ways in which we function in our various communities by sending out dozens of links to sites of interest or contestation. We compile hot lists or bookmarks that indicate which groups we choose to belong to at any given moment, and we can erase these lists as easily as we create them.

It is a truism that American culture encourages individualism and therefore breaks with the European traditions of many of its immigrants. In the 1980s, before the explosion of interest in the Internet, the authors of *Habits of the Heart* saw contemporary, though not perhaps postmodern, individualism as the culmination of this historical process:

[T]he colonists [to America] brought with them ideas of social obligation and group formation that disposed them to recreate in America structures of family, church, and polity that could continue ... the texture of older European society. Only gradually did it become clear that every social obligation was vulnerable, every tie between individuals fragile. Only gradually did what we have called ontological individualism, the idea that the individual is

203

the only firm reality, become widespread (Bellah, Madsen, Sullivan, Sundler, & Tipton, 1985, p. 276).

But if individuals become indeed "the only firm reality," this does not mean that American individuals would no longer form groups. Americans may well form more groups than ever, because they feel so much freer to associate and break off their associations as they please. Individuals now regularly join and quit jobs, neighborhoods, clubs, political parties and action committees, and even churches several times in their lives. These affiliations are all seen as voluntary, and they are usually horizontal rather than vertical. The network is displacing the hierarchy. The culture of interconnections both reflects and is reflected in our new technology of writing, so that, with all these transitions, the making and breaking of social links, people are beginning to function as elements in a hypertextual network of affiliations.

Electronic communication is increasingly the medium through which we form and maintain our affiliations. E-mail, chat rooms, and the World Wide Web have become sites for highly mediated versions of community. These new technologies join earlier ones that have promoted visions and versions of community: television, radio, and film as well as print. However, if our culture has chosen to exploit these earlier technologies largely for their ability to unify and homogenize cultural difference, we seem today to prefer to deploy electronic technologies in other ways, as interactive applications that allow individuals to talk back and talk to each other.

There is nothing inevitable about the construction of our network culture. We could have chosen to exploit computers to reinforce traditional notions of community—perhaps by strengthening communication channels for existing institutional structures. What we have come to valorize in electronic communication, however, is largely the capacity to promote multiplicity, heterogeneity, and immediate, if temporary, connections. The popular writer Fred Rheingold argued in *Virtual Community* (1994) that news groups and bulletin boards could both reconstitute local communities and forge new groups from those who share common interests but are separated in space. He pointed to thousands or millions of users who have shared the vision of the virtual community since the prototype of such a community, the WELL, was formed in the San Francisco Bay area in the 1980s:

> People in virtual communities use words on screens to exchange pleasantries and argue, engage in intellectual discourse, conduct commerce, exchange knowledge, share emotional support, make plans, brainstorm, gossip, feud, fall in love, find friends and lose them ... To the millions who have been drawn into it, the richness and vitality of computer-linked cultures is attrac-

tive, even addictive. There is no such thing as a single, monolithic, online subculture; it's more like an ecosystem of subcultures, some frivolous, some serious (p. 3).

Clearly what Rheingold values is the diversity that finds expression in these virtual environments, a diversity that is for him ultimately liberating on a political as well as personal level:

> The technology that makes virtual communities possible has the potential to bring enormous leverage to ordinary citizens at relatively little cost—intellectual leverage, social leverage, commercial leverage, and most important political leverage. But the technology will not in itself fulfill that potential; this latent technical power must be used intelligently and deliberately by an informed population. More people must learn about that leverage and learn to use it, while we still have the freedom to do so, if it is to live up to its potential (pp. 4–5).

For those, like Rheingold, who see the Internet and Web as enabling new forms of community or democratic empowerment, there remains the key problem that the technology is not universally available. Although it is called the "World Wide Web," this global hypertext system is largely limited to North America, Europe, Israel, and the developed countries of the Far East. As it continues to expand, the Web will likely remain limited to the middle and upper classes in the third world as elsewhere, so that the virtual communities that the Web and Internet mediate will remain exclusive as well. To say that these virtual communities will be exclusive, however, is not to say that they will be elite in the traditional sense. In developed countries, millions of users find on the Web expressions of their popular culture (from fan sites for film stars or country music divas to sites on weight loss or astrology) as well as their commodity culture (in online marketing and sales sites offering everything from books and CD-ROM to fine wines or used cars). Traditional high culture is also represented, but has no special claim to the user's attention.

CULTURAL UNITY

One consequence of this networking of culture is in fact the abandonment of the ideal of high culture (literature, music, the fine arts) as a unifying force. If there is no single culture, but only a network of interest groups, then there can be no single favored literature or music. Nor is there a single standard of grammar or diction in writing. Elizabeth Eisenstein (1979) has argued that printing was used to promote cultural unification during the centuries when the modern nation states were being formed. "Typography arrested linguistic drift, enriched as well as standardized vernaculars, and paved the way for the more deliberate purification and codification of all major European languages" (vol. 1, p. 117). Today we are exploiting electronic writing to oppose standardization and unification as well as hierarchy. The World Wide Web is a famously chaotic distributed system, in which individuals or their organizations are free to create new pages and sites and to add them to the global hypertext without the approval or even the knowledge of any central authority. The Web offers as a paradigm a writing system that changes to suit its audiences of reader–writers rather than expecting that that audience to conform to some predetermined authority or standard.

As we rewrite our culture into a vast hypertext, each of us as readers becomes free to choose to explore one subnetwork or as many as she wishes. It is no longer convincing to say that one subject is more important than another. Today even highly educated readers, humanists as well as scientists and social scientists, may know only one or a few areas well. Such ignorance of any shared textual tradition is in part the result of the specialization of the sciences that has been proceeding since the 17th century. But even the humanities are now utterly fragmented, so that a student of postcolonial literature may know very little about Renaissance poetry or ancient epic. The Web itself with its millions of pages is far too large and disorganized for any individual to encompass it, and the Web is still small in comparison with the verbal and visual information stored in a large research library, where the materials are much better organized but vastly beyond the scale of an individual reader.

Through the last decades there has remained some uneasiness about this situation: hence the traditionalist's plea for a canon of great authors, his call somehow to reestablish a core of textual knowledge that everyone must possess. But the specialization in the sciences and the humanities and social sciences has gone far too far to be recalled. The academic world, like the rest of our culture, is now defined by its numerous "special interest groups." Although all the groups are interconnected—some grew out of others, and each sends out runners (links) into other camps—nevertheless, an over-arching unification is no longer even the goal. In *After Virtue*, published in 1981, just prior to the advent of electronic writing, Alasdair MacIntyre was already complaining about the fragmented state of moral philosophy and drew the following analogy (MacIntyre, 1981). Imagine an environmental catastrophe that causes human society to turn against modern science. Scientists are persecuted, and science texts are torn up or destroyed. Then imagine a later generation trying to reassemble these fragments ("half-chapters from books, single pages from articles, not always fully legible because torn and charred") into a single system. The result would be a mish-mash of incoherent theories and misunderstood facts. Of course, this disaster has not happened to modern science, but it is, according to MacIntyre, exactly what happened to the great systems of moral philosophy (pp. 2–3). For MacIntyre, the disaster was the Enlightenment. MacIntyre's analogy can be extended beyond moral philosophy to almost all humanistic fields today: each is an incomplete and disorganized hypertext that no one knows how to read in its entirety.

To call this fragmentation a disaster, however, is to assume that unity is an achievable and desirable goal. In fact, the fragmentation of our textual world is only a problem when judged by the standards of print technology, which expects the humanities, including metaphysics and ethics, to be relatively stable and hierarchically organized. Postmodern culture values instead the heterogeneity and spontaneity of shifting positions—the ability to form small groups that fit local circumstances (= > p. 167). Ironically, the global hypertext of the World Wide Web affords small groups just such an opportunity: groups with interests in dead languages, in local or national political problems, in any imaginable disease can each have Web sites. The tiniest political organization or interest group can afford to purchase space on a Web server somewhere in the world and to make that space available to its members. Hypertextual publication can and does accommodate all the mutually incomprehensible languages that the academic and political worlds now speak. Within the hypertextual libraries that are now being assembled, individual communities can retreat into their subnetworks and operate with as much or as little connection to each other as they desire.

On the World Wide Web, as elsewhere, the distinction between high culture and popular culture has all but vanished. If one click of the mouse will take a Web surfer to Project Gutenberg, a textual repository of the "classics" (www.gutenberg.net September 6, 1999), another click will take her to sites for current Hollywood movies or popular music on CD or to ostensibly marginal sites for body art or homeopathy. The ease and equality of access to all the various forms of cultural representation (including pornography) appall traditionalists, who want to see a hierarchy that reinforces the distinction between respectable literature and forbidden images. On the Web, however, none of the familiar indications of quality apply. A site on body piercing may be far better designed than the ASCII format of Shakespeare's plays available through Project Gutenberg. An unwillingness to distinguish between high art and popular entertainment has long been a feature of American culture, and we have chosen to confirm and accelerate this trend in the Web and other new media forms.

THE REMEDIATION OF CULTURE

Electronic forms of communication give us the opportunity to redefine cultural ideals inherited from printed genres and forms. We have been discussing one such redefinition: the breakdown of the distinction between elite and popular literature (and art in general). This breakdown was not determined or predetermined by our shift to electronic communications. It is rather that our network culture, which rejects such hierarchical distinctions, finds in the Internet and the Web media that it can shape to express its preference for popular forms. More generally, our network culture is construing new media as radical forces that disrupt the traditions of print.

For hundreds of years, we had associated with print an ideal of stability: print was supposed to preserve and promote a stable, authoritative, and yet vital literate culture, in which tradition and innovation were in balance and in which verbal representations were of a higher order than visual. This is the ideal espoused in the late age of print by cultural traditionalists or political conservatives from Sven Birkerts (1994) and Mark Slouka (1995) to William Bennett (1984). Just as there are many cultural constructions for electronic writing, however, there have also been many constructions for print. At various historical moments, print technology could in fact have been used to radicalize culture. The most obvious example would be the publication of printed tracts by Reformation theologians and polemicists (Eisenstein, 1979, pp. 303–450). Historian Carla Hesse (1996) has explored another historical moment, pointing out that Condorcet and other Enlightenment thinkers also saw printed newspapers and periodicals as instruments of revolution:

> The best way to spread knowledge, according to Condorcet, was through authorless and open-ended texts, circulating freely between all citizens: he imagined the periodical press supported through the mechanism of subscription rather than through the institution of royalties to authors or monopolies to publishers. Indeed, what Condorcet conceived of as an ideally transparent

mode of exchange through the deregulation of print publishing looks a lot like a mechanical version of the Internet (p. 24).

Although in the past print could be construed as radical, this is not its role today, according to either the critics of or the enthusiasts for electronic writing. In the late age of print, electronic technology defines itself as remediation, and print technology defines itself as resisting that remediation. Some enthusiasts for electronic writing still believe that it can radicalize our culture by providing that transparency that Condorcet ascribed to print publication. For these enthusiasts, the goal of perfect or authentic communication has not changed; they are simply pursuing the goal with new technological means. For them, electronic writing in chat rooms or by e-mail is more diverse and democratic, because unlike print, electronic writing can be published without the intervention of authorities (publishers and editors) who will decide on its commercial or intellectual value and therefore enforce cultural norms and biases. The traditionalists, too, still believe in authentic communication, but authenticity for them is defined differently. They favor their construction of print, with its traditions, its hierarchies, and its unidirectional form of communication. For them the authenticity of print derives from the privileged nature of the dialogue it fosters—a dialogue in which the author is necessarily dominant. As Laura Miller put it, in terms almost of sexual domination, readers in print crave "the intimacy to be had in allowing a beloved author's voice into the sanctums of our minds" (NY Times, 1998, p. 43) (= > p. 44). For Miller this "intimacy" is what constitutes an authentic reading experience.

To what extent do the technologies determine these different qualities that our culture is assigning (= > p. 19)? It seems clear that communication on the Internet could have evolved differently. Instead of diversity and distribution, communications systems on the Internet could have been designed to emphasize uniformity and central control. Computer systems after all can easily produce identical copies of data and establish and monitor the hierarchical control of information. In the 1980s, however, the Internet matured through the efforts of dedicated computer specialists, mostly graduate students and faculty in universities. They constructed a technology that was congenial to their culture, in which individual autonomy was highly prized. That the World Wide Web grew out of that same culture explains its distributed architecture, lack of security, and use of the hypertext model of associative linking. We can easily imagine a World Wide Web protocol in which all sites had to be registered and validated by a central authority, but that protocol would have contradicted the ethos of the Internet community at the time. By the time the Web had become a cultural phenomenon and attracted the attention of the corporate and government bureaucracies, it was too late to change its architecture radically. Control issues continue to the raised: for example, the questions of censoring pornography on the Web and of protecting intellectual property (or the economic interests of the entertainment industry). These questions are often met with the answer that the technology itself will defeat almost any method of censorship and that any means of protecting intellectual property must be evaluated in terms of what the technology, as constructed, will permit. The hierarchies of previous information technologies do not seem to be easily grafted onto the network technologies of today.

Theorists in the humanities and social sciences would, however, argue that hierarchies based on gender, race, and economic advantage remain strong in our culture. The late age of print is like late capitalism in this respect. It is a well-known irony that global capitalism is flourishing at the very time when it is being condemned by theorists to senescence. Similarly, in the late age of print, books and other printed materials are more abundant than ever: laser printers and copying machines are largely responsible. Once again, the term "late" does not mean that print technology is necessarily about to disappear: it may continue to survive and even prosper for an undetermined future. The term refers instead to the relationship of print technology to our literate culture. The printed book is no longer the only or necessarily the most important space in which we locate our texts and images. For all our communicative purposes, print is now measured over against digital technology, and the ideal of perfect communication that our culture associated with print is under constant challenge.

That ideal is deeply ingrained, however, and may not be easily overturned. The recent history of intellectual property shows us how tenacious the standard can be. The modern legal concepts of intellectual property and the ownership of ideas and their expression grew up in the 18th century and have developed since that time in the context of print technology (see Woodmansee & Jaszi, 1994). Many of these concepts fit comfortably into our current world of print, but do not seem to make sense for new media forms. In print, the words and images are determined once and for all in the process of publication, so that the expression of an idea fixed in words and images can be copyrighted. In the electronic writing space, as we have seen, words and images are not necessarily fixed; instead, they are called forth through the interaction of the author(s), the computer system, and the readers. Electronic documents can also be copied and altered with remarkable ease. On the World Wide Web, for example, every time a reader visits a page, she is in fact making a copy of that page, with all its images, in her computer. Although she cannot modify the page at its source (on the server), she can always save and even revise the version that she has captured on her machine.

If technologies really determined cultural values, then the notion of copyright would already have been severely curtailed, if not abolished, at least for electronic publication. Hypertext certainly seems to suggest a different economic and social model (e.g., Samuelson & Glushko, 1991). And it could be argued that popular notions of intellectual property are in fact changing: people use copying machines, VCRs, and computer storage to make the copies that they require without much concern for legal propriety. Nevertheless, powerful economic forces (of late capitalism) are seeking to extend the notion of ownership of verbal and especially audiovisual materials throughout the realm of electronic media. They are seeking to set even stricter limits on the rights of readers and viewers to make fair use of copyrighted materials (Samuelson, 1997). Tyanna Herrington sees an ideological struggle around the question of intellectual property—a struggle between those who want to use electronic technologies to distribute information and entertainment for what they see as social benefit and those who want to insure economic gain for the (corporate) owners of information and entertainment. Rather than acknowledging that the notion of intellectual property is socially constructed, economic interests, with the help of the government, are insisting that electronic text, graphics, audio, and video are all property in a strict sense, sanctioned by a long legal tradition (see Herrington, forthcoming). Instead of withering in the electronic age, the notion of intellectual property seems to be strengthening and extending itself into new domains.

Our late age of print is characterized by such struggles, as economically dominant groups and forces attempt to define the new technology to their advantage, usually by extending definitions appropriate to earlier technologies that they already dominate. Notions of intellectual property are extrapolated from those appropriate to print and the music and film industries. Entertainment giants have been trying to "converge" new media around the model of commercial, broadcast television. Electronic commerce on the Internet has focused on re-establishing familiar genres and services: newspapers and magazines, bookstores, auctions, pornography, and so on. On the other hand, other constructions of new media are working subtly against the extension of older models of economic and cultural control. Our culture continues to find in these new forms, particularly in the Internet and on the World Wide Web, qualities of decentralization, local autonomy, and flexibility. It is for this reason that politicians from across the spectrum, at least in the United States, speak of the democratic and educational potential of the Internet: they are simply developing a rhetoric to which their constituents respond.

Thus, the reforming or remediating potential of the new writing space has probably not been exhausted. It would be foolish to doubt the power that entrenched hierarchies will bring to bear in forcing new media technologies into traditional formal, legal, and economic structures. Nevertheless, it seems likely that these traditional structures will be changed even as they attempt to assimilate new media. For example, those in the television and computer industry who are trying to promote Web television must find something to distinguish their product from pure broadcast television. So they are envisioning ways in which the Web could serve as an information resource for traditional television programs. They imagine a viewer watching a sporting event on television, having a question, and then using her browser to access a database of sports information while the television broadcast proceeds. As unimaginative as this scenario is, it nevertheless defines a changed relationship between the viewer and the viewing space. It presents an opening for the viewer to intervene in the flow of traditional television and suggests, however timidly, a myriad of other possibilities, other ways to arrange the act of communication.

It seems likely that our heterogeneous culture will choose to explore many of these possibilities—revised relationships between the media that we have known and the new media in which we are rediscovering the familiar. The future of text as a remediator of culture is uncertain, even if text (as hypertext) continues to serve a variety of functions in cyberspace. Textual forms such as e-mail, chat facilities, and even MOOs remain popular precisely because of their role in defining electronic community. Teachers and scholars continue to promote these electronic textual forms as refashioners of the traditional sense of community that was (and is) mediated by face-to-face meetings and conventional mail. E-mail and chat facilities still provide most users with their best means of "talking back" in cyberspace. Although millions of World Wide Web participants now have the skills and opportunity to create their own Web sites combining graphics and text, a far larger number of the hundreds of millions of Internet users can still only be consumers of Web sites and other multimedia forms. That far larger number, however, can be producers as well as consumers of verbal e-mail. In other words, multimedia remains a somewhat privileged mode of communication within the already privileged world of the Internet.

This situation may change. Even for users at home, it is becoming easier to generate as well as receive multimedia. When most users gain fast access to the Internet and have the software and hardware needed for audiovisual communication, will they continue to type e-mail messages? Will they not seek to recapture the immediacy of phone and face-to-face conversation through real-time, video and audio conferencing over the Internet? Will they not look to other audiovisual media (television, film, and radio) as defining the authenticity of communication that they wish to capture and refashion in new media? Will written verbal communication come to be regarded as an ancillary form, to be used when microphones or cameras fail or when the Internet connection is degraded?

It is fair to wonder whether the late age of print may also become the late age of prose itself.

11

The Web Site

The first edition of this book was accompanied by a hypertext version on a diskette. It was a stand-alone hypertext that used links to attempt to define a shadow text—a text that confirmed, elaborated on, and sometimes reversed the printed version. The second edition has an associated Web site instead: (www.lcc.gatech.edu/~bolter/writingspace/). It has become a fairly common practice to accompany a printed book with a Web site, often to provide ancillary material that the book omitted due to limitations of space or the limitations of the printed medium itself. A Web site can also contain multimedia features, such as digitized audio and video, that the book cannot. As a respectful remediation, the Web site for *Writing Space* does not seek to render the printed version unnecessary. Much of the text is not included in the site. It is rare for a site to include more than a fraction of the text, perhaps one chapter, for fear that readers may choose not to buy the book if they can read the text online. That fear is probably unjustified, because at present most readers prefer reading extended texts on paper rather than at a desktop computer. Perhaps the main reason for having a Web site is simply to extend the reach of the text, to establish a colony in the new territory of cyberspace. There is a feeling among publishers and authors, as among so many others in the industrialized world, that it is important to have a presence in this new writing space.

If the hypertext diskette for the first edition was meant to provide a shadow text, a metaphoric replacement of the printed text, the Web site is instead an extension, and a remediation, of the printed text, containing additional information, corrections, and improvements. It also remediates the printed text by making a modest claim to interactivity, in the sense that visitors to the site can register comments and criticisms, which will be recorded and made available to subsequent visitors. Although the visitors cannot intervene directly in the text, they will be able to affect the reading and interpretation of both the Web and to some extent the printed text by others.

REFERENCES

Aarseth, E. (1997). *Cybertext: Perspectives on ergodic literature.* Baltimore, MA: Johns Hopkins University Press.

Abrams, M. H. (1953). *The mirror and the lamp: Romantic theory and the critical tradition.* New York: Oxford University Press.

Alberti, L. B. (1972). *On painting and on sculpture: The Latin texts of de pictura and de statua* (C. Grayson, Trans.). London: Phaidon.

Alexander, J. J. G. (1978). *The decorated letter.* New York: G. Braziller.

Bacon, F. (1955). Advancement of learning. In H. G. Dick (Ed.), *Selected writings of Francis Bacon* (pp. 157–392). New York: Random House.

Baker, G. P., & Hacker, P. M. S. (1980). *Wittgenstein: Understanding and meaning.* Chicago: University of Chicago Press.

Balestri, D. P. (1988). Softcopy and hard: Wordprocessing and writing process. *Academic Computing, 2*(5), 14–17, 41–45.

Barnes, S. B. (1997). Douglas Carl Engelbart: Developing the underlying concepts for contemporary computing. *IEEE Annals of the History of Computing 19*(3), 16–26.

Barth, J. (1967). The literature of exhaustion. *The Atlantic, 220*(2), 29–34.

Barthes, R. (1974). *S/Z* (Richard Miller, Trans.). New York: Hill & Wang.

Barthes, R. (1979). From work to text. In J. V. Harari (Ed.), *Textual strategies: Perspectives in post-structuralist criticism* (pp. 73–81). Ithaca, NY: Cornell University Press.

Barthes, R. (1981). *Camera lucida: Reflections on photography* (R. Howard, Trans.). New York: Hill & Wang.

Beach, R., & Lundell, D. (1998). Early adolescents' use of computer-mediated communication in writing and reading. In D. Reinking, M. C. McKenna, L. D. Labbo, & R. D. Kieffer (Eds.), *Handbook of literacy and technology: Transformations in a post-typographic world* (pp. 93–112). Mahwah, NJ: Lawrence Erlbaum Associates.

Bellah, R. N., Madsen, R., Sullivan, W. M., Swidler, A., & Tipton, S. M. (1985). *Habits of the heart: Individualism and commitment in American life.* Berkeley: University of California Press.

Beniger, J. R. (1986). *The control revolution: Technological and economic origins of the information society.* Cambridge, MA: Harvard University Press.

Bennett, W. J. (1984). *To reclaim a legacy: A report on the humanities in higher education.* Washington, DC: National Endowment for the Humanities.

Bernstein, M. (1998). Patterns of hypertext. *Hypertext '98 Proceedings* (pp. 21–29). New York: ACM.

215

216   **REFERENCES**

Birkerts, S. (1994). *The Gutenberg elegies: The fate of reading in an electronic age*. Boston: Faber and Faber.
Bloom, H. (1973). *The anxiety of influence: A theory of poetry*. New York: Oxford University Press.
Bolter, J. D. (1991, Spring). The shapes of WOE. *Writing on the Edge 3*, 90–91.
Bolter, J. D., & Grusin, R. (1999). *Remediation: Understanding new media*. Cambridge, MA: MIT Press.
Bolter, J. D., Joyce, M., & Smith, J. B. (1990). *Storyspace* [Computer software]. Watertown, MA: Eastgate Systems.
Borges, J. L. (1962). *Ficciones* (A. Kerrigan, Ed.). New York: Grove Press.
Brooks, P. (1984). *Reading for the plot: Design and intention in narrative*. New York: Knopf.
Bruckman, A. S. (1999). Gender swapping on the Internet. In Victor Vitanza (Ed.), *Cyberreader*, 2nd ed. (pp. 418–424). Needham Heights, MA: Allyn and Bacon.
Bush, V. (1945). As we may think. *Atlantic Monthly, 176* (1), 101–108.
Bush, V. (1999). As we may think. In P. Mayer (Ed.), *Computer media and communication: A reader* (pp. 23–36). Oxford: Oxford University Press.
Chartier, R. (1994). *The order of books: Readers, authors, and libraries in Europe between the fourteenth and eighteenth centuries* (L. G. Cochrane, Trans.). Stanford: Stanford University Press.
Chartier, R. (1995). *Forms and meanings: Texts, performances, and audiences from codex to computer*. Philadelphia: University of Pennsylvania Press.
Châtillon, J. (1966). Le 'Didascalion' de Hugues de Saint-Victor. *Journal of World History, 9*, 539–552.
Conklin, J. (1987). Hypertext: An introduction and survey. *IEEE Computer, 20*(9), 17–41.
Coover, R. (1992, June 21). The end of books. *New York Times Book Review*, pp. 1, 11, 24–25.
Coover, R. (1993a, August 29). And hypertext is only the beginning. Watch out! *New York Times Book Review*, pp. 1, 8–10.
Coover, R. (1993b, August 29). Hyperfiction: Novels for the computer. *New York Times Book Review*, pp. 1, 8–10.
Culler, J. (1981). *The pursuit of signs: Semiotics, literature, deconstruction*. Ithaca, NY: Cornell University Press.
Curtius, E. R. (1973). *European literature and the Latin Middle Ages* (W. R. Trask, Trans.). Princeton, NY: Princeton University Press.
D'Alembert, J. (1963). *Preliminary discourse to the Encyclopedia of Diderot* (R. N. Schwab, Trans.). Indianapolis, IN: Bobbs-Merrill.
Davies, W. V. (1987). *Egyptian hieroglyphs*. Berkeley: University of California Press.
Deleuze, G., & Guattari, F. (1987). *A thousand plateaus: Capitalism and schizophrenia* (B. Massumi, Trans.). Minneapolis: University of Minnesota Press.
Derrida, J. (1974). *Glas*. Paris: Éditions Galilée.
Derrida, J. (1976a). *Glas* (J. P. Leavey, Jr., & R. Rand, Trans.). Lincoln, NE: University of Nebraska Press.
Derrida, J. (1976b). *Of grammatology*. Baltimore: Johns Hopkins University Press. (Original work published in French in 1967)
Derrida, J. (1979). Living on. In J. Hulbart (Ed.), *Deconstruction and criticism: A continuum book* (pp. 75–176). New York: Seabury Press.
Descartes, R. (1960). *Meditations on first philosophy* (L. J. Lafleur, Trans.). Indianapolis, IN: Bobbs-Merrill.
Dickey, W. (1991). Poem descending a staircase: hypertext and the simultaneity of experience. In P. Delany, P. Landow, & G. P. Landow (Eds.), *Hypermedia and literary studies* (pp. 143–152). Cambridge, MA: MIT Press.

Douglas, J. Y. (1988) *Beyond orality and literacy: Toward articulating a paradigm for the electronic age.* Unpublished manuscript.

Douglas, J. Y. (1991, Spring). Understanding the act of reading: The WOE beginner's guide to dissection. *Writing on the Edge 2*(2), 112–125.

Douglas, J. Y. (1994). *I have said nothing* [Computer software] Watertown, MA: Eastgate Systems.

Douglas, J. Y. (2000). *The end of books—or books without end?: Reading interactive narratives.* Ann Arbor: University of Michigan Press.

Drucker, J. (1994). *The visible word: Experimental typography and modern art, 1909–1923.* Chicago: University of Chicago Press.

Drucker, J. (1995). *The century of art books.* New York: Granary Books.

Duguid, P. (1996). Material matters: The past and futurology of the book. In G. Nunberg (Ed.), *The future of the book* (pp. 63–101). Berkeley: University of California Press.

Eco, U. (1976). *A theory of semiotics.* Bloomington: Indiana University Press.

Eisenstein, E. (1979). *The printing press as an agent of change: Communications and cultural transformations in early-modern Europe (Vols. 1–2).* Cambridge: Cambridge University Press.

Eisenstein, E. (1983). *The printing revolution in early-modern Europe.* Cambridge: Cambridge University Press.

Encyclopaedia Britannica. (1974–1987). (P. W Goetz, Ed.). Chicago: Encyclopaedia Britannica.

Encyclopaedia Metropolitana (Vol. 1). (1849). (E. Smedley, H. J. Rose, & H. J. Rose, Eds.). London: John Joseph Griffin & Co.

Febvre, L., & Martin, H. (1971). *L'apparition du livre* [The coming of the book]. Paris: Editions Albin Michel.

Finnegan, R. (1977). *Oral poetry: Its nature significance, and social context.* Cambridge: Cambridge University Press.

Fish, S. E. (1980). Literature in the reader: Affective stylistics. In J. P. Tompkins (Ed.), *Reader-response criticism: From formalism to post-structuralism* (pp. 70–100). Baltimore, MD: Johns Hopkins University Press.

Foucault, M. (1977). What is an author? In *Language, counter-memory, practice: Selected essays and interviews* (pp. 113–138). (D. F. Bouchard & S. Simon, Trans.). Ithaca, NY: Cornell University.

Foucault, M. (1989). *This is not a pipe* (J. Harkness, Trans.). Berkeley: University of California Press.

Fox, E. A., & Marchionini, G. (Eds.). (1998, April). Digital libraries, global space, unlimited access. *Communications of the ACM 41* (4). [special issue on digital libraries]

Frank, J. (1963). *The widening gyre: Crisis and mastery in modern literature.* New Brunswick, NJ: Rutgers University Press.

Frank, J. (1981). Spatial form: Thirty years after. In J. R. Smitten & A. Daghistany (Eds.), *Spatial form in narrative* (pp. 202–243). Ithaca, NY: Cornell University Press.

Furuta, R., & Stotts, P. D. (1989). Programmable browsing semantics in Trellis. *Hypertext '89 Proceedings* (pp. 27–42). New York: ACM.

Gaggi, S. (1998). *From text to hypertext: Decentering the subject in fiction, film, the visual arts, and electronic media.* Philadelphia: University of Pennsylvania Press.

Gaur, A. (1984). *A history of writing.* London: The British Library.

Gelb, I. J. (1963). *A study of writing.* Chicago: University of Chicago Press.

Gellrich, J. M. (1985). *The idea of the book in the Middle Ages: Language theory, mythology and fiction.* Ithaca, NY: Cornell University Press.

Gergen, K. J. (1991). *The saturated self: Dilemmas of identity in contemporary life.* New York: Basic Books.

Gibson, W. (1984). *Neuromancer.* London: Gollancz.

Gombrich, E. H. (1982). *The image and the eye: Further studies in the psychology of pictorial representation.* Ithaca, NY: Cornell University Press.

Goody, J. (1977). *The domestication of the savage mind.* Cambridge: Cambridge University Press.

Grant, M. A. (1973). *Michel Butor L'emploit du temps* [Michel Butor: The use of time]. London: Edward Arnold.

Greco, D. (1996). Hypertext and its consequences: Recovering a politics of hypertext *Hypertext '96 Proceedings* (pp. 85–92). New York: ACM.

Groden, M. (1977). *Ulysses in progress.* Princeton, NJ: Princeton University Press.

Grossberg, L., Nelson, C., & Treichler, P. (1992). Cultural studies, an introduction. In *Cultural Studies* (pp. 3–22). New York: Routledge.

Grossman, M. L. (1971). *Dada: Paradox, mystification and ambiguity in European literature.* New York: Bobbs-Merrill.

Grusin, R. (1996). What is an electronic author? Theory and the technological fallacy. In R. Markley (Ed.), *Virtual realities and their discontents* (pp.39–53). Baltimore: Johns Hopkins University Press.

Guyer, C. (1992). *Quibbling.* Watertown, MA: Eastgate Systems.

Haas, C. (1996). *Writing technology: Studies on the materiality of literacy.* Mahwah, NJ: Lawrence Erlbaum Associates.

Hafner, K., & Lyon, M. (1996). *Where wizards stay up late: The origins of the Internet.* New York: Simon & Schuster.

Halasz, F. G. (1989). Reflections on notecards: Seven issues for the next generation of hypermedia systems. In *Hypertext '87 Proceedings* (pp. 345–365). New York: ACM.

Halasz, F. G., Moran, T. P., & Trigg, R. H. (1987). NoteCards in a nutshell. In *Proceedings of ACM CHI+GI'87* (45–52). New York: ACM Press.

Halasz, F. G., & Schwartz, M. (1990). The Dexter hypertext reference model. In J. Moline, D. Benigni, & J. Baronas (Eds.), *Proceedings of the Hypertext Standardization Workshop* (pp. 95–133). Gathersburg MD: National Institute of Standards and Technology.

Haraway, D. (1991). *Simians, cyborgs, and women: The reinvention of nature.* New York: Routledge.

Haraway, D. (1997). *Modest_Witness@SecondMillennium.FemaleMan©MeetsOncoMouse™: Feminism and technoscience.* New York: Routledge.

Harpold, T. (1991a, Spring). The contingencies of the hypertext link. Writing on the Edge 2(2), 126–37.

Harpold, T. (1991b). Threnody: Psychoanalytic digressions on the subject of hypertexts. In P. Delany & G. Landow (Eds.), *Hypermedia and literary studies* (pp. 171–181). Cambridge, MA: MIT Press.

Harpold, T. (forthcoming). *Links and their vicissitudes.* Ann Arbor: University of Michigan Press.

Havelock, E. A. (1982). *The literate revolution in Greece and its cultural consequences.* Princeton, NJ: Princeton University Press.

Hawisher, G. E., Leblanc, P., Moran, C., & Selfe, C. L. (1996). *Computers and the teaching of writing in American higher education, 1979–1994: A history (New Directions in Computers and Composition Studies).* Greenwich, CT: Ablex Publishing.

Hawisher, G. E. & Selfe, C. L. (Eds.). (1999). *Passions, pedagogies, and 21st century technologies.* Logan: Utah State University Press.

Hayles, N. K. (1999). *How we became posthuman: Virtual bodies in cybernetics, literature, and informatics.* Chicago: University of Chicago Press.

Haynes, C., & Holmevik, J. R. (Eds.). (1998). *High wired: On the design, use, and theory of educational MOOs.* Ann Arbor: University of Michigan Press.

Heim, M. (1987). *Electric language: A philosophical study of word processing.* New Haven: Yale University Press.

Herrington, T. K. (forthcoming). *Controlling voices: Dissonance at the intersection of intellectual property, the Internet, and humanistic studies*. Carbondale, IL: Southern Illinois University Press.

Hesse, C. (1996). Books in time. In Geoffrey Nunberg (Ed.), *The future of the book* (pp. 21–36). Berkeley: University of California Press.

Hiltzik, M. (1999). *Dealers of lightning: XEROX PARC and the dawn of the computer age*. New York: HarperCollins.

Hugo, V. (1967). *Notre-Dame de Paris, 1482*. Paris: Garnier.

Iser, Wolfgang. (1980). The reading process: A phenomenological approach. In J. P. Tompkins (Ed.), *Reader-response criticism: From formalism to post-structuralism* (pp. 50–69). Baltimore, MD: Johns Hopkins University Press. (First published in 1974)

Jackson, S. (1995). *Patchwork girl* [Computer program]. Watertown, MA: Eastgate Systems.

Jackson, S. L. (1974). *Libraries and librarianship in the west: A brief history*. New York: McGraw-Hill.

Jameson, F. (1991). *Postmodernism, or, the cultural logic of late capitalism*. Durham, NC: Duke University Press.

Jay, M. (1993). *Downcast eyes: The denigration of vision in twentieth-century French thought*. Berkeley: University of California Press.

Jensen, H. (1969). *Sign, symbol and script: An account of man's effort to write* (George Unwin, Trans.). New York: Putnam.

Johnson, S. (1997). *Interface culture: How new technology transforms the way we create and communicate*. New York: HarperCollins.

Johnson-Eilola, J. (1997). *Nostalgic angels: Rearticulating hypertext writing*. Greenwich, CT: Ablex.

Joyce, J. (1960). *Anna Livia Plurabelle: The making of a chapter* (F. H. Higginson, Ed.). Minneapolis: University of Minnesota Press.

Joyce, M. (1988). Siren shapes: Exploratory and constructive hypertexts. *Academic Computing, 3*(4), 10–14, 37–42.

Joyce, M. (1990). *Afternoon, a story* [Computer program]. Watertown, MA: Eastgate Press. (first published 1987)

Joyce, M. (1991). Woe-or a memory of what will be. Writing on the Edge 2(2) [Computer program].

Joyce, M. (1995). *Of two minds*. Ann Arbor: University of Michigan Press.

Joyce, M. (1996a). *Twilight, a symphony* [Computer program]. Watertown, MA: Eastgate Press.

Joyce, M. (1996b). *Twelve Blue*. Retrieved from the World Wide Web: *www.eastgate.com/TwelveBlue/* [website]

Joyce, M. (1999). *On the birthday of the stranger* [Computer program]. Watertown: Eastgate Systems.

Joyce, M. (2000). *OtherMindedness: The emergence of network culture*. Ann Arbor: University of Michigan Press.

Kaplan, N., & Moulthrop, S. (1994). They became what they beheld: The futility of resistance in the space of electronic writing. In C. Selfe & S. Hilligoss (Eds.), *Literacy and Computers* (pp. 220–237). New York: Modern Language Association.

Kendall, R. (1996a). Hypertextual dynamics in a life set for two. In *Hypertext '96 Proceedings* (pp. 74–84). New York: ACM.

Kendall, R. (1996b). *A life set for two* [Computer program]. Watertown, MA: Eastgate Systems.

Kenner, H. (1962). *Flaubert, Joyce and Beckett: The stoic comedians*. Boston: Beacon Press.

Kenny, A. (1984). *The legacy of Wittgenstein*. Oxford: Basil Blackwell.

Kernan, A., (1990). *The death of literature*. New Haven: Yale University Press.

Kirschenbaum, M. G. (1999). *The other end of print: David Carson, graphic design, and the aesthetics of media*. Paper delivered at Media in Transition conference held Massachusetts Institute of Technology on October 8–9, 1999.

Knowlson, J. (1975). *Universal language schemes in England and France: 1600–1800*. Toronto: University of Toronto Press.

Kolko, B. (1998). Bodies in place: Real politics, real pedagogy, and virtual space. In C. Haynes & J. R. Holmevik (Eds.), *High wired: On the design, use, and theory of educational MOOs* (pp. 253–265). Ann Arbor: University of Michigan Press.

Krieger, M. (1992). *Ekphrasis: The illusion of the natural sign*. Baltimore: Johns Hopkins University Press.

Kurzweil, R. (1999). The future of libraries. In Victor Vitanza (Ed.), *Cyberreader (2nd ed.)* (pp. 291–303). Needham Heights, MA: Allyn & Bacon.

Landow, G. P. (1989). Hypertext in literary education, criticism, and scholarship. *Computers and the Humanities, 23*, 173–198.

Landow, G. P. (1991). The Rhetoric of hypermedia: Some rules for authors. In P. Delany & G. Landow (Eds.), *Hypermedia and literary studies* (pp. 81–103). Cambridge, MA: MIT Press.

Landow, G. P. (1992). *Hypertext: The convergence of contemporary critical theory and technology*. Baltimore, MA: Johns Hopkins University Press.

Landow, G. P. (Ed.). (1994) *Hyper/Text/Theory*. Baltimore, MA: Johns Hopkins University Press.

Landow, G. P. (1997). *Hypertext 2.0: The convergence of contemporary critical theory and technology*. Baltimore, MA: Johns Hopkins University Press.

Lanham, R. (1989). The electronic word: Literary study and the digital revolution. *New Literary History, 20*, 265–290.

Lanham, R. (1991). *A handlist of rhetorical terms*. Berkeley: University of California Press.

Lanham, R. (1993). *The electronic word: Democracy, technology, and the arts*. Chicago: University of Chicago Press.

Larsen, D. (1994). Marble springs [Computer program]. Watertown, MA: Eastgate Systems.

Leggett, J. J., & Schnase, J. L. (1994). Viewing Dexter with open eyes. *Communications of the ACM 37*(2), 76–86.

Lemoine, M. (1966). L'oeuvre encyclopédique de Vincent de Beauvais [The encyclopedic work of Vincent of Beauvais]. *Journal of World History, 9*, 571–579.

Lentz, T. M. (1989). *Orality and Literacy in Hellenic Greece*. Carbondale, IL: Southern Illinois University Press.

Levin, H., & Addis, A. B. (1979). *The eye-voice span*. Cambridge, MA: MIT Press.

Liddell, H. G., & Scott, R. (1973). *A Greek-English Lexicon* (rev. by Sir Henry Stuart Jones). Oxford: Oxford University Press.

Liestol, G. (1996). Kontiki Interactive. [CD-ROM]. Oslo: Gyldendal Norsk Forlag.

Lord, A. B. (1968). *The singer of tales*. New York: Atheneum.

Llull, R. (1985). *Selected works of Ramon Llull (1232–1316) (Vols. 1–2)*. (Anthony Bonner, Ed.). Princeton, NJ: Princeton University Press.

Luesebrink, M. (2000). *Califia* [Computer program]. Watertown, MA: Eastgate Systems.

MacIntyre, A. (1981). *After virtue: A study in moral theory*. Notre Dame, IN: University of Notre Dame Press.

Mallery, G. (1972). *Picture writing of the American Indians (Vols. 1–2)*. New York: Dover Publications. (First published in 1893.)

Marchionini, G., & Schneiderman, B. (1988). Finding facts vs. browsing in hypertext systems. *Computer, 21*(1), 70–80.

Marshall, C. C. (1998). Towards an ecology of hypertext annotation. In *Hypertext '98 Proceedings* (pp. 40–49). New York: ACM.

Marshall, C. C., Halasz, F. G., Rogers, R. A., & Janssen W. C. Jr. (1991). Aquanet: A hypertext tool to hold your knowledge in place. In *Hypertext '91 Proceedings* (pp. 261–276). New York: ACM.

Marshall, C. C., & Malloy, J. (1995). *Forward anywhere*. Watertown, MA: Eastgate Systems.

Marshall, C. C. & Rogers, R. A. (1992). Two years before the mist: Experiences with Aquanet. In *Hypertext '92 Proceedings* (pp. 53–62). New York: ACM.

McDaid, J. (1991). Uncle Buddy's phantom funhouse [Computer program]. Watertown, MA: Eastgate Systems.

McLuhan, M. (1972). *The Gutenberg galaxy: The making of typographic man*. Toronto: University of Toronto Press.

McLuhan, M. (1964). *Understanding media: The extensions of man*. New York: McGraw-Hill.

Meggs, P. B. (1998). *A history of graphic design (3rd ed.)*. New York: Wiley.

Miller, J. H. (1991). Literary theory, telecommunications, and the making of history. In M. Katzen (Ed.), *Scholarship and technology in the humanities* (pp. 11–20). London: British Library Research / Bowker Saur.

Miller, L. (1998, March 15). *www.claptrap.com*. In *New York Times Book Review*, p. 43.

Mitchell, W. J. T. (1994). *Picture theory*. Chicago: University of Chicago Press.

Moulthrop, S. (1988). *Text, authority, and the fiction of forking paths*. Unpublished manuscript.

Moulthrop, S. (1989). In the zones: Hypertext and the politics of interpretation. *Writing on the Edge* 1(1), 18–27.

Moulthrop, S. (1991a). Beyond the electronic book: A critique of hypertext rhetoric. In *Hypertext '91 Proceedings* (pp. 291–298). New York: ACM.

Moulthrop, S. (1991b). Victory Garden [Computer Program]. Watertown, MA: Eastgate Systems.

Moulthrop, S. (1992). Towards a rhetoric of informating texts. In *Hypertext '92 Proceedings* (pp. 171–180). New York: ACM.

Moulthrop, S. (1994). Rhizome and resistance: Hypertext and the dreams of a new culture. In G. P. Landow (Ed.), *Hypertext/Text/Theory* (pp. 299–322). Baltimore: Johns Hopkins University.

Moulthrop, S. (1997a). Pushing back: Living and writing in broken space *Modern Fiction Studies* 43(3): pp. 651–674.

Moulthrop, S. (1997b). *Hegirascope*. Retrieved from the World Wide Web: <raven.ubalt.edu/staff/moulthrop/hypertexts/hgs/hegirascope.html>

Moulthrop, S., & Cohen, S. (1996). *The color of television*. <raven.ubalt.edu/features/media_ecology/lab/96/cotv/>

Mullins, P. (1988). The fluid word: Word processing and its mental habits. *Thought* 63(251), 413–428.

Murray, J. (1997). *Hamlet on the holodeck: The future of narrative in cyberspace*. New York: Simon and Schuster.

Myers, J., Hammett, R., & McKillop, A. M. (1998). Opportunities for critical literacy and pedagogy in student-authored hypermedia. In D. Reinking, M. C. McKenna, L. D. Labbo & R. D. Kieffer (Eds.), *Handbook of literacy and technology: Transformations in a post-typographic world* (pp. 63–78). Mahwah, NJ: Lawrence Erlbaum Associates.

Nakamura, L. (1999). Race in/for cyberspace: Identity tourism and racial passing on the Internet. In V. Vitanza (Ed.), *Cyberreader (2nd ed.)*; (pp. 442–452). Needham Heights, MA: Allyn & Bacon.

Neel, J. (1988). *Plato, Derrida and writing*. Carbondale, IL: Southern Illinois University Press.

Nelson, T. H. (1974). *Dream machines*. Theodor H. Nelson.

Nelson, T. H. (1984). *Literary machines*. Theodor H. Nelson.

Nelson, T. H. (1987). *The Xanadu paradigm*. San Antonio, TX: Project Xanadu. Published broadsheet.

Nielson, J. (1990). Hypertext and Hypermedia. Boston: Academic Press.

Nordenfalk, C. (1951). The beginning of book decoration. In *Essays in honor of Georg Swarzenrki* (pp. 9–20). Chicago: Henry Regnery Co.

Norman, D. (1999). *The invisible computer: Why good products can fail, the personal computer is so complex and information appliances are the solution.* Cambridge, MA: MIT Press.

Nunberg, G. (Ed.). (1996). *The Future of the Book.* Berkeley: University of California Press.

Olson, D. R. (1986). The cognitive consequences of literacy. *Canadian Psychology, 27*(2), pp. 109–121.

Ong, W. J. (1958). *Ramus, method and the decay of dialogue: From the art of discourse to the art of reason.* Cambridge, MA: Harvard University Press.

Ong, W. J. (1982). *Orality and literacy: The technologizing of the word.* London: Methuen.

Paulson, W. (1989). Computers, minds, and texts: Preliminary reflections. *New Literary History 20,* 291–303.

Peers, E. A. (Trans.). (1972). *Complete works of St. Teresa of Jesus (Vols. 1–3).* London: Sheed and Ward.

Peirce, C. S. (1934). *Collected papers of Charles Saunders Peirce (Vol. 5).* (Charles Hartshorne & Paul Weiss, Eds.). Cambridge, MA: Harvard University Press.

Plato. (1919). *Plato in English (Vol VI).* (H. N. Fowler, Trans.). London: William Heinemann.

Poster, M. (1990). *The mode of information: Poststructuralism and social context.* Chicago: University of Chicago Press.

Proulx, E. A. (1994, May 26). Books on top. *New York Times* p. A23.

Rabkin, E. S. (1981). Spatial form and plot. In J. R. Smitten & A. Daghistany (Eds.), *Spatial form in narrative* (pp. 79–99). Ithaca, NY: Cornell University Press.

Reinking, D., McKenna, M. C., Labbo, L. D., & Kieffer, R. D. (Eds.). (1998). *Handbook of literacy and technology: Transformations in a post-typographic world.* Mahwah, NJ: Lawrence Erlbaum Associates.

Rheingold, H. (1991). *Virtual reality.* New York: Simon & Schuster.

Rheingold, H. (1994). *The virtual community: Homesteading the electronic frontier.* New York: HarperCollins.

Reynolds, L. D., & Wilson, N. G. (1978). *Scribes and scholars: A Guide to the transmission of Greek and Latin literature.* Oxford: Clarendon Press.

Rosenberg, J. (1996). The structure of hypertext activity. In *Hypertext '96 Proceedings* (pp. 22–30), New York: ACM.

Rouet, J., Levonen, J. J., Dillon, A., Spiro, R. J. (Eds.). (1996). *Hypertext and cognition.* Mahwah, NJ: Lawrence Erlbaum Associates.

Rouse, R. H., & Rouse, M. A. (1989). Wax tablets. *Language and Communication, 9* (2/3), 175–191.

Saenger, P. (1982). Silent reading: Its impact on late medieval script and society. *Viator, 13,* 367–414.

Sampson, G. (1985). *Writing systems, an introduction.* Stanford, CA: Stanford University Press.

Samuelson, P. (1997, May). The never-ending struggle for balance. *Communications of the ACM 40*(5): 17–21.

Samuleson, P., & Glushko, R. J. (1991). Intellectual property rights for digital library and hypertext publishing systems: An analysis of Xanadu. In *Hypertext '91 Proceedings* (pp. 39–50). New York: ACM.

Saporta, M. (1963). *Composition no. 1: A novel by Marc Saporta* (Richard Howard, Trans.). New York: Simon & Schuster.

Sawhney, N., Balcom, D., & Smith, I. (1996). Hypercafe: Narrative and aesthetic properties of hypervideo. In *Hypertext '96 Proceedings* (pp. 1–10). New York: ACM.

Scholes, R. (1986). Aiming a canon at the curriculum. *Salmagundi 72,* 101–117.

Scott, G. F. (1993). Review essay: Ekphrasis. *European Romantic Review 3*(2): 215–223.

Scribner, S., & Cole, M. (1981). *The psychology of literacy.* Cambridge, MA: Harvard University Press.

Seaman, D. W. (1981). *Concrete poetry in France*. Ann Arbor, MI: UMI Research Press.

Shaw, J. (1988–1991). *The legible city* (Interactive installation).

Shklovsky, V. (1965). Sterne's Tristram Shandy: Stylistic commentary. In L. T. Lemon & M. J. Reis (Trans.), *Russian formalist criticism: Four essays* (pp. 25–57). Lincoln, NE: University of Nebraska Press.

Siegel, D. (1997). *Creating killer web sites: The art of third-generation site design*. Indianapolis, IN: Hayden Books.

Slatin, J. (1991). Reading hypertext: Order and coherence in a new medium. In P. Delany & G. Landow (Eds.), *Hypermedia and literary studies* (pp. 153–169). Cambridge, MA: MIT Press.

Slatin, J. (1999). *This will change everything: Computers and English studies*. Unpublished manuscript.

Slouka, M. (1995). *War of the worlds: Cyberspace and the high-tech assault on reality*. New York: Basic Books.

Smith, J. B., & Weiss, S. F. (Eds.). (1988). Hypertext [Special Issue]. *Communications of the ACM, 31*(7).

Smith, J., Weiss, S. F., & Ferguson, G. F. (1989). A Hypertext writing system and its cognitive basis. *Hypertext '87 Proceedings* (pp. 195–214). New York: ACM.

Snell, B. (1960). *The discovery of mind: The Greek origin of European thought* (T. G. Rosenmeyer, Trans.). New York: Harper & Row.

Solt, M. E. (Ed.). (1970). *Concrete poetry: A world view*. Bloomington, IN: Indiana University Press.

Sontag, S. (Ed.). (1982). *A Barthes reader*. New York: Hill and Wang.

Spencer, S. (1971). *Space, time, and structure in the modern novel*. New York: New York University Press.

Spiro, R. J., Feltovich, P. J., Jacobson, M. J., & Coulson R. J. (1991). Cognitive flexibility, constructivism and hypertext: Random access instruction for advanced knowledge acquisition in ill-structured domains. *Educational Technology, 31*(5), 24–33.

Steinberg, S. H. (1959). *Five hundred years of printing*. New York: Criterion Books.

Sterne, L. (1965). *The life and opinions of Tristram Shandy, gentleman* (I. Watt, Ed.). Boston: Houghton Mifflin.

Stone, A. R. (1991). Will the real body please stand up? In M. Benedikt (Ed.), *Cyberspace: First steps* (pp. 81–118). Cambridge, MA: MIT Press.

Street, B. V. (1984). *Literacy in theory and practice*. Cambridge: Cambridge University Press.

Streitz, N., Hanneman J., & Thüring, M. (1989). From ideas and arguments to hyperdocuments: Traveling through activity spaces. In *Hypertext '89 Proceedings* (pp. 343–364). New York: ACM Press.

Streitz, N., Haake, J., Hanneman J., Lemke, A., Schuler, W., Schütt, H., & Thüring M. (1992). SEPIA: A collaborative hypermedia authoring environment. In *Proceedings of the ACM Hypertext '89* (pp. 11–22). New York: ACM Press.

Strickland, S. (1997). True north [Computer program]. Watertown, MA: Eastgate Systems.

Thomas, R. (1992). *Literacy and orality in ancient Greece*. Cambridge: Cambridge University Press.

Tiffin, J., & Rajasingham, L. (1995). *In search of the virtual class: Education in an information society*. London and New York: Routledge.

Trigg, R. H., & Irish, P. M. (1989). Hypertext habitats: Experiences of writers in Notecards. In *Hypertext '87 Proceedings* (pp. 89–108). New York: ACM.

Tufte, E. R. (1983). *The visual display of quantitative information*. Cheshire, CT: Graphics Press.

Tufte, E. R. (1990). *Envisioning Information*. Cheshire, CT: Graphics Press.

Tufte, E. R. (1997). *Visual explanations: Images and quantities, evidence and narrative*. Cheshire, CT: Graphics Press.

Turing, A. (1963). Computing machinery and intelligence. In E. A. Feigenbaum & J. Feldman (Eds.), *Computers and thought* (pp. 11–35). New York: McGraw-Hill. (First published in 1950)

Turkle, S. (1995). *Life on the screen: Identity in the age of the Internet.* New York: Simon & Schuster.

Ulmer, G. (1989). *Teletheory: Grammatology in the age of video.* New York: Routledge.

Ulmer, G. (1994). *Heuretics: The logic of invention.* Baltimore: Johns Hopkins University Press.

VanHoosier-Carey, G. (1997). Rhetoric by design: Using web development projects in the technical communication classroom. *Computers and composition 14:* 395–407.

von Hallberg, R. (1983). Canons [Special issue]. *Critical Inquiry, 10.*

Weitzmann, K. (1970). *Illustrations in roll and codex: A study of the origin and method of text illustration.* Princeton, NJ: Princeton University Press.

Welch, K. E. (1999). *Electric rhetoric: Classical rhetoric, oralism, and a new literacy.* Cambridge, MA: MIT Press.

Wenk, R. (1984). *Indiana Jones and the legion of death.* New York: Ballantine Books.

Williams, R. (1975). *Television: Technology and cultural form.* New York: Schocken Books.

Wills, F. H. (1977). *Schrift und Zeichen der Völker: Von der Urzeit bis heute* [Writing and signs among peoples: From primitive times to the present]. Düsseldorf: Econ Verlag.

Winspur, S. (1985). Poetry, portrait, poetrait. *Visible Language, 19,* 426–438.

Wittgenstein, L. (1953). *Philosophical investigations* (G. E. M. Anscombe, Trans.). Oxford: Basil Blackwell.

Woodmansee, M. (1984). The genius and the copyright: Economic and legal conditions of the emergence of the author. *Eighteenth Century Studies 17,* 425–448.

Woodmansee, M. (1992). On the author effect: Recovering collectivity. *Cardozo Arts and Entertainment Law Journal 10*(2), 279–292.

Woodmansee, M., & Jaszi, P. (Eds.). (1994). *The construction of authorship: Textual appropriation in law and literature.* Durham, NC: Duke University.

Wysocki, A., Grimm, N., & Cooper, M. M. (1998). Rewriting praxis (and redefining texts) in composition research. In C. Farris and C. M. Anson (Eds.), *Under construction: Working at the intersections of composition theory, research, and practice* (pp. 250–281). Logan, UT: Utah State University Press.

Yates, F. A. (1964). *Giordano Bruno and the Hermetic tradition.* London: Routledge and Kegan Paul.

Yates, F. A. (1966). *The art of memory.* Chicago: University of Chicago Press.

Year 2000 Grolier multimedia encyclopedia. (1999). Danbury, CT: Grolier Interactive.

Ziegfeld, R. (1989). Interactive fiction: A new literary genre? *New Literary History, 20,* 341–372.

Zuboff, S. (1988). *In the age of the smart machine: The future of work and power.* New York: Basic Books.

Index